Teacher Lore and Professional Development for School Reform

Teacher Lore and Professional Development for School Reform

&

Written and Edited by
Gretchen Schwarz and Joye Alberts

BERGIN & GARVEY
Westport, Connecticut • London

Library of Congress Cataloging-in-Publication Data

Schwarz, Gretchen, 1952–
    Teacher lore and professional development for school reform /
written and edited by Gretchen Schwarz and Joye Alberts.
      p.   cm.
    Includes bibliographical references and index.
    ISBN 0–89789–509–6 (alk. paper)
    1. Teachers—United States.   2. Teachers—United States—
Biography.   3. Storytelling—United States.   4. Teachers—In
-service training—United States.   5. Educational change—United
States.   I. Alberts, Joye, 1951– .   II. Title.
LB1775.2.S38   1998
371.1′00973—DC21   97–48624

British Library Cataloguing in Publication Data is available.

Library of Congress Catalog Card Number: 97–48624
ISBN: 0–89789–509–6

First published in 1998

Bergin & Garvey, 88 Post Road West, Westport, CT 06881
An imprint of Greenwood Publishing Group, Inc.

Printed in the United States of America

The paper used in this book complies with the
Permanent Paper Standard issued by the National
Information Standards Organization (Z39.48–1984).

10 9 8 7 6 5 4 3 2 1

To my parents, Margaret and Al Schwarz (1923–1996)
and my Aunt Mary, teachers all
G. S.

For Van and Thelma Jones, my parents
J. A.

Contents

Acknowledgments

Teacher Lore and Professional Development for School Reform is a book written in honor of teachers. We first thank all of the teachers and soon-to-be teachers who share their stories with us and listen to our own stories about teaching. These include preservice teachers in Gretchen's classes, the teachers connected to the Oklahoma State University Writing Project, and those colleagues throughout the National Writing Project network whose dedication and enthusiasm for teaching are sources of inspiration. We owe a special thank you to Toni Pantier, author of "Apart from the Rest" in Chapter 3 of this volume, our colleague in the Writing Project and our friend, who believed in this project from the beginning and allowed us to share her story of Jody with publishers to illustrate the power of teachers' stories.

We are indebted to all the teachers whose stories and reflections on their teaching lives appear in this book. Each contributor willingly took the risk that comes with sharing the truth. Likewise, we are indebted to the participants in the Mid-Del Teacher Lore class whose writing and thinking about teaching inspired us.

Many colleagues have been a source of encouragement and support throughout the process of writing this book . We are grateful to Kathryn Castle who urged us to write a book and shared her own experiences with using teacher lore. Pam Bettis provided an excellent and careful critique of an early draft of the book. David England, Gretchen's school chair, acknowledged the time this kind of project takes out a professor's work life. Ron Brandt and the ASCD Publications Board gave us early support and showed the first sign of interest in the project.

We are especially grateful for the day-to-day support provided by Shea Thomas, student assistant in the Oklahoma State University Writing Project office, who organized manuscripts and correspondence and cheerfully did whatever was needed to keep us on schedule.

Betty Ann Sisson's help with editing the final manuscript was invaluable. She is a thoughtful, precise editor, and we were fortunate to have her nearby whenever we needed advice. Chris Moody's work with the index was a tremendous help, and we appreciate his willingness to take on the task.

We also appreciate the help of Greenwood Publishing Group editors Lynn Taylor and Rebecca Ardwin who gently taught us the ins and outs of book publishing. Copy editor Linda Robinson gave us clear direction for getting the manuscript into final form.

We are grateful for the support of our friends and families. Joye thanks her children Abby and Sam for waiting patiently while she worked at the computer. Most importantly, she is grateful to Marty for his support, understanding, and acceptance.

Preface

The vocation of teaching does not offer security, stability, or comfort; it offers adventure, an invitation to remain open and vulnerable, and occasions to reshape and recompose the story of our life. (Huebner, 1987, p. 21)

School reform in America is as old as schools. Still, the rate of change, the political rhetoric of crisis, and the proliferation of movements and panaceas have increased dramatically in the last half of the twentieth century. Just since we began teaching 25 years ago, we have been through Back to Basics, *A Nation at Risk*, career ladders, Outcomes Based Education, Effective Teaching, Total Quality Management, and numerous other programs and policy pronouncements. Reform topics have varied from curriculum to dress codes, from block scheduling to state competency testing. Whatever the concern, however, teachers clearly lie at the heart of any genuine and ongoing school improvement. Although many factors affect ultimate educational outcomes, the quality of schooling depends on what goes on in the classroom with children and teachers. Thus, the focus of much reform discussion has shifted to professional development. In 1994, for example, "teacher education and professional development" was added to the original six National Education Goals. States have increased their focus on professional development, as well. America's classrooms now are more diverse, the family is tremendously altered, technology changes daily, and Americans expect more of their schools. Given the growing pressures, expectations, and changes facing teachers in the twenty-first century, not to mention the call for ongoing school improvement, successful teachers need more support and better educational opportunities than ever before.

Our own experience with professional development, both as preservice and especially as inservice teachers, is probably typical. In the last 25 years, we have been subjected to an almost complete preoccupation with technique, procedure, and behavior: teacher groups assigned to write behavioral objectives; experts holding forth with little idea as to what life is like in any real school; cute but quickly forgotten workshops; lectures offering prescriptions for "effective teaching"; talks by generic "motivational speakers"; and research results from those who know nothing of our subjects, our schools, or our students. Seldom has school reform begun with us and what we know as teachers. Seldom have teacher education courses or professional development sessions called on our best talents and ideas, on our abilities and desires to reflect on our own practice, on our best and most caring selves. Fortunately, teacher lore, an alternative to the usual professional development, can help teachers create and propel school reform.

The purpose of this book is to describe the power of teacher lore to prepare and move teachers to become agents of change. We have experienced the power of teacher stories ourselves—with Writing Project teachers, with future secondary teachers, with our colleagues, and in our own professional lives.

Teacher narratives are an essential means to school reform. First, teacher stories can reveal what really goes on in the classroom, offering rich insights into teacher thinking, student needs and behaviors, curriculum issues, and school climate. Authentic school change must build on the realities of school life. Teacher lore is a fundamental source of information. Second, teacher lore both validates and challenges teacher knowledge. Teacher lore honors teachers as the dedicated educators they are, empowering them to see themselves as part of a larger professional community in which their knowledge counts. Teacher lore also motivates teacher growth. Teachers who read, write, and discuss narratives of teaching must look at their own thinking, beliefs, and practices. Questions emerge, old issues are seen in new ways, struggles are recognized, and research is required. Story is a powerful medium for learning, and school reform in the twenty-first century demands teachers who never stop learning. Ultimately, teacher lore honors teaching itself. Teacher lore portrays teaching as something much more than technique or technology. Banner and Cannon (1997) use teacher lore to illustrate their findings about teaching, reminding us that "teaching is not for the faint-hearted, nor for those who consider it just a means of diffusing knowledge. It requires a fullness of self, braced by consciousness of the effect each teacher has or ought to have on students, and this breadth of character is demanded of few, if any, other callings" (p. 6).

The audience for this book then is, first of all, teachers—current and future. Teachers across levels and of diverse backgrounds will find stories which confirm their own knowledge and engage them in questioning that knowledge as well. We also offer practicing teachers ideas on using teacher lore for professional development; teachers can use this book to demand more appropriate inservice for themselves. Possibilities for reflection, growth, and change need to begin in teacher education programs. In addition to the stories themselves, teacher educators will find a wealth of ideas about using teacher lore. Clearly, administrators and those working with professional development in the schools will find this a valuable book, offering concrete ideas and provoking thought. The message to policy makers at all levels is clear: the teacher's voice must be heard if school reform is to be successful and meaningful. Finally, parents and the public will find in this book more than the superficial rhetoric which all too often passes for the truth about education in the media. Anyone who cares about schools and school reform will find worthwhile issues, information, and understandings through teacher lore.

Narrative has been increasingly a topic of study across disciplines. Many voices in the field of education have been promoting teacher lore as a medium for teaching and learning in the last 15 years—Jerome Bruner, William Ayers, Nancie Atwell, and Nel Noddings, to name a few. Excellent books have emerged such as *Teacher Lore* by Schubert and Ayers (1992) and *Teachers' Stories* by Jalongo and Isenberg (1995). This volume is the first, however, to make clear the connection between teacher lore, professional development, and school reform. This volume is also unique in that the teachers in the collected stories are speaking for themselves; we have not attempted to interpret or comment on the stories we included. We did look for diversity and clarity, but we invited the teachers to reflect on their own stories in their own ways. The only framework we have imposed is to categorize the kinds of stories. Authentic teacher voice is key to our understanding of development and reform.

We begin this volume with an introduction to teacher lore in Chapter 1—what it is and the theory behind it. Following in Chapters 2, 3, 4, and 5 are stories about teaching from teachers all over America, addressing in powerful ways a variety of experiences and issues in schooling. In Chapter 6 we survey methods for using teacher lore in inservice professional development. Likewise in Chapter 7 we address methods for using teacher lore in teacher education for preservice teachers. In Chapter 8 we bring together theories of change, professional development, and teacher lore to offer a clear rationale for using teacher narrative in the service of school improvement. We converse about teacher lore and how we came to appreciate it as teachers ourselves in Chapter 9. At the end we offer further resources in teacher lore, film and book titles.

We are fortunate in that we have the opportunity to work with so many wonderful teachers and future teachers in our own professional lives. It is their example and their stories which have moved us to develop this book. We hope this work will support and aid teachers everywhere.

REFERENCES

Banner, J. M., Jr., & Cannon, H. C. (1997). *The elements of teaching*. New Haven, CT: Yale University Press.

Huebner, D. (1987). The vocation of teaching. In F. S. Bolin & J. M. Falk (Eds.), *Teacher renewal: Professional issues, personal choices* (pp. 17–29). New York: Teachers College Press.

Teacher Lore and Professional Development for School Reform

Chapter 1

The Power of Teacher Lore

Stories . . . invite us to remember that we are in the business of
teaching, learning, and researching to improve the human condition.
(Witherell and Noddings, 1991, p. 280)

School reform efforts nationwide continue to focus on the improvement of
teaching. Teachers remain at the center of reform, whether the topic is site-based
management or learning styles, the Copernican plan or middle school teaming.
Reformers strive to improve teacher education, as well. And rightly so. Learning
happens, or does not happen, in classrooms where teachers and students live and
work together. It has become commonplace, however, to note that top-down
prescriptions have failed to make a lasting difference in teaching, that one-shot staff
development programs delivered by outside experts are ineffective, and that most
teacher evaluation systems have failed to help most teachers. Yet little has come
along to replace all these programs and policies. Change remains elusive.

We believe in an alternative receiving growing attention and showing
great promise—teacher lore. We argue that teacher lore may serve as a basis for
professional growth among teachers, engendering genuine and ongoing school
reform. Teacher lore has been defined by Schubert (1992) as follows:

Teacher lore includes stories about and by teachers. It portrays and interprets ways in
which teachers deliberate and reflect and it portrays teachers in action. Teacher lore refers
to knowledge, ideas, insights, feelings, and understandings of teachers as they reveal their
guiding beliefs, share approaches, relate consequences of their teaching, offer aspects of
their philosophy of teaching and provide recommendations for educational policy makers.
(p. 9)

Teacher lore involves reading, hearing, viewing, writing, telling, and discussing stories of teaching, both fictional and true. Teacher lore exemplifies a way of knowing or learning Bruner (1985) calls the narrative mode of thought. In this book, we will examine the nature of teacher lore, a rationale for its value, and its uses in professional development for both pre- and inservice teachers. We will further elaborate the need for a new kind of professional development to generate continuous school reform.

We believe in the power of teacher lore because of our own stories, of course. Gretchen has been using teacher lore with preservice secondary English teachers and graduate inservice teachers to engage and challenge thinking. Journal responses and class discussions are articulate, focused, and significant when students think of teaching in terms of lived experience—their own and others'. Films, case studies, and teachers' stories (oral and written) aid preservice teachers in making theory-practice connections and in trying out new ideas when they teach. Joye has been encouraged by the involvement and sense of ownership inservice teachers acquire when asked to begin the Summer Institute of the OSU Writing Project with their own teaching stories. In addition, most of the teaching methods and techniques shared in the Project are embedded in stories. Project teachers go on to change their own classrooms and to bring new ideas to others. Joye and Gretchen also experienced the community-building power of teacher lore in an extension course for inservice teachers as we describe in Chapter 6. We share more of our own stories in Chapter 9 of this book.

At the center of this book stand true stories, teacher lore which teachers from across the nation have chosen to reflect on and share. The power of teacher lore is evident in these narratives of educators dedicated to the improvement of the human condition. Teacher lore can energize teachers as educators and as agents of change in schools, leading to meaningful and positive reform.

BACKGROUND

Teacher lore is as old as teaching itself. In the first century A.D., Quintilian, a successful teacher and the first rhetorician to set up a public school in Rome and to receive a state salary, wrote his *Institutio Oratoria* (1980, p. vii). This opus includes ideas about the education of a great orator; it is rich in teacher lore from Quintilian's own life as well as from other authorities. Leaping over the centuries, from Cicero to Erasmus and beyond, we find many stories of teachers in the history of the novel, from Dickens' *Hard Times* in the nineteenth century to Hilton's *Goodbye, Mr. Chips* in the first half of the twentieth century. Teachers serve as both villains and heroes in fiction. Television has found teachers comical and admirable as in *Our Miss Brooks* in the 1950's, *Welcome Back, Kotter* in the 1970's, and *The Head of the Class* in the 1980's. Hollywood loves inspirational teacher stories, fictional or based on nonfiction, such as *To Sir with Love* (1967) and *Teachers* (1984). The 1960's were an especially prolific time for teacher lore in the form of autobiographical teacher writing, including Sylvia Ashton-Warner's *Teacher* (1963), John Holt's *How Children Fail* (1964), Jonathan Kozol's *Death at an Early Age* (1967), Herbert Kohl's *36 Children* (1968), and James Herndon's *The Way It Spozed to Be* (1969). During a decade of change and experimentation in schools, the 1960's saw a rebirth of progressivism with humanistic educational philosophies having some impact; personal insights of teachers were highly regarded. Such writing is again finding a wide audience as evidenced by the well-received *My Posse Don't Do Homework* (1992) by LouAnne Johnson, which was transformed into *Dangerous Minds,* the movie and TV show. Despite its popular appeal and long history, however, teacher lore has not been taken seriously as a tool for educators and educational reform in America until recently.

Individual works of teacher lore like Wigginton's *Sometimes a Shining Moment* (1986), describing the birth of Foxfire, and Atwell's *In the Middle* (1987), heralding the use of writing and reading workshops, have had a significant impact on teachers and curriculum, especially in the language arts. Nevertheless, teacher lore has only become more widely respectable since Witherell and Noddings' *Stories Lives Tell* (1991) and Schubert and Ayers' *Teacher Lore* (1992). Interest in teacher lore is currently soaring as reflected in articles, books, and research. Why now? Is teacher lore just another passing fad? We believe teacher lore is here to stay as the educational climate changes and new paradigms for educational thought gain credence. Feminist perspectives on education, for example, encourage teacher voice and invite active teacher participation in school change; most teachers in America remain women. Teacher lore empowers women in particular because teacher stories demonstrate the value of the affective in understanding the classroom. As Witherell and Noddings (1991) remark, "Stories can join the worlds of thought and feeling, and they give special voice to the feminine side of human experience—to the power of emotion, intuition, and relationships in human lives" (p. 4).

Commitment to justice and democracy in schooling recommends teacher lore, both for professional development and for educational insight and policy. For example, *Black Teachers on Teaching* (1997) by Michele Foster is a collection of narratives by a variety of black teachers. Foster explains as follows:

Life history and the associated techniques of oral history and personal narrative are forms of analysis that can bring the experiences of blacks, including teachers, into view in ways that reveal the complexity of their experiences. Life history not only provides material about individual lives but also offers the opportunity to explore how individual lives are shaped by society. . . . First-person accounts have long been employed by individuals to encode and record the experiences of blacks, and such accounts have served as a valuable source of information for both scholars seeking to understand the black community and for the black community itself. (pp. xx–xxi)

Black Teachers on Teaching contributes to our understanding of the downside of desegregation as black teachers lost their jobs to white teachers in integrated schools and to our appreciation of the outstanding achievements of black educators. As we shall discuss again, teacher lore is a tool for crossing cultures and valuing diversity. Teacher lore enables a view and a language of education which get at the humanity of the educational undertaking. As Thomas (1992) says, teacher narrative allows an "opportunity for the silent and silenced. In narrative studies a countervailing discourse is generated producing an alternative vocabulary, which in many ways is agonistic to current modes of educational discourse which seek to portray education as a commodity" (p. 17). Teacher lore explores the human realities.

School reform has been moving, in some circles, towards a greater appreciation for teachers and their knowledge in general. Shulman (1987), for instance, recognizes the "wisdom of practice" as basic to what teachers know and how they become experts in their fields (p. 11). As many researchers and authorities move away from a "deficit model" of teaching, teacher lore is seen as a worthwhile resource for researchers and reformers. Teacher lore can be viewed as part or partner of the teacher researcher movement. As Cochran-Smith and Lytle (1993) say of teacher research in general, teacher lore "is concerned with the questions that arise from the lived experiences of teachers and the everyday life of teaching expressed in a language that emanates from practice" (p. 59). In their own language the teachers in this volume reveal their questions and realizations, doubts and passions, struggles and triumphs. Michael Burns in "The Screening" in Chapter 2 of this book, for example, reveals his self-doubts and confusion as he interviews for a teaching job, and Sheryl Lain in "Teaching Is a State of Mind" in Chapter 3 describes the lack of preparation and emotional overload that shadowed her first teaching experience on a reservation. Such teacher lore demonstrates the potential power of qualitative and action research in increasing understanding of teaching and students. Human, educational significance replaces statistical "significance" as the goal.

Along with a new respect for the classroom teacher, teacher lore reflects the influence of constructivist thought. Teachers, like their students, do not learn and change simply because they are threatened with regulations, rewarded by career ladders, or "deskilled" by teacher-proof curricula. Teachers learn when they feel the need to learn. They, like their students, construct new knowledge based on present understandings and concern over what does and does not work, over what is puzzling or disturbing in their own lives. In teacher lore, we can see one way teachers build new knowledge about teaching, we can encourage that process, and we can also share the insights with all concerned about school reform and the improvement of teaching.

RATIONALE FOR TEACHER LORE

Teacher lore, particularly in the form of teachers' own true stories such as we share in this book, has much to say to anyone concerned about teaching and schooling. First, teacher lore can reveal teachers' work from the inside, holistically, within real life contexts. Narrative is perhaps the most natural way for humans to make sense of their work and lives and to share that sense, as scholars in many fields argue. Sacks (1987), for example, examining the lives of patients with severe neurological disorders, argues for the "spiritual priority" of the narrative mode of thought. He observes, "It is this narrative or symbolic power which gives a *sense of the world*—a concrete reality in the imaginative form of symbol and story—when abstract thought can provide nothing at all" (p. 184). Atwell (1987) notes, "The word *story* can be traced to the Greek word *eidenai*, which means 'to know.' As a reader, I look to stories to help me understand and give meaning to my life. As a writer, I tell stories so I may understand, teaching myself and trying to teach others " (p. 3). Teacher lore lays bare the "real stuff" of life in schools, not generic abstractions, not an outside observer's fragmented interpretation, not ungrounded theory. In teacher lore we can see real kids, classrooms, and everyday problems, the feelings and thinking of teachers. Florio-Ruane (1991) declares that "teachers' stories are a largely untapped source of information about teaching" (p. 242). Paying attention to teacher lore simply makes sense in ongoing efforts to improve schools, in efforts to know more about teaching and learning. Cohn and Kottkamp (1993) argue the following:

The absence of teachers from the dialogue and decision-making on reform has been a serious omission. It has yielded faulty definitions of problems, solutions that compound rather than confront the problem, and a demeaned and demoralized teaching force. . . . If reform is to be successful, their voices and views must be included in any attempts to improve and alter their work. (p. xvi)

The second important thrust of teacher lore is to validate teachers as knowers, as thinking, feeling human beings engaged in purposeful work, and as members of a professional community. Contrary to the media's negative depiction of teachers, especially since the national report *A Nation at Risk* in 1983, teachers do know a great deal. They know their subjects, their students, and their communities. Good teachers always continue to learn on the job; their knowledge is grounded in daily experience. Teacher lore validates this knowledge in the field of education. Teacher lore invites teachers to view themselves as makers of knowledge and not merely recipients of wisdom handed down by university researchers or outside consultants. Miller (1992) describes this knowledge below:

The term "lore" captures the intuitive, the informal, the spontaneous and subjective undersides of what, in recent years, have been codified as planned, predictable, controllable, and objective elements of "effective" teaching. Lore is what we know to be similar in our teaching experiences, even as we tell our stories in order to point out the differences among us. And, over time, the telling of our stories allows us to hear our own changing and evolving understandings of ourselves as teachers. (p. 14)

Teacher lore elevates what practicing teachers know to an acknowledged status—here in the form of the written word. When teachers see themselves positively, as knowledgeable, they are empowered to act on their knowledge, to seek more understanding, to value themselves and their work. People who do not value what they themselves bring to their work can hardly be expected to welcome others' reform mandates. As Schubert (1991) puts it, teachers' stories give "credibility to teachers themselves as creators of knowledge and theory that can illuminate an understanding of curriculum, teaching, and the educative process" (p. 214). We cannot but be impressed by the knowledge and expertise revealed by the teachers in this book, from relative newcomers like Steffie Corcoran to retired, but still very active educators like Elaine Greenspan. Teacher lore captures a wealth of knowledge.

Not only are individual teachers validated through teacher lore, however; storytelling is a communal activity which generates communal knowledge and collegiality. Schubert and Ayers (1992) recognize the source of teacher lore as "an oral tradition among teachers who exchange and reconstruct perspectives together. This reflection on experience, this reconceiving of meaning and purpose of one's life and contribution as a teacher, is the essence of teacher lore" (p. vii). Teacher lore can bring educators together. A book such as this one celebrates collegiality and invites every reader to become part of the ongoing professional conversation. Here teachers, administrators, policy makers, and others who care about children can read stories from a variety of teachers, elementary to college, rural and urban, older and younger. The usual boundaries which separate educators can be broken down when a university professor reads the story of a kindergarten teacher and learns how much they have in common. Educators will recognize themselves in these stories. Readers will want to talk to each other about the stories, too. Certainly a story like Ruth Givens' "Teacher Lure" in Chapter 4 of this volume, which explores the dark side of teaching and the ambiguity, will stir thought and discussion. Witherell and Noddings (1991) capture the sense of professional community teacher lore offers:

Stories and narrative, whether personal or fictional provide meaning and belonging in our lives. They attach us to others and to our own histories by providing a tapestry rich with threads of time, place, character, and even advice on what we might do with our lives. The story fabric offers us images, myths, and metaphors that are morally resonant and contribute both to our knowing and being known. (p. 1)

Teacher lore validates teachers but it also challenges them to consider new and multiple perspectives on classroom life, to construct new knowledge, and to enact change. If teacher lore had nothing more to offer than a good read or a warm feeling, it would not be the significant tool for school reform we think it can be. Teacher narrative offers one avenue for "members of the teaching profession [to] develop their own systematic and intentional ways to scrutinize and improve their practice," as Cochran-Smith and Lytle express it (1993, p. 101). Rosen (1985) declares, "Story telling may be discovery learning" (p. 35). Reflection builds on validation; teachers are free to become self-critical without feeling defensive. We asked the teachers in this book to write reflections on their stories. The depth of discovery and resulting analysis points to the power of teacher lore to precipitate reflective practice.

In their own stories and those of others, educators can come to question their own work. We assume, in Dewey's formulation that Gretchen puts in capital letters on a course syllabus, experience plus reflection equals growth. Teachers may discover a fear never before acknowledged or a philosophy that makes sense, a weakness previously unidentified, or a strength on which to build. Stories require higher level thinking—making connections, remembering experiences, analyzing character and theme, making judgments. Because stories are so engaging, emotionally and cognitively, they invite deep reflection. For example, such stories as Carolyn Thomas's "Sally's Story" in Chapter 4 and Gloria Nixon-John's "Crossing the Highway" in Chapter 5 of this book challenge us to think carefully about what kinds of places schools are and what kinds of places they should be. White (1991) describes the power of teacher lore in this way:

Teachers' narratives or "war stories" encode their specific experiences and go beyond them. Teachers tell stories for reasons other than being expressive, being entertaining, or "letting off steam." When they tell stories, teachers are beginning a process of reflection on their practice. When teachers tell stories, they make claims about the premises of teaching, theoretically argue about priorities, inculcate those moving into the profession and cause others to reflect on their own practice. (p. 226)

Teacher lore challenges us to ask what Joye calls the "hard questions": What is education for? What do students need to know? How do children learn? What should schools look like? Who should make decisions? What is my role as a teacher? In this book, as in the growing literature on teacher lore or narrative, we respect "war stories" as a formal means for professional development. We will examine specific applications in Chapters 6 and 7.

Reflective practice is sharpened by the consideration of new ideas and situations encountered in teacher lore as well as tacit knowledge made explicit. By seeing not only the familiar but the different, readers as well as writers of teacher lore may learn about diverse cultures, different kinds of schools, new ways of being in the classroom. As Witherell and Noddings (1991) observe, "Through . . . writing . . . and listening to life's stories—one's own and others—those engaged in this work can penetrate cultural barriers . . . and deepen their understanding of their respective histories and possibilities" (p. 4). For instance, as described in Chapter 7 of this book, Florio-Ruane at Michigan State University has been using teacher lore to prepare future teachers to embrace diversity. Stories and reflections of diverse teachers can be found in this book. These stories challenge the reader to think about educational problems in different ways. They offer experiences other educators may not have had. They build empathy across differences.

Moreover, teacher lore challenges educators to consider teaching as an ethical, moral undertaking. Connelly and Clandinin (1990) elaborate, "Narrative explanation and, therefore, narrative meaning, consists of significance, value, and intention" (p. 9). Florio-Ruane (1991) adds, "Stories are representations of knowledge that do not dodge moral consequences" (p. 242). Stories present difficult dilemmas, hard decisions, and choices. Stories go beyond teaching as technology, challenging us to ask ourselves what is best for children, what do we believe, and whether the status quo is the best we can offer. Furthermore, Jalongo and Isenberg (1995) state that "Teachers' stories promote the 'ethic of caring'" (p. 146). Teachers care enough to share their stories, and their stories often emphasize the reason they went into teaching—to benefit young people. We are inspired by Coles (1989) and his use of narratives in graduate courses in law, medicine, and education. He says that "a compelling narrative, offering a storyteller's moral imagination vigorously at work, can enable any of us to learn by example, to take to heart what is, really, a gift of grace" (p. 191). Professional growth demands that educators reflect on the values which motivate them and think carefully about the ethical dimension of the decisions they make.

One of the important ways in which teacher lore challenges teachers and other educators lies in the power of stories to problematize the familiar and to resist simplistic answers. Teacher lore gives us permission to move beyond the prescriptive and reductive in school reform efforts. Teacher stories capture and respect teaching as does Ayers (1993) in his own teacher story—"exhausting, complex, idiosyncratic, never twice the same, at its heart, an intellectual and ethical enterprise. . . . Teaching begins in challenge and is never far from mystery" (p. 127). Real stories tell us that there are no quick fix-its or generic panaceas in educational reform. The Hunter Lesson Plan is no answer to better teaching when the teacher's aim is to have students leaving the classroom puzzling about a poem. Classroom management tips from effective teaching research are useless when a distressed student is troubled by abuse at home. No teaching method works for all students—or all teachers—all the time. Curriculum "alignment," discipline "plans," national standards and certification—none of these attend to the complex realities of teaching. Teacher lore, on the other hand, depicts teaching as the value-laden, complicated, multilayered, context-dependent, and uncertain work teachers know the calling to be. In this volume of stories we share the vision of teaching expressed by Ayers (1992). "There are moral myths and heroic accounts, subversive parables and standard homilies, women's stories as well as men's stories, black and white narrative, tales of humiliation and of triumph, tragedy and transcendence. . . . The key is that teaching and teachers are never quite summed up, never easily reducible to a simple story" (p. 155). Teacher stories are open-ended, requiring interpretation and analysis. Such stories invite us to identify new problems and ask deeper questions because they refuse to offer surefire prescriptions. Teacher lore offers no simple stories or simple solutions.

Teacher lore does more than challenge thinking, though. It is praxis centered, connecting theory/philosophy and practice/experience. With its special ability to engage readers and writers intellectually and emotionally, teacher lore may actually accomplish significant reform. A story can motivate change in practice. As Schubert (1990), speaking of the Teacher Lore Project, declares, "The powerful moment, the moving insight (though just from one person or even a handful) is sometimes enough to create dynamic improvement in those who have access to it" (p. 100). Stories engage us in unique and moving ways. Jackson (1987) expresses the motivating power of stories in the following words:

Stories . . . sometimes change us in ways that have relatively little to do with knowledge per se. . . . They leave us with altered states of consciousness, new perspectives, changed outlooks, and more. They make us wish for things we have not wished for before. They gladden and sadden, inspire and instruct, not by transmitting facts and principles, but by acquainting us with aspects of life that we heretofore had not experienced. (p. 313)

Readers and writers of teacher stories want to learn more, to talk to other educators, to do things better or differently, perhaps to do research in their own classrooms. In Chapter 6 of this book, we look at ways teacher lore can lead to change and professional growth through teacher research, teacher evaluation, and other means.

In addition to personal change and contributions to educational research, teacher lore can lead to school reform through communication with the public and parents. All too often educational innovations and school life are misunderstood by parents and community members who know only what they read in the paper, hear on TV, or hear from someone else. Thus, the whole language movement has been demonized in some communities, or using calculators in math class is seen as suspect, leading only to weak math skills. Teachers as responsible professionals need to do a much better job of communicating with families and the public; teacher lore is a natural way to communicate. Strieb (in Threatt et al.,1994), author of her own teacher journal, observes, "I believe it is partly through the sharing of stories about classrooms, in our own words, that teaching and teachers will come to be valued by the public at large" (p. 227). Teacher narrative offers an engaging invitation to the public, to policy makers and legislators, to understand schools from the inside. Parents and the public must become partners if school reform is to succeed. We offer this book to all who care about public education.

We must be careful in our enthusiasm, however, not to imply that teacher lore is the new panacea for teacher growth and development. It is not; we do not believe "the answer" exists. In addition, teacher lore has its critics, too. For example, Grumet (1987), a pioneer in using autobiographical studies of educational experience, comments that "my neighbors, the marxists, [have] identified autobiography with bourgeois individualism" (p. 320). Likewise various critical theorists and education reformers warn that teacher lore may be too much "navel gazing" and too little connected to the larger political, social, and economic issues of American education. Zeichner (1992), for example, argues that teacher development efforts must be connected to questions of equity and social justice. Such critics argue that teacher lore may not prod teachers into considering or acting upon larger notions of social justice and societal reform. Teacher lore is not radical enough for some.

This argument has some validity. We certainly offer no guarantees that teacher lore *will* change teacher thinking or teacher practice at all. Some teacher lore may ignore the social contexts for educational problems although, as the list of topics (in Chapter 6) emerging from a teacher lore course demonstrates, thinking and caring teachers *do* concern themselves with political issues, with race and poverty and neglected students. In response to this kind of criticism, we must say that our view of teacher lore is dependent on a faith in practicing teachers, that teachers can and do make a difference in the lives of children. We consider our view perhaps even more radical than that of critical theorists or others in that we have tried to avoid imposing any political agenda on teacher development. We believe that most teachers, if given the time and support and materials with which to work, can develop into reflective practitioners and agents of change through the use of teacher lore. We cannot tell what this change will look like, what political and social aspects it will include, but the caring which lies at the heart of teacher narrative demands attention to social justice and democratic pedagogy. Teacher lore is not "the answer," but it holds great potential for engendering some answers.

Ultimately, we argue that as teacher lore strengthens teachers as knowers, inquirers, and doers; builds community and communication; and challenges the power of the outside researcher or removed bureaucrat to hand down reform mandates, lasting and ongoing change can result in schools. Students will benefit most as excited and renewed teachers share their knowledge and enact new ways of being and working in the classroom.

REFERENCES

Atwell, N. (1987). *In the middle*. Portsmouth, NH: Heinemann.

Ayers, W. C. (1993). *To teach: The journey of a teacher*. New York: Teachers College Press.

————. (1992). In the country of the blind: Telling our stories. In W. H. Schubert & W. C. Ayers (Eds.), *Teacher lore: Learning from our own experience* (pp. 154–158). White Plains, New York: Longman.

Bruner, J. (1985). Narrative and paradigmatic modes of thought. In E. Eisner (Ed.), *Learning and teaching the ways of knowing* (pp. 97–115). Chicago: National Society for the Study of Education.

Cochran-Smith, M., & Lytle, S. L. (1993). *Inside outside: Teacher research and knowledge*. New York: Teachers College Press.

Cohn, M. M., & Kottkamp, R. B. (1993). *Teachers: The missing voice in education*. Albany, NY: State University of New York Press.

Coles, R. (1989). *The call of stories*. Boston: Houghton Mifflin.

Connelly, F. M., & Clandinin, D. J. (1990). Stories of experience and narrative inquiry. *Educational Researcher, 19* (5), 2–14.

Florio-Ruane, S. (1991). Conversation and narrative in collaborative research: An ethnography of the written literacy forum. In C. Witherell & N. Noddings (Eds.), *Stories lives tell* (pp. 234–256). New York: Teachers College Press.

Foster, M. (1997). *Black teachers on teaching*. New York: The New Press.

Grumet, M. R. (1987). The politics of personal knowledge. *Curriculum Inquiry, 17,* 319–329.

Jackson, P. W. (1987). On the place of narration in teaching. In D. C. Berliner & B. V. Rosenshine (Eds.), *Talks to teachers* (pp. 307–328). New York: Random House.

Jalongo, M. R. (1992). Teachers' stories: Our ways of knowing. *Educational Leadership, 49* (7), 68–73.

Jalongo, M. R., & Isenberg, J. P. (1995). *Teachers' stories: From personal narrative to professional insight*. San Francisco: Jossey-Bass.

Miller, J. (1992). Teachers' spaces: A personal evolution of teacher lore. In W. H. Schubert & W. C. Ayers (Eds.), *Teacher lore* (pp. 11–22). White Plains, NY: Longman.

National Commission on Excellence in Education. (1983). *A Nation at Risk*. Washington, D. C.: U.S. Government Printing Office.

Quintilian. (1980). *Institutio Oratoria* (H. E. Butler, Trans., 1920). Cambridge, MA: Harvard.

Rosen, H. (1985). *Stories and meanings*. Sheffield, England: National Association for the Teaching of English.

Sacks, O. (1987). *The man who mistook his wife for a hat*. New York: HarperPerennial.

Schubert, W. H. (1992). Our journeys into teaching: Remembering the past. In W. H. Schubert & W. C. Ayers (Eds.), *Teacher lore* (pp. 3–10). White Plains, NY: Longman.

————. (1991). Teacher lore: A basis for understanding praxis. In C. Witherell & N. Noddings, (Eds.), *Stories lives tell* (pp. 207–233). New York: Teachers College Press.

————. (1990). Acknowledging teachers' experiential knowledge: Reports from the Teacher Lore Project. *Kappa Delta Pi Record, 26,* 99–100.

Shubert, W. H., & Ayers, W. C. (Eds.). (1992). *Teacher lore: Learning from our own experience*. White Plains, NY: Longman.

Shulman, L. (1987). Knowledge and teaching: Foundations of the new reform. *Harvard Educational Review, 57,* 1–22.

Thomas, D. (1992, April). *Putting nature to the rack: Narrative studies as research.* Paper presented at the Teachers' Stories of Life and Work Conference, Liverpool England. (ERIC Document Reproduction Service No. ED 346 461).

Threatt, S. (organizing author); Buchanan, J.; Morgan, B.; Strieb, L. Y.; Sugerman, J.; Swenson, J.; Teel, K.; and Tomlinson, J. (1994). Teachers' voices in the conversation about teacher research. In S. Hollingsworth & H. Sockett (Eds.), *Teacher research and educational reform* (pp. 222–244). Chicago: University of Chicago Press.

White, J. J. (1991). War stories: Invitations to reflect on practice. In B. R. Tabachnik & K. M. Zeichner (Eds.), *Issues and practices in inquiry-oriented teacher education* (pp. 226–252). London: The Falmer Press.

Witherell, C., & Noddings, N. (Eds.). (1991). *Stories lives tell.* New York: Teachers College Press.

Zeichner, K. (1992). Connecting genuine teacher development to the struggle for social justice. Opinion Paper. (ERIC Document Reproduction Service No. ED 344 881).

Chapter 2

Beginnings

We all have a basic need for story, for organizing our experiences into tales of important happenings. (Dyson and Genishi, 1994, p. 2)

Chapters 2–5 are collections of stories by teachers about teaching. The best information about teaching comes from the teachers themselves, from their stories of practice (Jalongo, 1992; Schubert & Ayers, 1992). The settings of the stories that follow vary—an elementary classroom, a college professor's office, a boarding house in New York, a central administrator's office, an Indian reservation. We collected the stories in a variety of ways. Many came in response to a call for manuscripts for this book which proposed to "offer readers a window into what really happens in the minds and hearts of teachers and their relationship with students and colleagues." One was written as a capstone paper at the end of student teaching. "Apart from the Rest" by Toni Pantier (Chapter 3) was originally written for a writing response group in the Oklahoma State University Writing Project's 1994 Summer Institute. Several authors originally wrote their stories during Summer Institutes of National Writing Project's affiliate sites. "Monique's Gifts" by Steffie Corcoran (Chapter 3) was written during an extension course described in Chapter 6.

After each story was completed, the author was asked to write a reflection on issues embedded in the writing connected to the daily challenges of teaching. Together, the story and reflection invite readers into the classroom and into the process of reflecting on the meaning of the story. Administrators, parents, teachers, and university educators have a new way of looking at the classroom through teachers' stories. Readers are challenged to reflect on their own beliefs and practices, to look at old issues in new ways, and to ask questions brought up by the experiences and responses of others.

Stories are loosely divided into four categories: Chapter 2, "Beginnings," includes stories of student teaching, a job interview, and the early years of teaching; Chapter 3, "Changes," includes stories of teachers who were changed by taking a close look at the lessons taught by their students; Chapter 4, "Perplexities," includes stories about difficult students and the hard questions teachers must ask themselves; and Chapter 5, "Empowerment," includes stories about teachers finding their own voices and sharing them as part of the ongoing professional conversation.

The stories are set in both urban and rural schools, in elementary, secondary, and college classrooms. While each selection offers its own unique insights, the thread running through the collection is each author's quest to make sense of his or her teaching practice through story. We purposefully chose a variety of stories written in different styles.

According to Jalongo and Isenberg (1993), good and useful teacher narratives, like these, have the characteristics that contribute to education:

- A teacher narrative should be genuine.
- A teacher narrative should invite reflection and discourse.
- A good teacher story is recursive and reinterpreted.
- A teacher story is the antidote to a "technological mentality."
- A good teacher narrative is powerful and evocative. (p. 261)

The stories in the following chapters each offer the reader a real-world look at the joys, struggles, and challenges of the teaching life. As Jalongo and Isenberg (1995) state, "The good teacher's life is not an orderly professional pathway; rather, it is a personal journey shaped by context and choice, perspective and values. Narrative is uniquely well suited to that personal/professional odyssey. It is primarily through story, one student at a time, that teachers organize their thinking and tap into the collective, accumulated wisdom of their profession" (p. xix). The stories in Chapters 2–5 add to collective wisdom and represent a willingness on the part of the authors to offer themselves and their teaching practice to examination by others. The writing here requires each author to take a risk as a teller of stories. Grumet (1987) reminds us that "even telling a story to a friend is a risky business" (p. 321).

The stories collected in the following chapters are interesting reading in their own right. Preservice teachers in methods classes and teachers in education courses or study groups will find the stories effective as a catalyst for discussion and reflection. While many of the selections raise more questions than answers, each provides an honest look into the mind and heart of the author.

REFERENCES

Dyson, A. H., & Genishi, C. (Eds.). (1994). *The need for story: Cultural diversity in classroom and community*. Urbana, IL: National Council of Teachers of English.

Grumet, M. R. (1987). The politics of personal knowledge. *Curriculum Inquiry, 17,* 319–329.

Jalongo, M. R. (1992). Teachers' stories: Our ways of knowing. *Educational Leadership,*
        49(7), 68–73.
Jalongo, M. R., & Isenberg, J. P. (1995). *Teachers' stories: From personal narrative to*
        professional insight. San Francisco: Jossey-Bass.
Jalongo, M. R., & Isenberg, J. P. (1993). Teachers' stories: Reflections on teaching,
        caring and learning. *Childhood Education, 69*(5), 260–263.
Schubert, W. H., & Ayers, W. C. (Eds.). (1992). *Teacher lore: Learning from our own*
        experience. White Plains, NY: Longman.

Assembled in Chapter 2 are stories about entry points into teaching. The collection begins with Penelope Palmer's story "Awakening the Boy," which recollects her experience with one student during her student teaching experience. In "The Screening" Michael Burns uses stream of consciousness to let readers in on his quest to answer the question "Why do I want to teach?" as he interviews for a teaching job. "Settling In" is Sharon Robbins' remembrance of finding a new teaching job in New York City and the challenges faced by new teachers wherever they may teach. Also in Chapter 2 Linda Powers reflects on her first year of teaching in the story "1973 in Review." She shares how, nearly 25 years later, she is applying some of the lessons learned in 1973 to a mentoring program she and her colleagues use to support beginning teachers.

Awakening the Boy
Penelope Palmer

There was a great deal to take in on that first day of student teaching. Our assignment was to "observe" for the first few days; we were to acquaint ourselves with our new surroundings and new students. The student population in this rural Oklahoma school was uncommonly diverse. About half were Native American, although from many different tribes, and the non-Native students came from a range of backgrounds including China, Russia, Mexico, and rural Oklahoma. Dress and grooming styles included everything from the traditional cowboy boots to the latest MTV fashions, from shaved heads to pink mohawks. Against this background of rainbow kids and individual fashion statements, it was difficult for any student to stand out in physical appearance, but one student in particular did capture my attention on that very first day.

Anato Cervantes looked like he should be walking the streets of Los Angeles instead of the halls of a rural school in the middle of the Oklahoma prairie. His eyes engaged nothing as he sauntered into the classroom, put his head down, and went to sleep. No one bothered him. At the end of the period he awoke at the commotion of shuffling papers and feet of fellow students, got up, and left—towering past the teacher who only gave him a wary glance. I wondered if he always slept during class, or if this was an unusual occurrence. It was not his oversized shirt, sagging pants, short ponytail, or even his walk that made him unique. There was something about Anato's eyes, an unusual hardness that aged him beyond his years, that made him stand out to me.

When I asked the teacher about him, she said, "Anato has only been here for about a month. I really haven't had a chance to get to know him yet. I was hired after school started, and with such a difficult teaching load, I really haven't had as much individual time with students as I would like to have, even the ones who have been here all year. That is why I wanted your help. So far, Anato hasn't done much work, but I think he's pretty bright."

The next day, some of the sophomore students stayed in the classroom to work with the teacher on revising their papers while I accompanied others to the computer lab next door. Anato came into the lab, sat at a side table, and went to sleep. I thought it over and, even though it was only my second day as a student teacher, I decided to break into his space. I knelt down next to him and laid my hand on his arm quietly asking him if he was feeling okay. He slightly raised his head and opened his eyes without looking at me. "Yeah."

"You're not sick?" I asked.

"No."

"Just really tired?"

"Yeah," and he put his head back down without ever looking at me.

"Okay, well, I'll leave you alone then." Smilingly I threw in, "I'll spare you my 'value of English speech' until you are awake enough to listen."

He mumbled a muffled "okay" into his arm.

We followed the same routine the next day. This time, I noticed that Anato was carrying a Tony Hillerman book with a marker about a third of the way through it. He went to a side table, but this time I made a determined effort to get to him before he could fall asleep. "Are you already finished with your paper?" I asked.

"No."

"Are you going to write one?"

"No," he answered without defiance or apology.

"I see you have a Tony Hillerman book. Are you reading it?"

"Yeah."

"Do you like it?"

"It's pretty good."

"I like his books, too. You know, Hillerman writes a lot about Native Americans as a non-Native; have you read many Native American authors?"

"No. . . . I don't know," he faltered and turned to look at me for the first time. Was it my imagination, or did I detect a glimmer of interest in—or curiosity about—me behind that protective, streetwise glare? He quickly turned away again, as if to dismiss me.

"Well, we'll be talking more about it . . . ," and I moved on in my circulating. I knew that it was totally "uncool" for a student to get too much attention from a teacher. Soon, I noticed that Anato was asleep again.

The following week I told him between classes that I had a list of Native American authors and some of their works for him. He followed me to the classroom, and after giving him a moment to look over the list, I asked if he had read any of these books. He indicated that he had read one of them and turned and walked away with the list. He did not smile or say thank you.

I took over the sophomore class that second week and gradually we watched Anato come alive in the classroom. He participated in the literature circle by taking a turn reading and listening as others read. During journal writing, he would write a few lines, then lay his head down and go to sleep.

After reading and discussing "Lather and Nothing Else" by Hernado Tellez, the students wrote a journal entry as though they were the barber making his defense to the other revolutionaries as to why he had not killed Captain Torres when the captain had come to him for a shave. Anato put his head down without writing. When asked why he wasn't writing, he answered, "Cause I'da killed him. There ain' no way I wouldn'a sliced 'im up."

"All right, then, you write a defense for killing him. Write down what you'd say when the military police came to get you."

Anato nearly filled a page. When we shared our entries, I specifically asked him to share his as the alternate voice. He read aloud about how it had all just been an accident and how the razor slipped in his nervousness. I could not help but be pleased that he had written so much and been willing to share it openly, but I was also very aware of the voice without conscience making flimsy excuses for deliberate actions in a very practiced manner.

That day seemed to be a turning point for Anato. He began to stay awake. The day of the first visit from my university supervisor, he decided to cause a fierce argument with the Chinese exchange student during the presentation, throwing papers in the other boy's face. As the days passed, he began to talk loudly to other students during class, flick people with rubber bands, or shoot them with paper wads. Some days I began to question whether I should have just left him sleeping. Was this disrespect some sort of payback for waking him up? I wondered if he really wanted my attention (which he never seemed to appreciate), or if he was just beginning to adjust to the new surroundings. Was I being tested to see if my interest in him was genuine, or was he just struggling to balance the "boy" inside with his tough protective outer veneer? Was he choosing negative attention over lack of attention when I tried not to appear partial or overly attentive, or was this a power struggle, just plain face-value manipulation? One thing was for certain: he was certainly more difficult awake than asleep.

On day I met Anato coming out of the office while everyone else was in class.

"Where were you yesterday, Anato?"

"Oh, I had a funeral," he was actually looking at me as he spoke.

"I'm sorry. Was it family?"

"No. It was a friend of mine in town."

"What happened?"

"He got burned in a fire. The house burned."

"How'd that happen? Was he drinking?"

"Yeah, I think so," Anato kind of smiled.

"My husband did that—years ago. I woke up to a house full of smoke. Really scared me." I detected a moment of engagement and went on to ask about where he lived, who he lived with, and where he had come from. For once he was talking to me. Eventually, I told him in a teasing way that he was in a bad position because we knew he was smart, a very capable student. "I know you can do the work if you just want to . . . is there anything I can do to help you *want* to?"

He looked down at me and answered thoughtfully, "I don't know."

I decided to leave him thinking, and said, "Well, I'm really sorry about your friend," and continued on into the office. I knew this kid was tugging at my heartstrings, but for the first time I realized how much he reminded me of my brother . . . my little brother who died eighteen years ago . . . my little brother who never got away from the tough street scene . . . away from drugs . . . my little brother that I did not/could not help. I had to determine that I would not put up a protective guard around my own feelings to keep Anato out, nor would I hinge great hopes on his survival; I would simply continue to drop little morsels here and there in hopes that he would continue to pick them up and follow without feeling threatened in any way. I could not help but hope that the death of his friend would cause Anato to re-evaluate those adolescent feelings of immortality and think seriously about what he wanted his future to be like.

The following week the students gave speeches about someone they liked or admired. Anato sauntered up to the podium, leaned down on it and said, "There is no one that I admire more than my Poppy." He went on to relate the story of his father growing up in Los Angeles, getting involved with gangs, and going to prison. In prison he got involved with the politics of the day. When he came out, he worked to organize farm laborers in California, and later became involved with the American Indian Movement, taking part in both the Alcatraz and Wounded Knee takeovers. No wonder this kid had to be tough, I thought. Like any other son, he wanted his father's love, respect, and approval.

Those glorious moments of connection with Anato were few. On a daily basis he kept himself somewhat aloof from me. He seemed to get annoyed when I nagged him about assignments. When I spoke quietly to him, he answered in a loud voice, yet when he wanted something from me, he used the traditional Indian quiet voice of respect. Anato was also becoming a discipline problem for other teachers. At one point Anato was sent to in-house suspension for use of foul language. However, in Anato's own mind, he had strictly adhered to acceptable euphemisms and was totally "innocent" of wrongdoing.

While he was in isolation, Anato had to take a test over part of a novel we were reading in class. The novel concerned a Paiute Indian who had been raised in a traditional manner and was then thrust into an Indian school in the early part of the century. The answers were to be in complete sentences. Anato's answers were the best in the class. His insight into the character, the situation, and even the author's portrayal were beyond my most hopeful expectations. However, his writing included no punctuation or capitalization. I took off points and reminded him that he had to write in complete sentences using proper punctuation. There were four tests, and Anato continued to give insightful, comprehensive answers in his own writing style. I was puzzled . . . was this rebellion or ignorance?

Once more I talked to Anato about his tests. I explained to him that even though he had a great analytical mind and could express his ideas very well, if he did not use standard English, he would never be respected for those ideas and would be looked upon as uneducated; "poor grammar destroys your credibility—no matter how much you really know." He finally admitted that he did not know basic punctuation rules. Finally, an important piece of the puzzle was revealed. I offered to give him a workbook to develop these skills. He adamantly refused. I told him it wouldn't be to carry around school but to take home. He calmed down and said he would think about it.

I could not help but marvel at this revelation. Here was a student who was not only a good reader but an avid one. This was the student who thought every student should be required to read *Bury My Heart at Wounded Knee* and was nearly always carrying around a book that he was reading for his own enjoyment. Usually good readers develop good grammar and punctuation skills just from seeing them modeled on the page. Although I was still puzzled, I felt good about seeing a clear goal to work toward.

Unfortunately Anato made some poor choices that caused him to be suspended from school soon after. By sleeping through classes, Anato had been able to barely pass by turning in a minimal amount of work. Awake, however, he was unequipped to deal with the stresses of everyday school life in an effective or successful manner.

Before he left school, I made sure that Anato had a basic skills workbook for punctuation and capitalization. I wondered who would help him with the "basic skills" for successful everyday living.

REFLECTION ON "AWAKENING THE BOY"

I wrote about Anato because, even though I tried very hard not to be partial with my energy and attention in the classroom, I knew that, within myself, I gave him more mental and emotional energy than any other single student. Once I made the decision to wake him up, I felt that I owed it to him to stick with him and not lose interest. I felt that I had willingly stepped into the ring of his battlefield and said, "I'm here to help you; we can beat this," and that I better not flinch. It seemed that he was going to put me through a kind of streetwise test of loyalty. I also had a sense that some of his other teachers had not made that mental commitment. They may have only seen that this kid was a lot of trouble.

I reviewed some information about "unmotivated students" that I had from my language arts methods class and thought that the list of characteristics might all fit Anato. From day to day I never knew whether he was going to be hyperactive and aggressive or withdrawn and sullen. In the section about families, I guessed that his parents were probably permissive, but I had no idea as to their expectations of him or whether they were neglectful or protective. I did not know for sure what Anato's learning style or modality might be. I did think that his needs were not being met in the classroom. I wondered how I might get some answers to the many question marks I was forming around Anato.

When Anato received "D's" on his report card, his father contacted the school and wanted weekly reports on how Anato was doing. Great, I thought. I thought back to my list of strategies for unmotivated students. First thing on the list, ensure that each of these students is emotionally connected with an adult (e.g., parent or mentor) who is supportive of the value of the student's schoolwork, and social and emotional welfare. In my experience few Native American parents would take that kind of stand and get involved with their child's schoolwork.

Unfortunately, other teachers seemed to think of this request from Anato's father as just one more paperwork burden on already overloaded shoulders instead of an opportunity for real communication. Instead of letters, only Anato's grade point average was turned into the office each week. Since I knew we had his father's attention, I began to look for things we might discuss with him about Anato. Each of my suggestions to my cooperating teacher that we call his father were kindly negated. I wondered why we were wasting this great opportunity for parent involvement.

This was one of the most frustrating points of student teaching. I had to try to force myself to be objective about how other people felt because I realized I was in a protected position. My job was not on the line; no one could fail to renew my contract. In this politically tense community, I could afford to make mistakes because, after all, I was just a "student teacher" and my naivete could easily be overlooked. Such was not the case for my cooperating teacher. Anato was not high on everyone's agenda, and there were too many agendas around for some people to want any unnecessary involvement with a community activist.

I was not completely prepared for all the trouble Anato caused in class, but I was aware that if he had been well adjusted, with well balanced coping skills, he probably would not have been sleeping in class in the first place. Problems like drinking, drugs, and "partying" all might may cause students to be sleepy in class but are in themselves indications of poor life skills. I am not sorry that I woke him up. He could not learn or make any progress while he was asleep. Anato's street-survival skills were not helping him in the classroom; they were hurting him. I have learned that no matter how hard I try to be impartial, there are always likely to be particular students who get their hooks into my heart. Everyone makes choices every day, and the quality of those choices greatly affects the quality of life. Education should equip students with tools to make good choices, to become wise decision makers. Anato needs that kind of education. For certain he should not be protected from the consequences of his poor choices. As long as he is awake, however, there is a possibility that Anato can learn to make better choices.

The Screening
Michael Burns

"Michael?"

OK. This is it. Remember to stand up straight and project confidence.

"Yes."

"Hi there, I'm Nancy Payne, Assistant Personnel Director for Cobb County Schools. It's nice to meet you."

I hate this. I never know how to reply to, "It's nice to meet you."

"Michael Burns. It's nice to meet you, too."

OK, she doesn't look like she's going to offer her hand. This is hell! With a man you usually get a handshake. A handshake seems to be completely optional with a woman; yet being a man, I feel an obligation to shake hands. It's what we're supposed to do.

"Come in and have a seat."

Which one should I sit in? Is this one of those psychological tests that identifies my weaknesses and strengths from the position of the chair I sit in? Remember to smile and show enthusiasm. Just pick a seat.

"Michael, that's where I've been sitting. Why don't you sit here."

"I'm sorry. OK."

I blew that. I am so good at being the fool, the person who gets sympathy for messing up. I feel comfortable playing the fool, the lackey. Do I want to teach so that I can get attention and sympathy from teenagers? Geez! My back and armpits are already starting to get soaked with sweat. Smile and sit up straight. Exude confidence.

"Michael, I see here from your resume and application that you grew up in Cobb County schools, so I'll give you the short version. After this interview, I'll forward my remarks and comments on your suitability to the county office, and from there all the principals will have access to your application."

Blah. Blah. Blah. Blah. Is she reading this? If this isn't her usual speech I shudder to imagine what is. Headline: *Young Man Bored to Death*. This speech sounds like it was canned during the Eisenhower administration, but I have to pretend like I'm hanging on her every word. What a performance! Mmm, she says she taught high school for 16 years. Does that mean I'll develop the ability to act excited about shit I don't care about? Do I have to develop that skill? Smile.

"For example, let's say a principal at Wallace—that's where you went, isn't it, Michael?"

"No, actually I went to Mill Grove."

"Oh, gosh. I'm sorry. It's just that I do so many of these interviews, it's hard to keep track of who's who."

Polite laughter—why am I laughing about this? There's nothing funny about her not knowing me from anyone else in a job interview.

"Anyway, the principal at Lancaster needs an English teacher so he requests the application files and schedules interviews . . . "

What can she possibly learn about me in a 20-minute interview? It would take at least an hour to cut through all the artificial bullshit and politeness. I should come up with a question about the system to show that I've been listening intently. Ask something to keep her talking.

" . . . this should take place around the mid-part of June when the principals . . . "

What am I gonna ask? She's almost done. Can she see any sweat on my face? I wonder if my eyes are red. It's these damn contacts. Kids in high school used to think I was always stoned—something about my "laid-back" personality and my "give-away" eyes. It was allergies and my contacts, but they didn't believe me. Keep making eye contact to let her know you're with her.

" . . . and then, if the fit is right, you've got a job."

More big hollow smiles. What the hell am I gonna ask her? Shit! Shit! Think!

"Well, I was wondering . . . "

Where are you going? What are you gonna ask her? Stall! Act like you're deep in thought.

"Was wondering about one of the county's approaches."

She's staring at me! How am I going to be a teacher when I can't even think of a decent question for an interviewer? Come on, what did I think of when I was practicing for this interview?

"What is the county doing with all the money generated from the Georgia Lottery?"

"The county is making a concerted effort . . ."

That ought to keep her busy. Give her a smile that says this is fascinating. Do I really want to teach in Cobb County? When I went to school in the system it was the epitome of a big, impersonal bureaucracy. Maybe I'll be the one to turn it around. Headline: *Burns Takes System to No. 1 in Nation*. I know I could do *something* to make it better. Do I really want to teach in Newt Gingrich's home territory? All my classmates at Agnes Scott think that teaching in Cobb County, home of soccer moms, never-ending strip malls, the anti-gay resolution and the white, homogenized, upper-middle class Republican, is like working for Hitler. Cobb pays well. They think you've got to be some conservative clone to want to teach in Cobb. I got a good education there, I guess. Maybe I just can't escape my roots. This is terrible. How much longer?

"Our emphasis is on getting computers into the schools at all levels, particularly the younger levels."

"Well, uh, the reason I asked that question is that I feel that writing and computing are many times inseparable."

Don't make everything sound like an apology. Have some backbone.

"Yes. I agree. Now let me ask you some questions, Michael. Start off by telling me about the best moment of your student teaching."

"Um . . ."

Say more than "Um." It's indecisive.

"Ah, well, that's a good question . . ."

What should I say? The best moment of my student teaching was either Spring Break or about 3:16 p.m. on my last day. I can't tell her that though. When I go to Agnes Scott for the Wednesday evening classes, I hear most of my fellow Masters in Teaching students talking about how much they love their students, and how they hated to see student teaching end. The other classmates moan about how much they dislike the students and teaching. I don't feel passionate either way. Student teaching was a great learning experience, but I never loved the kids. I think about them sometimes, sure, and I like to think that they think about me, but I don't ache for them the way others apparently do, nor do I think of teenagers as the enemy, like many of my classmates do. I've got so much time and money invested in this degree that I can't just give up on teaching. Still, I can't help but wonder if teaching isn't the wrong thing for me. Getting in front of a class for fifty minutes, five times a day was hard and rarely fun like I thought it would be. And it was more about disciplining than teaching English—I'm not good at telling people how to behave. I know that teaching is important, but is it worth the trouble? Come up with something to tell this woman.

"Well, I think the best moment of my student teaching came on my last day."

Honesty—the job loser!

"Mmm-hmm."

"It was in my seventh-period class, ninth graders, where I had been teaching a unit on poetry. I had, ah, asked the AP classes to fill out an evaluation of my uh, unit on All Quiet on the Western Front, *and I had some forms left over. I gave, um, the ninth-graders a test and, ah, as usual, my ability to time a lesson for that class was way off. I had, uh, about fifteen minutes left and no plans so I, ah, decided to give them a chance to fill out the forms."*

Stop the ah's and um's. Make up your mind and say something. Show some enthusiasm.

"At the end of the day, I read their comments, and I was, uh, touched."

Is that enough? Should I say that reading those evaluations made me feel like a god? It was how I envisioned teaching would be every day. They actually liked me for teaching them, or so they said. Remember to send this woman a thank-you note.

"Most of the class, uh, wrote about how much they enjoyed learning about poetry from me, and how much they learned about poetry. Uh, it felt really cool."

Felt really cool! Nice work, Beavis.

"The greatest thing was that this class was a source of great . . ."

Anxiety. Confusion. Doubt. Stop; be positive.

" . . . challenge for me. You know how ninth graders can be during the last period."

I needed to hear what they were saying a couple of times every day, rather than on my last day. I'll save those notes forever.

"Well, this class was all that and more, so to read that they had enjoyed my class and learned from me was a big thrill."

Did they really learn from me though? I'm haunted by the comment I wrote to Mrs. Edwards, my history teacher, whose class I didn't like: "Mrs. Edwards, you have been a very special teacher. I will never forget your class." She bought it and even made a special effort to say thanks to me after class for the nice note. Now I'm doing my penance for that sin. I've damned myself to never be able to fully enjoy compliments. Be positive and smile.

"That's one of the great rewards of teaching, Michael. I'm glad you got some positive feedback."

This is the kind of comment I will reply perfectly to when I'm in the car on the way home; now I just have to sit here with an expression that I hope says "Hire me! I'll be a great teacher!"

"Yes, I was walking on clouds for a couple of hours."

I can still remember what Earl said: "Mr. Burns, you've got a great teaching style. I'm sure you'll be a great teacher, just relax and peace out." I had somehow gotten through, I think. One girl from the AP class even gave me her address because she said she likes to keep in touch with her favorite teachers. When she handed me her address on a folded sheet of notebook paper, I wanted to cry. What is this woman writing on her paper? I feel so uncomfortable sitting here. Sit up straight. Smile.

"Now, Michael, tell me what your greatest challenge during student teaching was."

OK, I can't be too negative here or else I'll look like I don't want to teach. My greatest challenge? Getting up at 5:30 every morning and dragging into school. Learning how to exist on two hours of sleep and little or no contact with friends, family and fiancé. Kissing administrator ass. Having to enforce rules I found stupid. Trying to get the Xerox machine to work when I need 56 copies in three minutes. Grading papers until I fell asleep on them, then trying to conceal the drool spots. Enduring the endless pettiness in the faculty lunch room. Being treated as a pariah when I returned graded papers. Stop. Think of an incident that you can twist into something that makes you look good. Should I tell her about the fight in first period? About how I had absolutely no control over what was happening when Mark threw the open bottle of White-Out across the room, ruining backpacks and clothes along the way? Or how no one listened to me when I told them to sit down or to leave the room? What can I tell her?

"Um . . . that's another great question."

I'm drawing a blank. I have no idea what to say. The silence is killing me. I gotta say something just to break the tension. I want to run away and lock myself in a closet or something.

"Well, I guess the biggest challenge I faced during my student teaching . . . "

The answer is not written on your shoes or on the corner of the ceiling. Look at her.

"The greatest challenge of my student teaching would have to have been motivating the students. I had this idealized vision of little children who would sit down in an orderly manner each day and listen to what I would tell them about English and love me for telling them. I quickly learned that this was not the case. Each day was a battle to win their attention and respect. It was very frustrating to have some lesson plans that I thought were great go down the tubes because I couldn't get anyone to pay attention. I learned that in order for a lesson to go well, I had to show enthusiasm for it and show that I knew exactly what I was doing at all times. That's not easy. The frustrating part was knowing that each day was a whole new experience. Yesterday's perfect class, well-behaved and well-prepared, would remember nothing for today. Answers they had given me and concepts they swore they understood were completely foreign to them the next day."

She's smiling and writing something down. Nice answer. It's strange how comfortable and more articulate I am when I'm speaking about something in a negative way. I hate that about myself. I hope that was the kind of thing she wanted. Maybe I should say more? This silence is painful. I think my eagerness to please has a lot to do with why I want to teach. People always tell me I'd make a great teacher. Visions of a classroom often seep into my head. I see myself in front of the room, and the class is really getting into whatever I'm teaching. When I read a novel or a short story or even the newspaper, I think of how I would teach it to my imaginary class. In student teaching, I never saw even a shade of my imaginary class. Now, when I'm down about teaching, people keep telling me the same thing: "You'll make a great teacher," or "I'd love to have you as my teacher." I smile sheepishly and think about how dumb and inadequate I felt in front of the class. The part of me that wants to please people keeps me going though. She's taking an awfully long time to write. I wonder how she thinks this interview is going. I've got to say something to break this silence.

"Of course, I also found time management to be a challenge. No matter how much I planned or prepared, I couldn't judge how long it would take a class to get through the material, so I learned that it's much better to be over-prepared than under-prepared."

Arghh. Now I've basically admitted I couldn't plan a decent lesson. Of course, she's writing more, and I'm twitching in the silence. I'm not saying anything. Project confidence with your body language.

"One final question for you, Michael. Explain why you want to be a high school English teacher?"

"Um . . . ."

REFLECTION ON "THE SCREENING"

"Oh, really?" or "Wow! That's great," expressed with a look of "I can't believe anyone would subject themselves to that." Those were the reactions I would get when I met people and told them I was working on my Masters in Teaching Secondary English. I had never taught before and the program allowed me to get teaching certification while getting a graduate degree. Friends, who meant well and knew my tendency to jump from job to job, would ask all sorts of questions about school and teaching. The well-meaning subtext of those questions was "Are you sure that's what you want to do?" Before student teaching, I was sure. I was sure that my commitment to making a difference in young people's lives, my love of reading and writing, my skill in those subjects, my understanding of what teenagers liked, and my knowledge of good teaching were enough to make me a successful teacher. After student teaching started, I wasn't so sure. When I found a few moments in the day to get to the faculty restroom, I saw my brow wrinkled with a question, too: "Why do I want to teach?"

That question was the genesis for my story. Student teaching had ended a few weeks earlier, and it hadn't been awful, but it hadn't been good. Student teaching was much harder and much less rewarding than I expected. I had expected that student teaching would confirm that teaching was the right career for me, but instead it left me full of doubt. The school where I did my student teaching had a well-deserved good reputation—supportive administration, well-behaved students, and excellent resources—so I couldn't blame anyone other than myself for the less-than-magical experience. I couldn't help thinking that I had made a huge mistake by choosing to teach.

While I was warring with myself over my future as a teacher, all my classmates at Agnes Scott College in Decatur, Georgia, were happily plotting their careers or decisively swearing off teaching and looking for new options. When I would ask fellow students about how student teaching went for them, hoping to find some company for my misery, I usually got a small amount of complaining followed by enthusiastic talk of getting a real teaching job. I felt alone in my uncertainty.

One of the last classes in our program was an excellent writer's workshop for teachers taught by Christine Cozzens. The course required a final paper about an aspect of our student teaching experience and during peer-editing sessions, I would read classmates' papers about successes they had and students they enjoyed—all positive stories. I had no such stories. I struggled deeply with the assignment and went through many, drastically different drafts trying to find a way to voice my frustration and confusion. When I tried to copy my classmates' enthusiastic attitudes, I felt like a hoax, and when I expressed my feeling of disappointment I got depressed—I had invested too much time, emotion, and money to just walk away from teaching.

I was swimming in this doubt while a host of school systems were doing on-campus interviews. It was only after I had half-heartedly gone through a string of seemingly pointless, jump-through-the-hoop bureaucratic on-campus interviews that the premise of "The Screening" came to me. Using an inner and outer voice allowed me to express my inner confusions while outwardly I was still going through the motions of becoming a teacher.

"Why do we want to teach?" That question is the center of the story. It's a question we all ask ourselves in light of other choices which offer more pay and prestige, and less effort and time. The answer is usually something about "making a difference." But what does "making a difference" really mean in a society influenced by Hollywood's portrayal of teachers as superheroes—able to leap tall layers of bureaucracy in a single bound and transform wild classrooms into learning centers in a couple hours, i.e., *Dangerous Minds, Stand by Me,* and *Stand and Deliver*? I admit that I've watched these movies and television shows and wished that I could be like those teachers, but the real world doesn't open and close in tight, sound-tracked, two-hour chunks. It's messy and ambiguous and frustrating.

Making a difference isn't something that you can prepare for, either. Before student teaching, I didn't realize this. Making a difference means opting for the opportunity to do something positive in a negative world, to do the right thing even when it's the hard thing, to be the stepping stone to the achievement of others, to sacrifice money, time and self for the benefit of others, to return the favor of attention and support that someone gave to each of us.

Teaching isn't easy. After doing it for a while, it's still maddening and messy. I suspect it always will be. Committing myself to teaching is no longer a sure thing like it was in my days prior to student teaching. My experience has taught me that few things involved with teaching are sure—students, parents, administration. But I am still sure that teaching, despite its many difficulties, is important. That is a good enough reason for me to keep going.

Settling In
Sharon McCoy Robbins

I have never been a particularly capricious person, but in 1982 I decided to move to New York. Ostensibly, I reasoned that in a big city I could teach and pursue graduate school. Looking back, I am not sure what force propelled me, but I do know that once the decision had been made, my shattered life took form, and all my energies that spring and summer were spent to one purpose and one destination—New York City.

I checked into the Martha Washington Hotel for Women and went out to survey my new home. That night I walked and walked, blocks and blocks down Park Avenue to Grand Central Station, then over to Fifth by Saks with the elegant mannequins posturing in the windows, by the Gothic spires of St. Patrick's and by the bronze mirrors of Trump Tower flickering with lights. Seeing the Plaza bearing her genteel grace and the horse drawn carriages flanking Central Park, I decided to turn around and walk over to Lexington past the offices and shops down to the intimate quietness of Gramercy Square. I was no longer conscious of the stretch of my leg or the contact of my foot with the pavement as I tried to find the lyrics of the city, feeling like Joshua claiming the land.

The next morning the sun blasted through my window. I could not respond. I lay in that bed perfectly still—a mummy wrapped in fear. For the first time, I allowed myself a glimpse into the seriousness of my seemingly irrevocable step. All the stories I had ever heard: the opera singer who ended up living in a box, the tourists who were mugged, the woman who was assaulted on the subway, and others more hideous, crowded into my consciousness and violated my courage.

Somehow, I quieted those voices and headed in the general direction of Court Street in Brooklyn where I knew I would find the Board of Education for the five boroughs of New York City. I remember the old subway cars, burdened with graffiti, they reminded me of circus wagons. However, inside these cars, there were no festive spirits. It was hot and my dress stuck to my thighs. "Sweat" had a different connotation here beneath the asphalt of the city than there on the beaches of my home.

For the next three weeks, I filled my days with disheartening trips to Court Street and my nights with the impressive free cultural activities that New York offers, determined to compensate for my thirty years of deprivation as quickly as possible. I got the last standby ticket to the last performance of *A Midsummer's Night Dream* in Central Park. I traveled to the World Trade Center to hear Ntozake Shange read and personally autograph her newest book, *Sassafras, Cypress and Indigo*. And I became well acquainted with New York's fine art museums and galleries.

Until the next morning of each day when, once again, I would travel to Court Street. Never in my life had I encountered such a quagmire of bureaucracy as I encountered at the Board of Education in New York City. If I were told one thing one day, it would be contradicted the next. Nevertheless, one afternoon long after Labor Day, I stood in a long line feeling much less optimistic than I had on my first visit. A woman came through yelling, "If anyone wants to teach down, there are openings in District Five." I had no idea what "teaching down" meant, but I knew whatever it meant that I was ready and willing to do it!

I soon discovered that "teaching down" simply meant teaching at a Junior High or Intermediate school. I was given a list of schools that had openings. That night I discussed my employment prospects with an acquaintance I had made at the Martha Washington Hotel for Women and her friend, a native New Yorker. After he looked at the addresses of the schools, he informed me in a most condescending manner that District Five was in Harlem, and that not anyone he knew would consider taking the train into Harlem. I hated his superior attitude. No warning of his could dissuade me. I needed a job!

The next day in triple A fashion, I looked at a subway map and plotted my trip into Harlem. I ended up almost traversing the island of Manhattan on 125th Street in my very high heels and very Floridian clothes. I was vaguely conscious of how conspicuous I looked and acutely conscious that I was an interloper in this uptown setting.

I finally reached I.S. 195, the Roberto Clemente School, where I was greeted warmly, even cheerfully. The school secretaries were joking and laughing. I had determined long ago that the attitude of the school secretaries was an accurate barometer for the climate of any school. A friendly gentleman escorted me to my interview. On the way he showed me a beautiful atrium planted with all varieties of lilies; splashes of yellow and orange and all shades of green exploded before my eyes, lively and fresh like children's first crayola sketches, right there in the middle of that school, right in the middle of Harlem. A very professional woman interviewed me and hired me "just like that." I was to report the next day and begin teaching drama and French to eighth graders at I.S. 195. Finally, I received the school tour where I took note that in the teacher's cafeteria, grits were being served for breakfast.

After teaching in New York only a few weeks, I began to really believe that certain members of the Board of Education in New York literally stayed awake at night scheming ingenious ways to torment their teachers. One way was to pay their teachers a salary on which they could not possibly subsist. Another was to give teachers half their summer pay at the end of June when New York City schools dismissed and the other half when they returned after Labor Day. Another particularly unkind practice, an unwritten law in New York, was to invariably give new teachers the lowest academic achievers, repeaters if possible, the most troubled, the worst disciplinary problems in the school. So it was when I went to I.S. 195. An infamous class known as 351 came to me twice daily, once for drama and once for French. I don't know how much drama they learned that year—we certainly had some drama—and I'm not sure what French word they could remember today. I can tell you, though, we all learned a lot that year.

Besides the usual tricks: giving false names, changing the clocks, switching desks, the students had some very inventive ways of having fun with the new teacher. For example, one day I took them out, and after some secret cue was given, they all hopped on a bus and disappeared. There they went—my entire class on a bus to who knows where. That was the last time we went out.

The first day of class they came in snickering. "She talks funny. She's from the country. She rides horses." I knew it was no use saying that I wasn't from the country—that there were malls and high-rises in my hometown. Maybe if I ignore them, they will tire of these jokes, I thought. I didn't understand about the horses, though. After a few days of listening to them talk, it dawned on me—the television show Dallas! They watched it on Friday nights and that was the most they knew about the South. If I had a drawl, then I must have lived on a ranch and must have ridden horses.

My most vivid recollection of that first day was of this very "smart-mouthed" boy. He sat in his desk, legs out in the aisle, leering at me and challenging me with his brown eyes flashing. Other students told me his name was Artie, and then they told me he was Ralph. He was the strongest in the class and appeared to be a bully. The other students silently reverenced him.

Those first few weeks we had some good days, and we had some not so good ones. The students started saying "Y'all" and "Hey" and I started saying "Yo." I learned what it means to be "dissing" someone and what "buggin-out" meant. To be "dissing" was being "disrespectful" and "buggin-out" meant to lose control.

After teaching for several weeks, I was talking about Ralph with his homeroom teacher and discovered that Ralph was one of the best basketball players to ever come through I.S. 195, and that Ralph was not Ralph at all but a girl, named Yolanda, who had been having a very good time with the new teacher from the country. On some days, Yolanda would be the nicest student in my class. On other days she would be the wildest, the meanest, the most difficult to handle.

I had deceived myself into thinking that I could empathize with these children until one day two girls volunteered to stay after school to wash my boards. They sponged and wiped all of the streaks off those old blackboards until they glistened and shined, but still they kept sponging and wiping, not wanting their task to end. I found myself listening to them to talk. "Last night, my brother got shot. He came home and he was bleeding real bad. His face was so bloody I couldn't recognize him and all over his shirt—red blood. Mama said we'd have to find a doctor—it wouldn't be safe to take him to the emergency room, but the police came before we had a chance. They just took him off. I hope they fixed him up!" At first, I thought they were teasing the new teacher, but as I listened, I realized that they were completely unaware of my presence.

For one brief moment, I tried to see through this open window into the homes, the families, the lifestyles these students led. After that afternoon, I knew I could be kind to these students, I could be the best teacher that I knew how to be, but I could not really relate to their lives outside the red brick walls. There was nothing in my background that could remotely compare with what these students faced everyday when they left my classroom.

One day I returned to class after lunch to hopefully teach drama to 351. When I entered the class, they were particularly stirred up. Students were out of their desks, engaged in some "inappropriate" name calling, shoving, pushing. The intercom in my room was broken. Panicked, I ran out into the hall. In the past, I had always been able to find some authority figure patrolling nearby to assist me, but there was not one person in sight. All of a sudden, I felt helpless. I was defeated; they had won. I started crying. I stood there humiliated by the hot tears blotching my face. All the frustrations of the past few weeks came shouting to me, "You're a failure! You're not accomplishing anything! You were a fool to move here!"

Then to my amazement, I heard Yolanda yelling at the class. "You go too far . . . you made the teacher cry . . . you need to be nice to her . . .you shouldn't be mean to her . . . you went too far!" I pictured her standing on my desk barking out orders to the class. In a few moments Yolanda came out into the hall and said, "Miss McCoy, it's okay. You can come back into the class now." Somehow, I knew despite our dubious beginning, I could trust her. I went back into the classroom, and we had drama class. I had previously assigned an exercise to mime some everyday chores: carrying groceries to the front door, catching a cab, boarding a subway. I was amazed at their control and focus. The class was a textbook success.

I don't recommend spontaneous crying as a regular pedagogical practice, but it worked! Class 351 was very well-behaved for many weeks. And Yolanda became my protector, one of the many guardian angels I would have in New York. If the class became too disruptive, she would quiet them down. If a student talked back to me, she would straighten them out. Once during a particularly brutal fight outside my classroom, I jumped in, horrified at the way the students were hitting each other in the face. She pulled me out. "Miss McCoy, they'll mess you up!" And there were many other times when Yolanda intervened for me.

In June, the eighth grade graduated, and I was busy moving into my new apartment. I had joyfully relinquished my efficiency at Lexington and 33rd for a spacious, one bedroom, Westside apartment with panoramic views of Central Park for $350 a month! I had acquired an evening teaching job with the Teamster's Union in their education department. This added an extra $200 to my weekly income and meant that I could consistently afford food and shelter in the city, a great comfort to me and my faraway family. I had my books and beloved art posters sent and eventually my furniture. I had become intimate with a handful of bright, interesting people. I had "settled in."

On the day of graduation, Yolanda came into the teacher's lounge to say her good-byes. Her hair was fixed—a hint of pink blush and lipstick. She was beautiful! She wore a pastel blue print dress that complemented her creamy, cocoa brown skin. Other students gently teased her about her changed demeanor. Faculty members expressed their praise. She just smiled, a little sheepishly, savoring the compliments, seeming to have found reconciliation within herself and to have traveled at least part of that very complex and chaotic passage from adolescent to young adult.

Looking back, I cannot imagine what made that pretty young woman hide her femininity that year to dress and act like a boy or what made her want to bully the boys and dominate the class or what familiar chord was struck in her life when she saw me crying. Had there been another woman who cried? I do know that two very dissimilar lives intersected that year, and I believe we were, forever, the better for it.

REFLECTION ON "SETTLING IN"

I was inspired to write "Settling In" when enrolled in the Writing Project at the University of North Florida, also known as "JaxWrites." During "author's chair," time set aside each day for reading aloud original pieces, several teachers read personal narratives about their teaching experiences and lives. It occurred to me that I had many stories about living in New York and that, in fact, the whole time I was there I was mentally writing stories. I read this story at our JaxWrites graduation and then again when I visited the project during the summer of 1996. During a discussion following the reading, three topics emerged which seemed to be of the most interest to educators.

First, several teachers stated that they appreciated my writing about losing control in the classroom. Individually, they related their own stories about feeling helpless in a classroom. One teacher spoke of the shame a teacher feels when unable to "teach" because of discipline problems. Most said that when they had found themselves in a situation where they were not "in control," they had experienced feelings of failure, thinking no other educator had ever lost control of a class. More than one teacher admitted that they had never felt free to discuss their "situation" with another educator. As new teachers, we often feel as though we have to prove ourselves, and we are reluctant to ask for help. When we are new to teaching, we are particularly vulnerable to feeling isolated and helpless. The real defeat of a new teacher comes, then, not in losing control of the classroom but in remaining isolated and succumbing to those voices that tell us we are failures.

Another issue which, I feel, is significant in the story is the "human" element. Yolanda and I made a connection. Even though I wrote, "There was nothing in my background that could remotely compare with what these students faced everyday when they left my classroom," we are all human beings regardless of our different socioeconomic backgrounds. Somehow, across those vast differences, a bridge was formed—a bridge founded on trust and mutual respect. Surely, trust is one of the most crucial elements to the classroom climate, and only when it is present can teaching be effective.

When Yolanda asked me back into the classroom, at least three changes occurred. First, I put myself into Yolanda's hands, and she responded to the trust I gave her. Second, the class saw any bravado I had tried to maintain crumble. Third, I believe when 351 saw me crying, they saw that this Southern girl, who talked funny, was a person who cried and laughed and dreamed just as they did. And, finally, I knew that Yolanda and this class were worth whatever hardness I had endured. I could not relate to living in Harlem, and they could not know what it meant to grow up in a North Florida coastal town. Nevertheless, we found each other that day.

When I read this story aloud to teachers, the race/gender issue was raised. One teacher felt that when I said Yolanda's skin was "cocoa brown" that I was making a racial slur because the story had made it quite clear she was African American. Another teacher defended my statement referring to the Langston Hughes poem "Harlem Sweeties," in which Hughes describes the beauties of Harlem with various phrases, "Walnut tinted / Or cocoa brown . . . Caramel, brown sugar, / a chocolate treat . . . Ginger, wine-gold, / persimmon, blackberry." She used the Hughes lines to support my description. Certainly, I did not mean to demean Yolanda in any way by my description. She truly looked beautiful to me. Still, another teacher felt that she had only become acceptable to me when she dressed like a girl. I did not mean to suggest that Yolanda would never play basketball again or rough house with the boys. I think most girls go through some transition at that age. It is the "rite of passage" age for most young adults. I do believe Yolanda found a new pride in being a female, and I was, frankly, glad to see her dress and look like a girl!

Finally, there is one other issue which did not emerge from the discussion this summer. This concerns the teaching of writing. It was extremely beneficial for me as a writing teacher to again experience the process of writing, one feature of the Writing Project that makes it so valuable to teachers. I had not allowed myself the luxury of writing creatively since undergraduate studies. In graduate school, I had become bogged down with academic writing, and after writing my thesis, I felt as if I never wanted to write again. In the rewriting stages of this story, I found several passages where I had opted for easy, vague prose. The rewriting of these not only helped me as a writer but as a teacher of writing. I feel I am much more in touch with the process and plan to write with my students much more, so that I can stay in touch.

To conclude, I stayed in New York one more year. I then moved to the Chicago area, taught school, and obtained a master's degree in English from University of Illinois at Chicago. Then, through a series of events, I moved home and married a man with a home two blocks from where I grew up close to the Atlantic Ocean. Three and one-half years ago we adopted a baby boy who is now in the three-year-old program where I teach. We ride our bikes on the same streets and go to the same beach where I played and explored throughout my childhood. I always tell people, "You can come home!"

1973 in Review
Linda Powers

In August 1972, I began my teaching career in a small town within driving distance of Stillwater where my husband could finish his degree at Oklahoma State University. At this high school of less than 50 students in grades 9 though 12, I was the English department. Also I was senior class sponsor which meant I supervised the concession stand for basketball season; the proceeds funded the senior trip for the twenty seniors. I sponsored the pep club, the librarians club, directed the school plays, and served as the high school librarian. All this in addition to teaching 9th, 10th, 11th, and 12th grade English. However, being young and excited about teaching, I did not realize four preparations and five extra duty assignments were a lot of responsibility and would be a lot of work.

I found an even greater challenge in motivating the rural teens who had little interest in grammar, writing, and the canon that I believed was the curriculum that they needed. Armed with the *Warriner's* grammar text and literature anthologies full of wonderful classical pieces, I was determined to educate these youngsters!

I worked the students hard, and I worked hard. Believing I needed to cover every piece in the literature books, I often read the stories one night ahead of the students as I fought to keep up with grading the essay assignments I made every week, in addition to the countless grammar exercises I had the students do.

I constantly worried that I was not covering everything they needed to know. But the classes were so diverse. In my ninth grade class, for example, I had Jimmy, who no matter what I asked him to read or write, devoured the task eagerly and was ready for the next assignment. His writing style was far more sophisticated than that of his peers and his ideas were more insightful than most of the senior students' papers. There was Jana in whom I saw and encouraged natural creativity, especially in writing poetry. Today she is an English teacher.

But there were also Lester and Walter, twins who lived in a house with no running water and consequently had poor personal hygiene habits. Their parents had not expected twins so after the doctor delivered Lester, he laid the child aside to help birth the other baby, and as a result, Lester did not get oxygen for a few minutes. Brought up in a home life of illiteracy and poverty, the boys still printed in the 9th grade and read on a first or second grade level. They, of course, failed everything they did, except the creative writing assignments. I felt it was important to not discourage them completely. Though they never seemed discouraged. At Christmas Lester brought me a metal cube that he had made in Vo-Ag. I did not quite know what it was, but before I could guess, Lester said it was a paperweight. And a dandy one it was! Later I discovered from the Vo-Ag instructor that it was the product of an exercise they did in welding to practice running beads. Lester never got beyond the practice. But he was proud of what he made and he wanted to give it to his teacher. In the spring Lester brought me some jonquils one day, and I praised and praised him for the lovely flowers and immediately got a glass from the cafeteria to put them in water. The next day Lester came in with a large brown grocery bag. When I asked him what he had he said, "These are for you. You liked the flowers so much, I thought you might like the bulbs."

Night after night I worked on lesson plans or graded papers until midnight. I spent weekends grading. There was little life beyond school, especially during basketball season. Running the concession stand meant being at the gym at 4:00 p.m. and staying until 11:00 or 11:30 because there were boys' and girls' basketball teams in every grade, 4th through 8th, and each played a game. Next, the high school girls would play and finally the high school boys' teams.

Since the games began at 5:00, I had to unlock the booth about 4:00 so the Dr. Pepper man could unload the syrup and carbonated water and check the pop dispenser to ensure its good working order. This hour went quickly as I got the hot dogs out to defrost, checked the bun supply, displayed some candy bars and gum, and visited with the moms who brought sandwiches and cookies to sell. Before the first spectators arrived, I heated up the popcorn machine and made sure I had the first batch popping because the aroma of fresh hot popcorn was a traditional part of the atmosphere and it was a real draw to the concession booth. Because the games began so early, patrons would come straight from work and our concession stand provided their evening meal. Basketball games and other school activities were the hub of the social wheel in Billings. There was no movie house, arcade, or other source of entertainment. School activities provided entertainment as well as a time and place for people to visit, so *everyone* came to the games whether they had children in school or not.

I didn't work the stand alone, but I had to prepare it and make certain the crew was there and had plenty of change. At about 11:30 I had to collect the cash that would finance the senior trip to Fin and Feather Lodge on Lake Tenkiller in May. Before I could leave the gym, I had to clean the popcorn machine and lock up the goodies that did not sell.

During the ball games, I spent most of my time with the pep club because as the sponsor, I kept the official record of merits and demerits, and a complicated set of bookkeeping it was! There were demerits for being out of uniform, being late, sitting with a boyfriend, going to the bathroom more than twice a game and being gone for more than five minutes at a time.

Fridays were long and a lot of work, but I didn't mind because they were the only nights I didn't do paperwork. Grading papers was an endless job that year. All other nights I sat at our dining room table and checked grammar exercises, vocabulary quizzes, and pop quizzes over reading assignments and read stacks upon stacks of essays and poems. This endless task of paper shuffling went on all the time at all places; whenever I got into the car to ride somewhere, I took papers to grade. A National Council of Teachers of English bookbag full of assignments was my constant companion.

But besides all the work, I had a lot of freedom in that small rural school. If I wanted to take the kids outside for reading under the elm tree, I did. If we wanted to go into the auditorium to do a readers' theater presentation of *Our Town* with commercials between the acts, we did. If I wanted to take the students to the library, I had to check with no one, except myself, because I was the librarian. If I wanted a film, I ordered it. Of course, I also had to thread the 16 mm projector to show it. There were no department heads, curriculum guides, curriculum supervisors, or assistant administrators to get permission from. I enjoyed the freedom to do as I pleased.

On the other hand, I had no real support system either. As a beginning teacher I had no files or supplementary materials (except what I bought), and there were no other English teachers from whom to borrow materials or get advice. There was an experienced history teacher, Mr. Waggoner, to whom I would go for advice. There was also another first year teacher, Pat, with whom I became really good friends. We supported each other as we discussed school and teaching.

I really never missed a greater support system because I did not know I was supposed to have one. My confidence and enthusiasm compensated for the lack of guidance. In actuality I knew very little about teaching writing. That was something that just had not been addressed in my college courses, but I thought it was imperative that the students write all the time. So they did. I had the students enter every writing contest I could find; they were constantly sending off poetry and essays. In fact they had 10 or 12 pieces published in the *Noble County Poetry Anthology* that year, and Jana won first place!

I was thoroughly enamored with being a teacher, and I worked very hard preparing lectures, creating activities, exercises and tests, and grading papers. I ignored the butterflies that fluttered in my stomach some mornings. Perhaps I was fearful and would never admit it. Perhaps I was afraid I might not know it all, or some student might challenge my authority. But they never did. When I interviewed for the position, the superintendent told me some of the boys were serious discipline problems, and he wondered if I could handle them since I was only three to four years older than the seniors. I had assured him I could. Luckily, there were no serious discipline problems. I never questioned why. I just more or less expected the students to be good, and they were.

At first I pretended to have a rather stern demeanor, but I was never afraid to laugh with the students. Once during junior play practice, they played a prank of tying me to my director's chair, but they let me go; everyone laughed and play practice continued. They also bought me flowers after both the junior and senior plays because they knew how nervous I was that they might forget their lines. They gave me a corsage to wear the night of the plays and presented me with red roses after the curtain call. There were other gifts that year, like the little silver heart necklace from my first senior class.

It was a good first year, and though there had been a lot of work and stress, I had many good feelings about being a teacher. As I sat at graduation for the Billings High School Class of 1973, I felt great pride in their accomplishment and aching sorrow at seeing these people whom I was very fond of leave. I wondered if I had done all that I could do to help prepare them for the life ahead, but there was no doubt in my mind about my choice to be a teacher.

REFLECTION ON "1973 IN REVIEW"

Writing about my first year of teaching has awakened in me a myriad of conflicting feelings. I have been reminded that it is an exciting, but also a stressful and sometimes frightening time. The first year of teaching is in many ways like being thrown into a pool of water and being told to swim. Some people have had instruction to help them survive; some have not. Some have a love of the water and the problems swimming presents; some do not. Similarly, some beginning teachers have more desire and preparation than others. I was lucky in that I had both.

As a curriculum and instructional specialist for the last two years, I have worked with first-year teachers through our district's teacher induction program. Our district did much research on the entry-year experience before we implemented our program. My own experience bore out what we found. Factors contributing to a difficult first year teaching assignment include being assigned to an area that does not match the teacher's background and training, having multiple preparations, having time-consuming and demanding extracurricular responsibilities, working with remedial and/or unmotivated students, and having to "float" between classrooms. Few professions have the "day one" expectations that the teaching profession does; first-year teachers are expected to go into that classroom on the first day and conduct class like the veteran teacher across the hall. Beginning teachers are often reluctant to ask for help because they do not want to appear incompetent, and experienced teachers often forget what it is like to be a beginning teacher so a double barrier to assistance develops.

Simon Veenman (1984) from the Netherlands did a meta-analysis in which he identified 91 studies in which beginning teachers reported their problems and concerns. Classroom discipline was the key problem in 77 of the 91 studies identified. Most beginning teachers, because of their lack of confidence, feel a need to control the class and its learning. They may set themselves up in an adversarial situation with the students and invite conflict rather than letting a relationship develop. Because discipline is such a major concern with beginning teachers, my district has four days of training in positive discipline that focuses on building relationships as the foundation to effective classroom management.

Novice teachers often overwork themselves because they feel a responsibility and a need to control all the learning in the class. Additionally, they feel pressure from administrators who are perhaps keeping an especially watchful eye on the new teachers; administrators will be evaluating the first-year teachers to not only renew contracts, but to see if the teacher deserves certification.

My thoughts have turned to how we might help teachers during the crucial first year. Providing a mentor is ideally an excellent means to help an entry-year teacher, but in practice, mentorship does not always provide the support intended. Some mentors may not contribute the time the new teacher needs, or perhaps a relationship conducive to helping the young teachers does not develop.

Life for the first-year teacher can be isolated and lonely, especially in a large school district. Time should be provided for beginning teachers to come together to reflect on and discuss issues pertinent to them. Encouraging beginning teachers to keep a journal might be helpful. Rekindling the first-year experience for all teachers and administrators on staff, thus creating an awareness of the need for support from the staff for the beginning teachers, might be most helpful. I believe it is the responsibility, the duty of experienced teachers to support, inspire, guide, and nurture the growth of beginning teachers. My first year was without formal support; however, all twenty-five teachers in that small system were helpful. I sought out my own mentor, Dick Waggoner. Through discussion and reflection, Pat Carter and I constructed our own understanding of what teaching was and should be.

REFERENCE
Veenman, S. (1984). Perceived problems of beginning teachers. *Review of Educational Research, 54* (2) 143–178.

Chapter 3

Changes

> What I have learned from the teachers with whom I have worked is that
> . . . there is no simple answer to how to work with children in the
> classroom. It is a matter of being present as a whole person, with your
> own thoughts and feelings, and of accepting children as whole people,
> with thoughts and feelings. (Duckworth, 1987, p. 121)

The stories in this chapter focus on how change followed an epiphany or realization by the author, often as a result of reflecting on what a student has to teach the teacher. "Apart from the Rest" by Toni Pantier tells the story of Jody, who leads Pantier to reexamine her thinking about the effect of inclusion on her students and teachers.

"Teaching Is a State of Mind: Relationship—the Heart of Curriculum" by Sheryl Lain tells of two schools, one on a reservation, another a large "factory" school. Lain's story illustrates what she knows "in [her] bones that students learn better through relationships." David Pulling's "Imitation of the Living Voice: What I Learned from Quintilian and a Few Eighth Grade Student Writers" shares a lesson he learned about teaching writing from his students.

"Journal Writing" by Joanne Bergbom makes a case for journal writing for herself and her students. "Writing becomes my opportunity to examine and clarify," she writes. "Monique's Gifts" by Steffie Corcoran is another story about a student teaching her teacher a lesson about teaching and life. In "My, My, My Delilah" Carole Weigand narrates the story of a student she did not know how to reach and what she learned about the experience.

REFERENCE
Duckworth, E. (1987). *The having of wonderful ideas*. New York: Teachers College Press.

Apart from the Rest
Toni Pantier

Slowly faltering down the hall, she wove her way through a number of groups of sixth grade students engaged in exchanges of conversations about summer events and tidbits of gossip. At one time or another they all seemed to notice her, each in their own way. Some managed a casual glance or two, almost as if noticing her embarrassed them. Other stares were of the lengthy sort, requiring the buzz of conversation to stop. The gaping seemed to go unnoticed as she plodded on, limping on her right foot and veering in that same direction.

When she reached the two, side-by-side sixth grade classroom entrances, she spoke something very slowly to another student who also hesitated at the doors. Her mouth, partially contorted to one side, garbled the words. He nervously asked her to repeat herself, obviously not understanding what she had uttered. This time, more deliberately, she carefully asked, "How-do-you-know-which-room-you -are-in?" He studied her for several moments, as if processing her words, and suddenly replied, "Ohhh! Uhhh! Look on the list on each door." He then slid away quickly, probably to avoid additional conversation. Her hand shook as she ran her finger down the list on the other sixth grade classroom door.

Suddenly I felt almost suffocated with fear. What if her name is not on Mr. Raymer's class roster? Panic! That will mean that she is on my list! In my classroom! What will I do? What if I can't understand her? What if I have to ask her to repeat herself over and over in class? Please, please let her be on Mr. Raymer's list! Lack of confidence welled up inside of me as I quickly drew visual images of teaching a student whom I couldn't even understand.

Uneasily I glanced back at her just in time to catch a crooked smile. Then, sighing, she resumed her awkward movement into the other classroom. With tremendous relief, I quickly dismissed the intimidating thoughts that had raced through my mind. My panic was for naught. I greeted a few more of my own students, the bell rang, and we all busied ourselves with the usual first day of school activities.

Late that morning the two sixth grades changed classes for math just long enough for the teachers to explain rules and expectations. As some students filed in and others filed out, dread unexpectedly surrounded me again. The girl that I had observed in the hall limped into my room. Somehow it had not registered that I could have her for math. My mind raced with repeated thoughts from earlier in the day. However, no time remained to dwell on my fears. I talked, the students all sat in their seats, and they listened. Few questions came up.

As she slowly filed out of the room, the other students' impatience for her to hurry up was already becoming evident. Nevertheless, she stopped on her way out the door mumbling something to me and grinning her awkward grin. Panic burned inside of me. I didn't understand a word! But I grinned, since she grinned, and patted her on the shoulder. She remained in the doorway. Very carefully she said,"I-don't-think-you-understood-me.-That's-okay.-I-said-you're-nice.- I-like-you." How did she know I hadn't understood her? That dumb, embarrassed feeling that creeps all over me when I feel put on the spot must show! Telling her that I was glad to have her in my math class seemed the right thing to do next. Grinning, she plodded on back to Mr. Raymer's room. Could she tell I was lying? Did she know how panicked I felt about the entire situation?

Communicating with Jody was stressful for me. Patiently she would repeat things over and over again. Gradually I learned to understand her slurred speech more easily. Her extremely poor motor movements made her math papers a nightmare to read. Her assignments always lacked a number of finished problems. I decided to speak with her in private when the next opportunity arose. Several days later when I had playground duty, I visited with her.

Finding her was easy. She was alone, in a world by herself—too different for others to feel comfortable including her. Complimenting her on how hard she worked in math, I suggested that, since writing was so tedious for her, she could automatically do the "evens" any time I assigned an entire page and do every other one when I assigned "evens" or "odds." Looking at me in puzzlement, she responded, "I-can-do-as-much-as-anyone-else.-I-need-the-practice.-I'm- just-slow -at-it." Her reaction surprised me! I wasn't prepared with a rebuttal. Many times through the year she had incomplete assignments, but always she completed much more than half. I rewarded her efforts by quietly giving her full credit.

Board work made me nervous when Jody took her turn. It seemed to take her an eon to complete a problem. The kids had quickly learned that rude comments were not acceptable in our classroom, but they continued to fidget with impatience as we waited. Jody always seemed to enjoy teaching her messy masterpiece, beginning with something similar to "You'll-have-to-listen-carefully- to-understand-me." Unfortunately, I appreciated her efforts a great deal more than the class did. She was different, and they kept up those walls against her.

After lunch each day it always broke my heart to see Jody lumber in to math with food stains all down her front. Coming from a family where appearance was obviously very unimportant, the food spills just added to her already disarrayed look. The other children quietly made fun of her stained clothing. It was just another thing that set her apart from the rest. One day she came in at recess to make up a test wearing a blouse that looked a bit newer than most. Feeling unsure of how to approach the subject, I took a deep breath and thought, here goes! Telling her how pretty she looked in her blouse, I mentioned what a shame that she had gotten something on it (how about a lot!) from lunch. I suggested, "Let's go to the bathroom to try to clean off your blouse." It appeared to be a foreign idea to her, but she eagerly agreed. As I worked on her blouse, I prayed I wasn't adding to the hurt and lack of acceptance that she constantly lived with from the children.

Soap and water do amazing things, she discovered. The almost spotless blouse thrilled her, and she shared, "I-always-hate-to-eat-lunch-because-I-know-how-I-am-going-to-look-when-I-finish!" She stayed to admire herself in the mirror for a moment, combing her hair with her fingers and smiling her off-centered grin. Each day after our laundry venture, she came to math with a slightly wet, but rather clean front.

Jody was also in my science class, a difficult subject for her. She again insisted on trying to do all of the written work. Jody loved the hands-on activities, although no one ever acted particularly thrilled for her to join a group.

One winter day we had a discussion on the central nervous system. Somehow the class ended up on the topic of disorders, and many were eager to put in their two-cents worth. I felt a little uneasy with the subject since I had always assumed that Jody had a nervous system disorder. The discussion continued longer that I had planned, but the flow excited me. I hated to interrupt and move on, but the clock and my anxiety told me that I should. As I started to push on, I noticed a hand waving in the back of the room. Jody, the invisible discussion member of our science class, waved her hand. Had we, in fact, stepped on her toes? Could the class understand what she was about to say? Would they be polite? I really needed to move on to the rest of our lesson. But, on the other hand, thank God her hand was finally up! I hesitated as her hand continued to bobble as it waved back and forth, "Yes, Jody?"

"That's-what's-wrong-with-me," she spoke slowly.

In my uneasiness I didn't quite follow. "What, Jody?"

"You-were-talking-about-cerebral-palsy. That's-what's-wrong-with-me," she answered.   Apparently eager to share her first-hand knowledge, she began telling about her disability. Immediately some of the students looked around at one another, almost embarrassed to listen.

I felt uncomfortable, but Jody looked eager. She desired the opportunity. I was afraid to give it to her. I felt so unsure of the outcome. Was I opening up a bag of worms? A bag of snakes? But something inside of me offered, "Jody, would you like to come sit on my stool and tell us more?"

My stool was sacred. It had become the place for students to sit for recognition and limelight. The kids always loved their opportunity to perch on it. She proudly walked to the front of the class in her methodical way. With difficulty she settled on the stool with my help. She balanced herself awkwardly. She then took command of the situation. The class sat silently as she spoke from her heart. Jody explained how her mind was good, but her muscles did not obey the signals sent by her brain. She also explained convulsions, her medication to control seizures, and how she felt before and after they occurred. Then she shared with the class in a very kind way, "Do-you-think-I-like-being-locked-in-this-body? I-don't-have-a-choice.-I'd-give-anything-to-be-like-all-of-you.-You-are-all-so-lucky!" Some students sat there drop-jawed. Others had tears in their eyes. Their walls of discrimination came tumbling down as they asked all sorts of questions.

Towards the end of the period Jody went on to describe how it felt to try to control her muscles and make her body move. She equated her walking to when a person turns round and round and then tries to walk a straight line. We pushed the desks and chairs aside, put a piece of masking tape down the center of the room, and everyone took a turn walking that line after Jody had turned them around and around. Amazement filled their eyes. The bell rang, and the class hurried on its way. But this time Jody was a part of them, not an outcast.

News traveled fast, and my other science class begged for Jody to come speak the next day. The principal even came. Jody related her experiences again. And again the class reacted in much the same way. Midstream I saw the principal wipe his eyes and leave the room. Jody was terrific! What a teacher! What a natural! What if I hadn't called on her?

This young lady had spent some very miserable years living with the painful bluntness of children. More than anything she desired acceptance, and her teaching debut seemed to be her ticket into the edges of that world. Soon after, Jody went out for basketball. The other girls learned to encourage her efforts. She wasn't exactly the most valuable player, but she was the most determined one. I watched a beautiful young lady emerge because her schoolmates came to understand her and her disability. They slowly realized her beauty that came from within.

During the awards assembly the last day of school, Jody received the "Most Improved Player" award in basketball. She grinned ear to ear as the teary-eyed P.E. teacher handed it to her. At the close of the assembly, Jody received the "Most Determined to Succeed" award out of the entire sixth grade class. As she faltered down the bleachers and slowly across the gym floor to me to receive her award, every sixth grade student stood up and gave her a standing ovation. I turned her around so she could face them and seize the moment. Jody beamed. I cried. Not only was I proud of her, I was proud of every one of the kids! And as I stood there watching, I wondered. How could I have been so afraid of you, Jody Milburne? You taught me so much about determination and a positive attitude. I only wish your name had been on my roster that first day of school.

REFLECTION ON "APART FROM THE REST"

Educational "buzz words" float in and out of conversations among educators, oftentimes receiving heated debate, changing from year to year. Such has been the case with the word "inclusion," cousin of mainstreaming, integration, and normalization. The inclusion debate remains alive and well. Even the most limited review of the available empirical research on inclusion indicates that there is little agreement on the subject.

When asked to write a reflection on "Apart from the Rest," I wrestled with the request for several months. My story was one of inclusion, but I am not in favor of inclusion. Did I dare put those words on the blank page and admit my inner beliefs to all who might read them? If I am against inclusion, I asked myself, does that mean that I am for exclusion? Each time I wrestled with what to say, how to describe what I firmly believed, I invariably ended up thinking about that year with Jody. Each time those thoughts came to mind, my heart felt warm and an indescribable emotion welled up inside of me. Surely my time with her was proof that I was not an exclusionist. The mental tug-of-war finally ended as I realized that I had to write about what I felt, what I knew, what I am. Just as my story of Jody had first been written in my heart and later my pen copied down the words, my feelings on inclusion had already been etched there also.

"Apart from the Rest" could be misread as a story that stands in strong favor of inclusion. After all, it was a success story. The chemistry was right, the timing was right, the group of children was right. However, in Room 12 with her other sixth grade teacher, the chemistry was not right and the timing never became right. Jody did not meet with the same successes in that room next door.

Unfortunately in my own classroom in years since Jody, similar lack of chemistry, lack of time, timing, whatever it was, did not produce the same heart-warming results. The Michaels with muscular dystrophy, the Charleses and Alysons labeled as educable mentally handicapped, and the Brians and Jonathans with extreme giftedness in math—for some reason the school year did not "click" in the same way with them. Still I did my best, my best with whatever else was going on in the classroom with the other students, the best with whatever else was going on in my own personal life at the time. The cards had been blindly dealt. Although I had played the hand as best as I knew how, I question if it was best for all the students involved.

Inclusion means to include all children in the regular classroom setting. How could one setting be appropriate for all students? The term "special" in special education, which once included the gifted population also, speaks to the very fact that one setting is not appropriate for all. How can there be only one appropriate setting when so many different individuals comprise each classroom? Each child is a unique individual with unique and individual needs. Each year's classroom chemistry is unique with needs that are different from the year before and the year afterward. And each teacher has that same capacity for uniqueness and individuality. Each year of teaching has found me in a different place in my life with a different energy level and a different focus. All things must be considered before placing students. Our mission as educators must be to provide individualized education based on individual needs of students, keeping in mind all members of the class, not just one or two. This is my belief on inclusion.

The term "responsible inclusion" used in the Inclusion Forum, a conference sponosred by California State in 1994, by several speakers is a needed "buzz word" in the vocabulary of many educators. Responsible inclusion was defined as examining the effects of inclusion on all students in the classroom. Teachers choose to participate, adequate resources are made available, the service delivery model is continually evaluated and altered to meet the needs of *all*, and academic and social progress is examined on an ongoing basis. As suggested by the Alberta Department of Education Response Centre (1990), "the focus of investigations should not centre on whether integrated placements are more desirable than segregated settings. Rather, the emphasis should be shifted to the consideration of what variables account for effective practices in both settings" (p. 8). And with that emphasis, we as educators would be amiss if we did not examine all contributing factors rather than making across-the-board decisions for the education of children. Edwin Martin, Associate Commissioner of Education and Chief of the U.S. Office of Education Bureau of Education for the Handicapped (as cited in Decker & Decker, 1977), recommends that we take a hard look at removing barriers to ensure that teachers as well as students won't be left to sink or swim by one "sudden impulsive administrative judgment" (p. 333).

As we examine prospective education for students with diverse learning needs in general education classrooms, we must ask if the adaptations are not only possible, but feasible. Struggling to meet the academic needs of all students in my classes, I worry about meeting the needs of regular education students as appropriate adaptations for students with disabilities are being met. With Jody I was fortunate. Adaptations for Jody did not consume too much class time, prevent student learning, or obstruct content coverage. The main chunk of my time was given at recesses. Communication among special and classroom teachers was nil in this particular case. No one asked if I understood her needs, how I was succeeding with her, how she felt, or what kind of training I brought with me.

No—the stage is not set for effective inclusion in our classrooms yet and never will be as long as educators seek a "one for all, and all for one" approach to students with diverse learning needs. Susan Winebrenner (1992), nationally known educator and speaker on autonomous learning, summed the issue up in one sentence when she stated, "Justice Felix Frankfurter said it best when he observed, 'There is nothing so unequal as the equal treatment of unequals.' " (p.19)

Jody never asked to be treated equally. She longed for patience from people to be herself. As I wrote the ending to "Apart from the Rest," an image of Jody graduating from high school within the month filled my mind. I had moved and was no longer in touch with her, but there was no doubt in my mind that she would graduate on time. I could see her crossing the stage with the tassel on her cap swaying to her lumbering gait. I could see that off-to-the-side grin flash as she received her diploma. Somehow I felt I was there, standing up at her high school graduation, a part of a standing ovation, with tears trickling down my cheeks. I wished I could hug her. I wanted to tell her how proud I was of her determination—how much I admired her for demanding to be herself. I wanted to share with her the impact she had made on me as a teacher.

We have all had "Jodys" tug at our hearts. All of us have within ourselves a vast wealth of teacher lore—those things about teaching that cannot be taught in education classes—those things that no evaluation measures—those things that research cannot calculate—those things that we never can be prepared for or even anticipate. But those are the experiences that richly reward us. They wrap our hearts in a warmth like Jody's big smile and warm hugs did when she came back to visit me in junior high. It is those moments that keep us going, encourage us to reach into tomorrow. The question is not about inclusion or exclusion. The challenge is to take a step at a time, a day at a time, celebrating successes and giving ourselves permission for failures. The challenge is to see each child as an individual and, reading the whole class as a barometer, provide for individual differences. There are no educational "buzz words" for that.

REFERENCES

Alberta Department of Education Response Centre (1990). *Integrating exceptional students into the mainstream: Literature review.* (Clearinghouse No. CHN ED 180651D). Edmonton, Alberta, Canada: Education Response Centre, Alberta Department of Education. (ERIC Document Reproduction Service No. ED 343 345).

Decker, R. J., & Decker, L. A. (1977). Mainstreaming the l.d. child: A cautionary note. *Academic Therapy, 12*, 353–356.

Gugliemo, M. J., Snow, I., Vaughn, S., & McMillan, D. (May 1994). Inclusion Forum, California State, Los Angeles.

Winebrenner, S. (1992). *Teaching gifted kids in the regular classroom*. Greeley, CO: Alps Publishing.

Teaching Is a State of Mind: Relationship—the Heart of Curriculum
Sheryl Lain

I was a '50's girl. Poodle skirts, can-cans, bobby socks. In my hometown, a farming community in northern Wyoming, nothing rocked the boat that much. We were mostly white, frugal, well-fed, home-permed, and right. The "Ed Sullivan Show," which came to our farmhouse in '57, pushed at the edges of propriety when Elvis gyrated on the snowy screen. Our elementary school basal readers featured Alice and Jerry. They looked like us. Even Jip's canine grin was self-satisfied. *Warriner's* dominated our junior and senior high years; orderly, dependable grammar didn't shake our complacency.

Meanwhile, a hundred miles away, right dab in the center of the state, was a foreign country, the Wind River Indian Reservation. Here I held my first teaching job. Here my smug world view was shattered. Here I learned the mind-numbing exhaustion, the deep sense of purpose, the thin-ice feeling which would characterize the next 28 years of my teaching career.

Upon my graduation from college in 1968, my own family of four moved to Riverton, Wyoming, border town to the reservation. It was late August. Two men in suits and ties came to the stoop of my yellow rented house. Turned out they weren't vacuum cleaner salesmen, though they had that courteous, expectant, smiling air of men who wanted to sell me something. "We need an English teacher. Would you come out to Horton School, forty minutes west of town?" These fellows were the superintendent and principal of one of the smallest school districts in the state. They said I'd be the high school English teacher for 69 students grades 9 through 12. Thirteen kids were in the senior class; forty percent of them were Native Americans, mostly Shoshone.

The pay would be $4,000. My National Defense Student Loan was due and payable. I hated leaving my two little sons in day care, but I took the job, on one condition. That I could teach my four classes—bang, bang, bang, bang—and head home early to be with my kids.

So began my daily commute through some of the most beautiful country on earth. Every day I drove westward on U.S. Highway 26 heading toward Horton School. The snowcapped Wind River Mountains paralleled the road on my left. One of the peaks was Gannett, reaching 13,804 feet into the sky, the highest point in Wyoming. On my right Owl Creek drew a blue line against the sky.

Behind me the sun rose over the Gas Hills and Copper Mountains. Every time I glanced through my rear view mirror, I saw a different colored landscape, purple shadows shifting to orange and gold.

To the left, right, and straight ahead stretched the Wind River Indian Reservation, home of two Plains Indian tribes, the Shoshone and Arapaho. Sacajawea, of Lewis and Clark fame, was buried at Fort Washakie, not too far from the school. A hundred years ago, Shoshone Chief Washakie wrangled a deal out of the U.S. government and secured these lands, his people's home since 1700, for a reservation. This was the same warrior who'd fought a duel with a Crow chief, Big Robber, for the territory—and won. The story goes that Washakie, so impressed with his opponent's valor in this fight to the death, cut out Robber's heart and ate it—raw.

The view inside my classroom was almost as intimidating as the one out my car window. To my unschooled eyes, the kids' faces formed a sort of chaotic jumble. Though I didn't know them individually yet, I knew one thing for sure. They all came with a strong sense of place, a strong sense of history.

The first two planning days, five of us teachers carpooled from Riverton to Horton. The initiatory hazing began in the car. "Did you know they fired the last four English teachers?" Vincent Samson, the business education teacher, reminded me of Uncle Melvin, a merciless teaser.

I paled. "Why?"

"The last guy was fired during the year—played his guitar in class and sang hippie songs."

During orientation, I learned something about the culture of the school.

"Let's see. This year you'll have three, or is it four, Nelson kids. Every other one is retarded. The in-betweeners are geniuses. They must have 20 kids."

"If you think a kid has lice or if the body odor gets too disruptive, the nurse gives mandatory showers."

There were other lessons I *didn't* learn through this informal indoctrination. But I learned them on the job:

Contradiction. We said Christian prayers to start the day in Morning Assembly—everyone gathered in the auditorium. I wondered what the Indian kids thought of this ritual. The Assembly of God Church down the road was the central symbol in the white kids' lives, but the Tribal Council hall, up the road, was the central symbol for the Native Americans.

False assumptions. The Wind River Indian Reservation was cohabited by two distinctly different tribes—and the two were natural enemies. Just because the Shoshone and Arapaho children looked alike to an untrained eye, they didn't see themselves as similar. They weren't always friends.

Boundaries. I tend to touch people. When I touched Dana Smith, the Assembly of God minister's daughter, she smiled, her forehead unfurrowing. When I rested my fingers on Cody Summer's shoulder—a ninth grade Arapaho—his pores froze and his skin's message was as loud as a command: Don't touch me!

Censorship. The Grapes of Wrath wasn't appropriate, according to the school board dominated by white farmers who attended the church. It's a Pulitzer Prize winner? Who cares. It's not right for a book to have a minister out cavorting in the bushes with female parishioners.

Double standards. One performance was expected and graded for white kids. The Native American kids were held to another. I learned this dual system with the Nelson boys, Clay and Larry. Both were seniors, but Larry was making his third stab at graduation. The superintendent said to hold him to the Indian standard—figure out how to pass him no matter how many zeroes he racked up. Meanwhile, Clay was held to the white standard.

Cultural differences. I had this nagging feeling that something wasn't fair. What business did I have forcing my beliefs, and the opinions of the white culture in general, on all these children? The old Harcourt/Brace *Adventure* anthologies featured beliefs in Manifest Destiny and the right to conquer the New World; not a Native voice was heard in these pages. Furthermore, the Native American kids would not give speeches in front of the class—heck, they wouldn't even raise their hands to answer my questions. If they did speak, they wouldn't look at me, making me feel confused, out of my element. My assumptions about the world peeled away one after the other, kind of like sunburned skin. Often I felt a little red, itchy and raw.

Pride. Gary Gregorio sat in the Number One desk—front row, teacher's right. A handsome senior, he was part Shoshone and part Mexican American. The desk was pretty tight-fitting, physically and psychologically, for Gary. He thought of himself as a man, and he looked like one. We got along. He flirted with me, an old married woman, at the Homecoming Dance. Then a few weeks later near the end of October, Gary came to class sick. His head lolled from side to side, and he rested his forehead on his desk. Suddenly, so suddenly he was taken by surprise, he threw up all over the desk, down on the floor. He stumbled out and refused ever to return to school. I learned later that he got drunk on the bus. "Why won't he come back?" I banged on the counter in the office and screwed up my face at the principal. "Make him and his folks come in for a meeting. Gary needs a high school diploma!" I didn't understand why the principal and the other veteran teachers wouldn't fight for him.

The Gregorios humored me and came in for a meeting. Why did I have the feeling all of them, including Gary, felt sorry for me? They acted like they knew something I didn't know, something obvious as the nose on my face.

Later someone patiently, like she was talking to a child, explained to me that Gary *couldn't* come back. Not once he'd lost face. Getting drunk wasn't so bad, but not holding his liquor and barfing in my room, that was bad.

A student's death. Dean Rusk was on his way into school. He drove his own car because he helped his dad on the dairy farm and could make better time in his own vehicle. His car sped along the quiet two-lane every morning, up and down hills following the undulating golden ribbon of road paint. This one particular morning Dean, blinded for a second by the rising sun, hit a tractor crawling along the highway. He died instantly. I never got to show him the A on his poetry, the comments on the freshness of his language, his metaphors. "You are the first teacher who believed in me," he'd said only the week before. He always thought he was dumb in English because he couldn't spell.

Teacher training programs at our state's only four-year university could not teach me all of this. I didn't know I'd feel drained at the end of the day, over-stimulated by all the energies emanating from those kids. Nobody warned me that for an hour or more when I got home, I'd need to zone out, be alone, submerge in catatonia. Nobody told me that all night long their faces would haunt my dreams.

In spite of exhaustion and emotional overload, that small school taught me more about teaching and learning, more about politics and community, more about accountability and personal responsibility, and more about willingness to build relationships than any other job since.

My intuition was wide awake: Dump exclusive use of the *Warriner's* and *Adventure* world views. The students wrote their lives and buried me in an avalanche of papers. Individualize the reading. They read their own books, and I didn't have the record-keeping strategies to keep up with them. Personalize their research. They picked their own topics for personal research papers, and I found I needed a clone of myself to keep track of *both* their processes of learning *and* their products.

But the rewards! I still have copies of the students' writing. I was introduced to the rich world of adolescent literature. And their research—the memory of Annie's presentation about intuition still goose fleshes my skin. Her guest was Dooley Westwood, a shaman, and he told about seeing into the future. He talked in a clipped, monotonal voice about his grandfather's vision, that someday these lands would be crisscrossed with barbed wire fences and irrigation ditches. All the while, his hands moved in his lap, speaking a language of their own.

I didn't always know how to defend my radical ways. How to explain to Rachel, who asked, "When are we doing *real* English—you know, parts of speech, diagraming sentences?" Not for 20 years would I finally luck into the Wyoming Writing Project: teach them to write correctly *through* their own writing. The Project coached us: Build community. Have students write their lives, learn from one another. Facilitate instead of teach. Construct curriculum based upon the needs of the students. Honor diversity and heterogeneity.

Breaking into education like I did, the cold-water dunking at Horton School after my luke-warm life in middle America, I learned enough to chew on for a lifetime.

I'm sure I learned more lessons than I taught my students. The lessons weren't easy to learn. I came to know that teaching is a state of mind. *It's a willingness* to be jolted out of my white bread American mentality. *It's a willingness* to extend myself to Gary, foreign to me in world view, habits, even body odor. *It's a willingness* to be expended, daily in class and nightly with kids' papers strewn across the dining room table. *It's a willingness* to observe learners with clear eyes: What happens, or doesn't happen, to students as a result of my curriculum? Why do the kids in the back two-thirds of the room, the ones I try so hard to convince they don't hate English, grow vacant the minute I drag out grammar worksheets? How fair are spelling tests when Rachel gets an automatic A without even studying, and Dean fails even after I coach him seconds before his retake test. *It's a willingness* to run the risk of chastisement from the school board for picking a novel that shocks some of them. *It's a willingness,* especially in the case of writing teachers, to burn the midnight oil, knowing full well that their colleagues who teach other subjects go home unburdened with briefcases full of student writing. *It's a willingness* to create relationships—among students, between student and teacher, student and literature, student and his own need for self-expression. This relationship-building means that the boy with the sunburned arms, who rides a tractor all weekend in his dad's beet fields, gains a broader world view. He never has to leave the farm nestled in the valley to know that his life is connected to the past and the future.

Teaching is a state of mind, *a willingness* to be alive in the classroom year after year even though the educational system, modeled after an assembly line in a factory, begs for reform.

I'm glad I taught, and learned, at Horton. I'm glad I knew Gary well enough to fight for him, and Dean well enough to mourn his death. Three decades later, the gift of their lives is with me still.

REFLECTION ON "TEACHING IS A STATE OF MIND: RELATIONSHIP —THE HEART OF CURRICULUM"

Now, instead of teaching in a small school community, I teach in a large factory school. Instead of 160 students in the whole building from first grade on, 1,500 high schoolers inch along the conveyer-belt hallways after the bell rings.

Out in the hall, few kids seek eye contact—why run the risk of an insult or a jab in the gut? Anonymity is safer for the ego and the body. But the kids get bruised anyway. One girl shot herself in the restroom a few years ago, and a boy was knifed outside waiting for his bus. Shana, decked out in her wool cheerleader's uniform, got a Big Gulp full of Coke dumped over her head by a jealous rival. Jake ditches phys ed so he won't be embarrassed by his late-to-appear pubescence. Richard hangs out in the English room for an hour after dismissal to avoid the bully waiting to beat him to a pulp. Miserable at school, Moira set fire to all her books in the hall, a last-ditch effort to finally get kicked out of school once and for all. And this is the school on the *right* side of town.

"There is an illness abroad in the land" (p. 3), begins Peck's (1993) book, *A World Waiting to be Born*, in which he argues for a return to civility, to community. And lately, books and articles are sprouting up like spring grass: how to make the impersonal schools personal, the fractured schools whole. Wynne and Walberg (1996) point out that in the last fifty years, the number of districts has declined by 87 percent, the number of schools has declined by 69 percent, and the average per-school increase is 410 percent, from an average of about 170 kids to about 800 kids in a school (p. 53). The National Association of Secondary School Principals recently issued the resolution: smaller is better.

Alvin and Heidi Toffler (1994) in their book, *Creating a New Civilization*, say that the Third Wave, or Information Age, "brings a genuinely new way of life" (p. 19) which will result in "radically changed schools" (p. 20). They say the factory model, left over from the Second Wave, or the Industrial Revolution (p. 83), is hopelessly out of date and useless to learners.

But, we resist change—the principal, the guidance counselor, the gifted and talented coordinator, the varsity football coach, the shop teacher. What do all of us have to lose if we look at Sizer's plan in *Horace's School* (1992)? He breaks up the monolithic high school into smaller Houses with four teachers responsible for about 100 students. What is threatening about Waldorf schools with one teacher working with the same kids from first grade through eighth? Or the New Zealand set-up with primary children of various ages learning together? Or the neighboring school district's experimental middle school with self-contained seventh and eighth grades—just like elementary school? Their class sizes are small, 17 kids, like research recommends in "Smaller Is Better" (1995, p. 18). Goodman, Goodman, and Bird (1992) urge all of us to create classroom communities.

We know in our bones that kids, really, all of us, need to belong to a small enough community so we can know one another. So the teacher can know Greg's dad just died and Laura is on Prozac. So we can teach one another to care, to learn and grow together, to be responsible.

But such reform is just too mind-boggling. It's too all-encompassing. Some of us feel like we're too old. "I don't want to know the little f—ers that well anyway," growls Delbert, the advanced science teacher. He is five years away from retirement.

"That'll never happen." Charley, the woodshop teacher, wags his head as if the idea of reform comes from a hopelessly deranged mind.

Dr. Rita, the superintendent, just stares at some point on the back wall. She wants to keep the status quo, to maintain the pyramid power structure borrowed from the Roman army, and adapted to fit factories in the Industrial Revolution.

Whose salaries would be leveled? Whose special interest programs would be eliminated? What specialists would need to go back to school for broader endorsement? What would the college of education do with their teacher training programs that produce teacher-specialists of every stripe and description? Change one thing in such a huge system and all the parts rub together wrong.

But in the face of what the kids tell us and what the headlines scream about crime and incivility, we can't continue business as usual. We can't heal fractured lives with fractured school days. We can't teach higher order thinking and deep literacy in factory systems herding kids to and fro from one work station to another. We can't afford the old system because it doesn't work.

Since I can't humanize the whole system, I will do what I can to warm up my little corner of the factory. But sometimes I recall with a certain nostalgia the intimacy of the Horton School community. And I know in my bones that students learn best through relationships. Once enough teachers are willing, when will the system respond to change?

REFERENCES

Goodman, K., Goodman, Y., & Bird, L. B. (1992). *Whole language catalog.* New York: Macmillan/McGraw Hill.

Peck, M. S. (1993). *A world waiting to be born: Civility rediscovered.* New York: Bantam.

Ruenzel, D. (1995, October). The Waldorf way. *Teacher Magazine*, 22–27.

Sergiovanni, T. (1995). Small schools, great expectations. *Educational Leadership*, *53* (3), 48-52.

Sizer, T. (1992). *Horace's school: Redesigning the American high school.* Boston: Houghton Mifflin.

Smaller Is better. (1995, October). *Teacher Magazine*, 18–19.

Toffler, A., & Toffler, H. (1994). *Creating a new civilization: The politics of the third wave.* Atlanta: Turner Publishing.

Wynne, E. A., & Walberg, H. J. (1996). The virtues of intimacy in education. *Educational Leadership*, *54* (3), 53-54.

Imitation of the Living Voice: What I Learned from Quintilian and a Few Eighth Grade Student Writers
David Pulling

The fifth grading period had just begun and I was desperate. The voices of my eighth grade writers were muzzled by an epidemic of writer's block that had begun after the Easter holiday. When the symptoms first appeared, I dismissed them as signs of spring fever and hoped things would get better on their own. However, when grade time rolled around, the skimpy portfolios turned in to me were mute testimonies of my failure to motivate and inspire.

I used the first mini-lesson of the new grading period to accept my share of the blame and to encourage the kids to join with me in casting off apathy. I announced a personal essay assignment and boldly volunteered to write the piece with them. Like all good writing teachers, I was willing to provide the adult role model that young writers need.

I began to motivate them by modeling a clustering exercise in an introductory lesson, asking them to help me brainstorm my topic in class discussion as I mapped out the details on the chalkboard. Since their assignment was to analyze the resolution of a difficult personal problem, I used a recent example from my own experience: my decision to postpone putting up a new fence around my back yard. The classes joined in with surprising enthusiasm as I shared my narrative and plotted the web of my dilemma; at the end of the day, I was pleased with the response in all five classes as volunteers had eagerly shared topics they were planning to write about.

The next day, I used mini-lesson time again to review the assignment and motivate the stragglers. After I got workshop going in my first class, I found an empty student desk and sat down to work on my own piece about the decrepit fence and the dog that ran away because Uncle Sam was too slow with the tax refund earmarked for fence repairs. Like most writers, I agonized over the lead. My first take was a monumental stinker: "Just about every decision a person makes involves some risk. A recent incident in my own experience has given me a fresh awareness of this fact." I knew as soon as I jotted the last period that this was bland, artificial garbage, and I chuckled at how teachers like me, brought up through high school and the ranks of freshman composition by an Industrial Revolution–minded school of rhetoric, so easily relapse into mimicry of that phony voice for which we were so ardently praised in our formative years.

I chided myself and began anew: "Last October, I brought home a two-month-old puppy—a frisky, cuddly Labrador Retriever." I put my pen down and read my second effort—a little warmer than the first, but still unbearably corny. I sighed, tucked the page with my pair of bloopers in a folder, and lost myself wandering among the students to check their progress. The elusive lead continued to nag me, though, and even as I visited with the students, I was bouncing around different possibilities in the playground of my thoughts.

About an hour later, during the next class, I got out my folder and tried another lead—this time, the light came on: "The ugliest fence in Louisiana is in my back yard." I sensed I was onto something now, so I continued: "Its weathered brown one-by-twelve planks are split and cracked; termites have eaten meandering trails on the board surfaces; the once fresh redwood stain has faded beneath crusty layers of greenish mold and chalky mildew."

"Yes!" I confidently proclaimed to myself. Like all great inventors, I wanted to share my discovery with someone. I looked around for a potential audience and spotted Kellie, one of those devoted teacher-pleasers who would kill herself memorizing the *Encyclopedia Britannica* if a teacher assigned it. I called her over.

"Hey, Kellie, you got a minute to confer with me? I have these different leads for this piece, and I need some feedback."

"Sure," she agreed, apparently flattered that I valued her opinion.

She didn't know, of course, that my mind was already fixed on the third one, but I really was curious to see her reaction. I cleared my throat and, with consummate professorial pomp, read the first phony lead. I paused after reading and looked up expectantly for her reaction. Her eyes were placid, a polite smile pursed her lips, and she nodded, "That's good. I like it."

I wasn't sure if she was honest or just being polite, so I probed further. "You don't think it's a little phony?"

"No," she insisted. "It sounds good."

I sensed a real opportunity to teach here, so I called Casey and Kyle, a couple of Kellie's classmates who were nearby. They also seemed flattered that I sought their advice, so I repeated the first opener that Kellie liked. I figured I could depend on Kyle for an honest reaction, and he didn't disappoint me.

"It's boring," he said as soon as I read it. Casey was at first noncommittal, but after a quick round of discussion, she concurred. Even Kellie was willing by now to admit a reservation about her initial reaction. I continued by reading the second and third leads. As I read the last one, "The ugliest fence in Louisiana is in my back yard . . . ," I noted the grave, attentive expressions which attended the reading of the first two leads instantaneously melt into beaming approbation as they looked at each other and nodded. Noting their receptive reaction, I seized the moment to teach them about leads and how real writers have to buy extra garbage bags to dispose of the abandoned beginnings that overflow their garbage cans.

I was so pleased with this method that I used it in every other class for the rest of the day, deliberately moving among the writing groups, repeating my plea for help in choosing a lead. Time after time, I observed their polite nods to lead number one and their eager "yeah's" to the last one. They recognized what I had hoped they would and reaffirmed more than just the lead that I liked, for their response also indicated that they were growing in their critical ability to evaluate choices in writing. I really felt like a teacher, and the honor they felt in having their opinion solicited was surpassed only by the satisfaction that I felt in the enthusiasm of their response, even from several students whose writing workshop habits were rarely characterized by zeal.

Perhaps the ultimate compliment to my efforts came the following day when Cindy, writing about her problem involving a messy bedroom and an insistent mother, was having problems with her lead. She really didn't have one, so as I responded to her first draft I reminded her how I had solved my lead problem. "Oh, yeah," she recalled, and she went back to her seat. A few moments later, she came back to me and held out her revision: "The messiest room in my house is my bedroom," and she proceeded to describe the clutter in concrete detail.

"Blatant imitation! Unoriginal! This child has the heart of a plagiarist!" I can imagine those excited objections raised by a few of my former mentors; I can even recall earlier stages in my own pedagogical development when I would have joined the chorus. Fortunately, though, I realized that Cindy's imitative act illustrates the truth in the ancient Roman master Quintilian's observation that "a great portion of art consists of imitation"; accordingly, I recognized that responsible teachers have a serious obligation to act as writers worthy of imitation in the presence of their students.

As I subsequently considered the significance of this episode, it became apparent that what I stumbled into was a deeper understanding of what it means for the writing teacher to be a model writer for kids in the classroom. I had occasionally read pieces of my own to my classes; I had published some of my work on the classroom wall alongside their polished drafts; I had held my worked-over rough drafts before them as I tried to explain that revision is a messy process involving critical evaluation and change; I had even worked at my own writing during class occasionally so the students could see I practiced what I preached. In short, I felt satisfied that I was "the adult writer kids need to know" described in most of the contemporary "how-to-teach writing" texts. What I had missed, however, was the important distinction that needs to be drawn between a professional teacher-writer and a friendly peer writer, the latter owning the superior capacity to influence and motivate students.

In my former role, as a purveyor of models, the original work I shared was nearly as ineffectual as the model paragraphs in *Warriner's* English book. No matter how much the students admired the exegetical explanations and demonstrations of style from my pieces and occasionally borrowed some of my narrative ideas, they still regarded me and my work as some inimitable ideal exalted beyond them. By sitting down among them in conference groups, though, in spite of my ruse about needing help with a decision, I met them as a peer writer. They were no longer captive auditors of a polished pro showing them how writers write; they were co-participants in the social process offering advice to their colleague, the teacher. I learned from them, they learned from me, and, as in all aspects of the messy art of teaching composition, I discovered that imitation works best for the student when it becomes personal, immediate, and relevant. Really, Quintilian understood the central issue two thousand years ago in his *Institutes of Oratory* where he instructs teachers in the importance of serving as living models worthy of imitation for their students. The famous Roman teacher wrote, "For though he [the teacher] may point out to them . . . plenty of examples for their imitation, yet the living voice feeds the mind more nutritiously, and especially the voice of the teacher, whom his pupils both love and reverence. How much more readily do we imitate those whom we like."

I've grown up to teach high school and even college students since my middle school days, but what I learned from Quintilian and those eighth graders about the living voice that I have to share with students has remained a part of me. Nor do I believe it's vain or presumptuous to think of myself as a model writer, and neither should any teacher. After all, writing teachers are engaged in one of the most artistic educational endeavors; and, while no higher compliment is paid the artist than to be imitated, I am humbled in knowing that being worthy of imitation is just part of my job.

REFLECTION ON "IMITATION OF THE LIVING VOICE"

I composed the earliest form of this essay, "Imitation of the Living Voice," as an assignment for a graduate course in rhetoric in 1992 at the University of Southwestern Louisiana. My major professor was directing me in an independent reading and study course in composition theory and had asked me to write a paper connecting some method I was using in my classroom to some important theoretical issues or ideas that I had encountered in my reading.

I was working hard at the time to manage a learner-centered writing workshop classroom because I had grown dissatisfied with feeling marooned in an unflowering desert of middle school paragraph and essay writing. I had suspected for three previous years, as a newcomer to teaching, that the existence of this desert was at least partially the fault of the scientific-behavioristic set of teaching conventions that had been handed to me in the form of a curriculum guide and mastery skills list. As a result, I studied my graduate readings among rhetorical theorists with greater zeal than usual so that I could more articulately defend the *avant-garde* methods I was using in a basics-oriented, rural school district.

My reading led me into an interest in classical rhetoric, especially as I observed how many of the classical notions about teaching composition were being rediscovered and freshly appropriated by twentieth-century rhetoricians. Particularly interesting to me was the Greek and Roman concept of *imitatio*, or imitation, which for the student learning composition skills functions much the same as imitation works for infants in the language acquisition process. I reasoned that if an eighteen-month-old relies on imitation to learn and ultimately master the use of a complex linguistic system, there must be some effective means of employing those inborn linguistic instincts to help older students become better writers.

Of course, the narrative of my learning experience with imitation tells how I discovered from the Roman teacher Quintilian the truth of an added human dimension to imitation for which theories seldom account. To me as a teacher in the humanities, that human dimension imparts to the theory its most glorious significance.

Two works have been especially useful to me in learning about the theoretical issues that are at the center of my essay. One is Edward P. G. Corbett's *Classical Rhetoric for the Modern Student* (New York: Oxford University Press, 1965), a textbook presenting a comprehensive sequence of neo-Aristotelian methods and activities for teaching a composition course. Although the text is written for college students, the methods are adaptable to a wide range of grade levels. Particularly helpful for teachers are Corbett's historical notes and explanations about how classical students learned rhetoric (including an explanation of the role of imitation) and how those ideas are still relevant. The other work is James J. Murphy's essay "Roman Writing Instruction as Described by Quintilian" in a collection of essays edited by Murphy entitled *A Short History of Writing Instruction: From Ancient Greece to Twentieth-Century America* (Davis, CA: Hermagoras Press, 1990). Murphy demonstrates how Quintilian's methods and theories are remarkably contemporary in their conception of learning as a process. Murphy also cites important passages from Quintilian's major treatises on teaching and learning, which provide the contemporary reader with an introduction to the Roman teacher's major ideas without having to wade through the complete works.

Hopefully, my testimony shared here will encourage many teachers who have never studied rhetoric to explore the theoretical riches of this ancient discipline which spans the history of teaching from classical times to the present. More importantly, I hope that this experience demonstrates how the self-directed teacher-as-learner, properly motivated, *can* connect theory to practice in the classroom.

Journal Writing
Joanne Bergbom

Journal Entry: 7/21/94

Here I am once more trying to put my thoughts on paper as my students struggle with their own. I feel as though I have so much to write, but I'm having real difficulty concentrating. Rob is staring out the window; Carolyn is putting on mascara; Peter is tapping his pen; and Kris is arguing with Vinny. The Simon and Garfunkel lyrics to "Sounds of Silence" are anything but. Yet, I force myself to write, and I insist that they do as well.

Practicing my teacher version of self-deception, I rationalize that journal writing works for every student, that through this each student becomes real to me and therefore real to him or herself—at least in this classroom, at least for a little while. If that were true, then the image of the weary bag lady trudging to her car on the eve of a long weekend, laden down with canvas bags spilling over with black and white marblebound notebooks, wouldn't be merely a sight gag. The hours I spend at the dining room table pouring over the scribblings of my students at the expense of time for family, friends, and sleep would be valid. What teacher doesn't want to make her students feel special about themselves as people and as writers?

Does classroom journal writing to musical accompaniment accomplish this? If not, what is my goal? It does start them off writing about something. That has to be good practice. I do see their journal writing becoming more authentic, more free flowing, better expressed than their attempts at other assignments. Some just unburden themselves; others ask themselves questions about life and attempt to answer them. Sometimes they write themselves into a deeper understanding of the literature which we are experiencing together. Even Carolyn will feel better for this break from instructional time, because the face she shows the world will have both eyelashes on straight.

And my responses to them? I will read all their entries at some time in the nearest future I can manage, and I'll comment on several for each student. Some of my replies will be trite, but some will speak to the hearts of the students I try to reach. I hope that at least once during each year, I'll respond to each student with at least one comment to boost the sense of self.

If it weren't for the journals, I would not have had the chance to let Thomas know that beneath his happy-go-lucky exterior, I sensed his pain and understood some of his suffering. I could write him words of comfort which we couldn't share face to face, because those faces were always smiling, always laughing. Despite my best efforts to get him help, I wasn't able to save Thomas from himself (I don't think any of us could), but I was able to be real with him through our journal dialogues. Thomas took his life several years after graduation. That haunts me. Yet, there is small comfort in that I didn't let him pass through my class as just one more senior struggling through *Hamlet*, *Ordinary People*, and a term paper on "The Book of Job." In his journal I called him by name and understood.

And then there was Thomas's friend John, another senior with whom I didn't have much in-depth face to face conversation, but in his journal I was able to address his self-doubts, comment on his obvious strength and intellect, and offer praise and encouragement. Today, years later, he writes, "I am a different person. I intend to keep growing and evolving. Posterity is important but so is forward motion. I think the time has come for you to know me as I am and as I will become. You may be surprised and even disappointed but I feel that we are missing an interaction that could fill a certain part of our lives; because I don't know you either but I know you well enough to want to be able to call you a friend . . . I think of you too and all that we've never talked about."

I read all the many questions from students asking for advice about problems with parents, best friends, romantic interests, math teachers. For some, these become oral conversations; with others there is just this ongoing written dialogue. Often, I feel overburdened by their problems; frequently I regret not having read their entries sooner; and occasionally I am successful in putting an emotionally needy student in touch with the school social worker. I think I've helped more than a few through some rough times. Does this justify the time I spend at work and at worry? Does it justify my entrée into their private lives, even when I find myself wishing they wouldn't share quite so much of themselves? Does it justify the use of journal time for those students who never really want to write and do so only very superficially? And is it a valid teaching strategy? I do believe that it answers their needs as people, and as a high school teacher, of necessity, I must serve those needs. After all, there is only one social worker to deal with the most serious concerns of 1,350 students.

But what does it do for them as writers? As I struggle to complete this, my journal entry for today, I remember again and again how writing is thinking, how it forces me to question, clarify, and confront my thoughts. The process even allows me surprise in the direction towards which my ideas gallop. Even as reluctant journal writers, all my students did engage with themselves and their lived lives through their writing. I know I will continue the use of journals in my classes, but now I see that I still need to clarify their intended purpose and work out a system of reading and response that is workable in my life.

If I am true to the belief that writing is thinking, I can tackle those problems in my next journal entry.

Journal Entry: 9/28/95

It's me again, a new school year, exciting enthusiasm on my part and that of my students, new literature, new possibilities, and the same old demons. We're doing journals again. I believe in this writing. They look forward to it, but it's not yet October, and I'm already overwhelmed. As always, there is the volume of their writing which I feel compelled to read—partly to validate its importance and partly in fear that I'll miss something important, a cry for help, a sensitive issue that I should know. I tried to spread out the work load by collecting the journals of one row of students in each class per night, resulting in my meeting one goal, but never being free, not one single day, of their thoughts.

Actually, I really thought I had found a way to face my demon head on. This would be the year we'd focus on double-entry journals. The students would select those lines in the literature which called out to them, and they would respond in writing. We'd follow that with the exchange of journals with a writing partner who would comment on the first writer's response. Certainly, what I, the teacher, would read would be more literary, less a tale of personal crisis and anxiety.

One student selected a William Golding line from *Lord of the Flies* which used the word "gay" in a pre-modern context, and then explored his own concerns about sexual identity. Another student quoted a line from Judith Guest's *Ordinary People* and expanded on his own failed suicide attempt. Somehow they find a way to tell us what they want us to know.

It's not the medium of the journal that creates these feelings and these needs to share. After all, I remember a few final exam essays from seniors whom I might never see again, in which they exploded with what needed saying in response to a seemingly innocuous test question. They will write what's closest to their hearts because they need to. I think it wise for us to give them the opportunity early and often. What remains is how we deal with the content. After so many years of agonizing over this, I'm no closer to the answers, if there are any. Perhaps the uncertainty exists because whenever we teach and open ourselves up to the pain (and sometimes the joy) of our students, we carry them with us. It's not the shopping bag that holds the journals which weighs us down, but the recognition of the loss of their innocence which has been revealed to us—because we are teachers, and because our students must pass through childhood and grow up in their journals and right before our eyes.

REFLECTION ON "JOURNAL WRITING"

Another class of seniors, the Class of 1996, has graduated and moved on, some weighed down by very difficult personal circumstances. I know I'll never see some of them again. Those few who are truly disenchanted by the institution of school will never visit me there. Those with limited interpersonal skills won't feel comfortable using the address and phone number I provided. But each one left with his journal sprinkled generously with my comments. We had a good year together in English class, and I want them to remember their successes. My voice in their journals should summon up those memories as each student recalls his or her own link with that particular past and measures subsequent continuity and growth. Our class's use of journals enabled me to develop a more individual relationship with each student, and it gave them a "safe haven" amidst the chaos of their lives. As related in Peter Elbow's (1980) *What Is English?*, Candy Carter, a high school teacher, examines the pressures afflicting today's teens:

The pressures are there, but often the foundations are not. The implications for the teacher of English can be overwhelming. On the one hand, literature, writing, self-expression can provide the necessary "great truths" to help these courageous but confused adolescents make sense of their world. On the other hand, students often come to school with so much unfinished business from home that it takes a real master to bring art and life together. Most teachers try, some more than others. Others live in a time capsule dated 1965, in which Mom made lunch, took the kids to the library for research papers, and set a curfew at 10:00. Yes, kids are different but oddly and sadly the same too. It is the world around them that has changed rather than the students themselves. (p. 27)

Before students can begin to learn, they need to drop off some of this baggage. Their journal becomes that place. It continues to be true that, with increasing need, today's students require this "safe haven" as external pressures make their interior lives more chaotic. We teachers, who often have no training as counselors, daily face, side by side with our students, the issues of divorce, suicide, child abuse, teen pregnancy, drug use, AIDS, sexual identity, abandonment, hopelessness, to name a few. In addition, judgments about confidentiality and reporting practices plague us. We want to make the worlds of our students whole, and yet sometimes all we can provide is a blank page that listens and a response that doesn't always hit the mark.

I chose to write this piece because for me, as for my students, paper is patient, often more patient than I am willing to be with myself. Like my students, I seek answers and I try to strip those answers of their elusive qualities by committing words to paper. Writing becomes my opportunity to examine and clarify. In a reflection on my periodic need to confront the issue of journal writing in my classroom, I realize it is very much about my need for meaningful connections with my students. How often I've penned above my signature in their yearbooks, "Use your talents to make a difference in our world." I think I am making my difference by dialoguing with my students through their journals.

As Tracy Kidder (1989) closes his book *Among Schoolchildren*, Chris Zajac, the teacher whose career he chronicles, muses, "Within a few weeks this year's disappointments would begin to fade" (p. 331). Kidder continues:

Even the most troubled children had attractive qualities for Chris. Even the most toughened, she always felt, wanted to please her and wanted her to like them, no matter how perversely they expressed it. She belonged among schoolchildren. They made her confront sorrow and injustice. They made her feel useful. Again this year, some had needed more help than she could provide. There were many problems that she hadn't solved. But it wasn't for lack of trying. She hadn't given up. She had run out of time. (p. 331)

Fortunately for us teachers, there is always the next September with other students and their journals. When any of my past or present students look back on what they have written, as I've just done for myself, they will confront honestly the reality of who they are and what values they espouse as they become who they finally will be. Then, if they try to write another journal entry, the process of putting words on paper will begin to answer some of their life questions, this time without my help.

Therefore, I continue the practice of journal writing with my students. They write two to three times a week in class in a variety of ways: in response to a quotation selected by the student from a piece of literature which we are reading; in response to a quotation or topic I write on the board; in response to an activity or event which we have experienced as a class or a school; in response to a reading selected and read by a classmate; in response to the invitation to "dump what's on your mind." When appropriate, they exchange journals and dialogue with each other after my admonition to respect the privacy of all previous journal entries. (They always do.) I collect them each time and then read them and comment as frequently as I can manage, at least once a month. I monitor a youngster who seems to be wrestling with a tough problem or when the response is to a particularly sensitive subject. I always encourage students to hand me their journals personally if they have written something which warrants immediate feedback. Sometimes they do. Often the need was served by putting the thoughts down on paper. Each student is always told he can turn down any page he'd prefer I not read. He does; I don't; and a trust is strengthened. And so, the need for meaningful relationships inside the classroom is nurtured for us all.

REFERENCES
Elbow, P. (1980). *What is English?* New York: The Modern Language Association of America.
Kidder, T. (1989). *Among schoolchildren.* Boston: Houghton Mifflin.

Monique's Gifts
Steffie Corcoran

A real charmer named Monique is currently enrolled in one of my 7th grade English classes. Monique, 4'5" and weighing in at 70 pounds or so after lunch, seeks out learning opportunities and takes them very seriously. From essay organization to common vs. proper nouns to sensory details to the great action vs. linking verbs debate, Monique meets each new concept I introduce in class with the grim, determined concentration of an Olympic athlete preparing for a gold medal performance.

In fact, she is so stone-faced and harsh in her approach to learning that her beautiful, spontaneous, exceedingly rare smiles are flashlights after long blackouts; I've learned to treasure them as I would valuable gems.

Recently, my seventh graders were right in the middle of a unit on descriptive writing. I had started off by having them add sensory details, similes, and/or metaphors to the graded final drafts of their narrative essays. We were exploring the possibilities of using description like an additive to writing to make it spicier, so to speak.

But I also wanted students to know that with description, there are times when it's important to think small. For example, in advertisements or 911 calls, it is neither necessary nor appropriate to be flowery, gushy, or verbose. So as a way to bring this point home to them, we discussed classified advertising, and I gave them a journal assignment to write a personals ad of 30 words or less with a title of seven words or less.

The students thought this assignment was pretty darn exciting. Most had seen personals ads before or had grown-up relatives who had dabbled in them. I gave them a scenario: Del Crest was starting a personals column in the school newspaper as a way for students to meet other students with whom they might have some things in common. Other than the word limits, the only other rule I gave them was to keep it clean.

But after looking over their shoulders while they were working on the assignment, I noticed, surprised, that few were saying anything about how they wanted that special boy or girl to look. "Hey!" I announced. "Excuse me, excuse me." Pretty much everyone picked up their pencils to listen. "You guys must not be too picky, because you're not saying anything about wanting a good looking boy or girlfriend. Isn't how the person looks important to you?"

"Ms. Corcoran," Monique said gravely, her eyes round, "how someone looks on the outside isn't important. It's what their heart looks like that counts."

"Yeah, Ms. Corcoran!" several other members of the class shouted in response. (Did I mention that in addition to her other fine qualities, Monique is a born leader?)

Well, how naive! I thought to myself. That Monique is sure an innocent. It's easy to say looks aren't important when you're young and beautiful.

But I caught myself thinking about what Monique said over and over again during the weekend. Eventually, the truth of her words began to seep in. Once that happened, boy, did I feel chastised! How could I be so small, so vain, so shallow, and still pretend to lead the young to an understanding of how to distinguish between adverbs and adjectives?

Once I started third period the following Monday, I waited until all my students were diligently (okay, some more diligently than others) working on their daily write and strode over to Monique's desk. I knelt down next to her and said, "Monique, do you remember what you told me last Friday about looks not being as important as the way someone's heart looks?"

She nodded solemnly.

"Well," I continued, "I think you really taught me something important when you said that, and I really learned something from you. I feel like you gave me a present. Thank you."

"You're welcome, Ms. Corcoran," she replied, the corners of her mouth turned upward only slightly.

On Tuesday, Monique stopped by my desk on her way to hers. "I knitted you a yellow pot holder last night, Ms. Corcoran," she said nonchalantly, as though she were informing me that she'd completed her homework (which of course she always does).

Deeply touched, I thanked her and told her it was a beautiful pot holder, that it would add a splash of color to my grayish-blue and white kitchen.

Now I'm the kind of woman who actually uses her Magic Chef perhaps half a dozen times a year so the yellow pot holder doesn't have a great deal of practical use in my life. But I can't remember ever getting a gift that has meant more to me, especially since Monique had already given me one gift by teaching me a lesson as much out of the mouths of babes as anything I've ever heard (or at least listened to).

But I can tell you this, after every hell day at school, after asking myself for the millionth time why I'm doing what I'm doing with my life for slave's wages, I'll just go home and spy that sunny pot holder on a shelf in my kitchen, and I'll remember Monique and remind myself of what students can be, what they can do, and how much we have to learn from them.

REFLECTION ON "MONIQUE'S GIFTS"

I'm a naturally reflective person, probably partly because I live alone and spend scads of time in my own company and in my own head. I was surprised, however, when I found myself time and again avoiding this reflection. No such hesitation sullied the teacher story itself! From a psychological standpoint, I thought the avoidance was interesting and probably involved some unresolved childhood issues.

But now that some time has passed, I think maybe I just don't want to quantify or philosophize too much in this amazing, magical field of dreams that is teaching. I don't want to reduce teaching to mere theories or stances or schools of thought (real schools being ever so much more interesting). I remember critical theory almost ruined literature for me in graduate school, and I don't intend to let it do the same in a career where in such a short time I've found such professional happiness and satisfaction. But then again, maybe I'm just resistant to the idea of actually discovering what my assumptions and philosophies are, exactly. Whatever they are, I suspect they're working well, and I'm probably just afraid that somebody is going to come along and tell me that whether they're working or not, my assumptions and philosophies are wrong/unacceptable/dangerous or whatever.

But as I was thinking about the assumptions or philosophies that went into the writing of the Monique story, I do remember saying something about how guilty I sometimes feel that I'm the one doing the most learning in my classes. Even though teaching isn't a profession that pays much, I still feel greedy because it seems I'm the one getting the most insight. Often teaching is more about what I'm getting than what I'm giving, especially on days when I have to explain for the thirtieth time what I mean when I say it's time to revise.

So I guess what I feel is selfish. I'm also saying that in some ways, this is a pretty selfish field. Sure, teachers fish around all the time for compliments on their selflessness; their saintly virtues; their no-win, simultaneous roles of interim parent, educator, sympathetic ear, and moral center. But let's get real—most teachers really get a lot out of all this power and influence. I'm honest enough to admit that if students see me as a role model, part-time mommy, and influential person in addition to a writing teacher, I'm gratified. Better me than some of the wing-dings on the boob tube and silver screen who influence them in terribly negative, dangerous ways.

I get pretty close to my students. In fact, I'm probably truly "myself" with them in ways that, in real life, I am with only family and very close friends. In fact, it occurs to me that in many ways, my students know me much better and have experienced the essential Stef much more so than have my colleagues and friends at Del Crest. I'm not sure what this says about me, that I feel somehow "safer" with kids than with adults, but there it is.

I do admit that in many ways I prefer the company of kids to that of adults. Kids generally shoot pretty straight, and they don't require that you play sophisticated head games with them. I like this about them. Even though I understand from an adult standpoint that it's often necessary to be politically correct and put on different masks in order to keep the adult world running smoothly, I'm not good at it, and I don't like being expected to do it. In the world of my classroom, life is played by the rules, but these are rules my students and I agree on. They're the right rules for me and for my classroom, however well or poorly they might work in the larger world surrounding us. So basically it all rolls right back around to control issues, to my deep-seated need for self-determination. Those needs get met with a bullet for me through teaching.

All this admittedly causes me some distress. I'm not sorry I don't have a teaching persona, one I can put in the closet with my heels and suits once the work day is done. But I occasionally find myself concerned that I'm most secure, most grounded with kids, not adults. I just know I like the refreshing, genuine, and generally pretty accepting world of adolescence, raging hormones and emotional turbulence included.

Boy oh boy, have I ever strayed from Monique! In terms of reflection, I got a lot from that story the same way I got a lot out of her and her class every day. Things I received: a valuable moral lesson, a chance to tell a kid that I have a great deal of respect and affection for her, a pot holder, and a neat story. Some days it's all good.

My, My, My Delilah
Carole Weigand

The first thing that struck me was the name on the class roll: Delilah. What kind of parent would hang that on a kid? The question lingered as I unpacked boxes of supplies and dusted off piles of books. As usual, opening day was hectic, but not enough to distract me from noticing the faces as my new third hour class trickled into the room. I speculated as each girl entered and tentatively selected a seat. "How about that one," I wondered as the brash redhead with the trendy too-snug jeans and the exaggerated swing to her hips sashayed through the doorway. She was a stereotype of the Biblical temptress Delilah I expected to see. Maybe the name had somehow come to be reflected in her behavior. Or, how about the girl with the nervous eyes and compulsive nail chewing?

My speculation was cut short by the inevitable bell. Each name I called eliminated another possibility, and since Delilah's last name began with "W," the actual person matched to the name was painfully slow to emerge. No wonder I had not been successful in my mental game of match up. The resulting Delilah turned out to have stringy dishwater blond hair framing a face dominated by a high forehead which was furrowed from a myopic squint. Her pale eyes were set deeply into the sockets and seemed focused on nothing. The unfortunate girl's upturned nose would have been an asset on some other person, but in Delilah's case only served to emphasize the sunken cheeks and grim mouth.

Her unfashionable round-collared blouse had been white at some point in the distant past. Now uniform grime permeated the coarse fabric so completely that the various stains were nearly camouflaged, and her outdated skirt was merely a darker-hued echo. The picture was completed by a length of grimy leg leading down to frayed cotton socks and scuffed thick-soled brown shoes. No human could be a worse match to this girl's namesake!

That was all I had time to notice that first class period. In fact, Delilah was so personally unobtrusive that as the year got underway, it was easy to overlook her needs day after day. Like every other busy high school teacher, some brash miscreant first demanded my attention, then an engaging student's problem lured me into turning my focus there. So the class periods slipped away without ever focusing on Delilah as I daily resolved I would . . . tomorrow.

In the first few weeks as I observed the social groups forming within the school, I found Delilah was included in none. Even the so-called outcasts considered her a pariah. However, by the time I had noticed that fact I had also discovered the reason why. Delilah stunk. There was no delicate euphemism to change the truth. She just plain stunk.

Because Delilah was a freshman and new to our district, the other teachers in my building had no more background than I did on how long the problem had existed or how to handle it. She became a well-worn lunch topic with the conversation inevitably containing a version of the sentence, "How about if we have————talk to her." The name in the blank rotated as staff member after staff member backed away from the unenviable chore. The counselor of course was tapped first. He dispensed some platitudes and a take-along bag of soap and deodorant. Once a social worker became involved, we discovered that Delilah's home had no running water, so the soap became more decorative than useful. As for the deodorant, either she did not have the inclination to try it, or her clothes were so odor-permeated that it did no good.

So the marking period plodded on with no resolution to the problem. Delilah volunteered information neither in class nor in the rare personal conversations I had with her. Her academics proved to be as lackluster as her personality. She was just an unpleasant odor wafting through the classes and hallways, never touching nor being touched by anyone either physically or socially.

In my English class I tried to be compassionate, but had trouble because it was physically impossible to stand next to Delilah without retching. Indeed, a steady stream of students came to me with a request to be moved. "Honest, Miss Weigand," I heard time and again, "it isn't that I want to move to sit by my friends. I just can't stand being next to Delilah." Then came the hesitant pause and the remainder of the plea I heard repeatedly, "You know what I mean?"

Of course, I knew exactly what these teens meant. I, too, found excuses not to have to sit down for one-on-one writing conferences as I did with my other students. I was nice to Delilah . . . but always from a safe and odorless distance. Eventually I found myself arranging the seating chart to put Delilah by the window and in the very front. This was not particularly because she could see the chalkboard better from there. It was just easier to have only two students to arrange around her rather than dealing with four constant requests for a seating change.

Through it all, Delilah seemed oblivious to the unease of those around her. She gave no sign of wanting social contact, and staff members who had enough chutzpa to approach her about the problem reported that the unkempt, odoriferous girl was unperturbed even as they spoke with her. She neither said nor implied with any sign or action that she was unhappy with her lot. Neither did she seem offended, dismayed, outraged, amused, angered, or any other adjective that one can imagine. She simply, placidly, let the adult ramble on about the issue until she was dismissed.

At one point early in the school year the home economics teacher devised a new special hygiene unit that she swore couldn't miss . . . but it did! Delilah continued to overlook hand washing, tooth brushing, and hair combing even when it became part of the stated lesson plan. Then, just a few weeks before Delilah moved to another school district, came my personal coup de grâce. Having given up on making a social change in Delilah, the home ec teacher had moved on to a cooking unit, perhaps to mask any offensive odor by filling the room with the smell of pies and fudge. Maybe she simply thought the class could drown its smelly sorrows in milk and cookies. Whatever the reason, desserts and snacks began to appear regularly in the hands of the freshman who came from her class to mine.

My prep time came that late fall day as I grabbed my daily cup of supplemental coffee and snuggled into my chair surrounded by stacks of papers to correct. As usual, the door was open and the hallway was deserted. Then Delilah, silent as always, appeared. I remember looking up into the thin, normally pale face, which now betrayed her shy embarrassment by the blotches of red staining either cheek.

The focus of Delilah's eyes settled at a point somewhere just below my own eyes. That was the closest she had ever come to looking me full in the face as we spoke. The words tumbled out in jumbled and breathless fashion, "You can have these, we made 'em in home ec, I really like you, there are chocolate chip ones too, some are sorta' burned but Mrs. Lyde says it's okay." Then her gaze shifted to the handful of misshapen cookies held in her sweating palm.

This was the longest string of words I had heard Delilah utter, and the effort seemed to have exhausted her. "Oh gee, cookies," I burbled to cover my own embarrassment. "Just what I need to go with my coffee while I'm working."

As soon as the words were out I froze; but of course it was too late. I had committed myself to actually consuming the food this grimy but compellingly needy child offered. Worse yet, I had implied by my words that I planned to eat the cookies now, while she stood watching. Reason dictated that this was not the hygienically correct path to follow, but my heart demanded the opposite course.

Delilah nudged the small pile onto the corner of my cluttered desk. I would like to report that in fairy tale fashion Delilah's offensive smell miraculously disappeared, or at least that I was able to ignore it at this crucial point. That was not the case. Truthfully, I was even more aware of the matter than normal as I selected a crumbled cookie from the stack. I must also admit that my choice was based on where it lay; certainly not the bottom one that had rested in her palm!

I glanced up to find Delilah watching me hopefully. It was the first sign of animation I had ever found in her, and this gave me the courage to nibble the cookie's edge and fake a favorable reaction. Immediately I swilled an enormous mouthful of coffee to wash down the offering, and in that short moment Delilah turned and slipped out of the room. I fleetingly noticed that the satisfied look of acceptance remained, and that is what I dwell on as I recall the whole incident.

Neither at that point nor at this can I imagine what I might have said if she had not departed right then. The next day and for each successive one until her family left the district, I fumbled for a way to make further contact. I tried to involve Delilah in the classroom community more, but she again settled into her unresponsive behavior. We would trade an occasional pleasant glance or word, but nothing more.

I have never had another Delilah; either with the same name or that smell. The part of her that does stay with me is the realization that I did more for Delilah by accepting that one cookie than any discussion on hygiene ever could have. It is that learning which I carry with me as I face new students with new needs.

REFLECTION ON "MY, MY, MY DELILAH"

In the summer of 1994, after having completed 23 years of high school teaching, I became part of the National Writing Project. No experience has had as great an influence. Both personally and professionally I became immersed in a wave of new information, innovative techniques, and first-time-ever introspection of my role as an educator.

Until then I had alternately floated along or swum against the tide of new "quick fix" ideas that seem to wash over educators in waves. To continue the metaphor, it seemed that these new philosophies which were touted as a sure cure for the sinking ship of student apathy and parent animosity had me adrift for a quarter century in a sea of useless ideas. Then the Writing Project introduced me to the concept of the writing workshop and collaborative learning as ways to individualize instruction. This was accomplished both by immersing me in a working model, and by providing the time and means to do professional development research. Also, I was encouraged to reflect on my teaching and to write about the experience.

One of the fruits of this endeavor was my Delilah story. The main character is a real student and the facts are accurate as I remember them. I'm sure that time has blurred some memories while other aspects of the story have become crystallized as though looking at a still snapshot of a rapidly moving scene. However, the story is most important because it allows me to view Delilah as an archetype of all students who silently call out for individual recognition.

I like to believe that if Delilah walked back into my classroom today, if I were able to replay the scene, I could do better. Since I currently use the writing workshop format, students are freed from the old constraints of endless dry drills on spelling, punctuation, grammar, and form which so often robbed writing of its spark. Nonresponsive students such as Delilah now enter into meaningful written dialogue with me as well as peer writers. They become more open and more fluent as they gain confidence in selecting and developing their own topics.

I make clear to writing groups in my classroom that non-judgmental response is vital. I also invite students to share with me directly if they feel the topic is too sensitive or personal. That one simple step in individualizing instruction has opened the floodgates for numerous shy writers.

One example will serve to illustrate the point. Amy was a student recently placed with a foster family in our district. Writing response groups had already formed, and for the first few assignments Amy "sat out." Actually she refused to submit any piece of writing except an antiseptic daily journal delivered directly to me. These I responded to with profuse written comments and questions. Gradually her writing lengthened and drifted into more personal narratives. This gave me an avenue for developing a relationship that paid off for me and Amy both academically and personally. Writing about the past abuse she endured helped start the healing process for Amy as I was also able to guide her to stronger writing skills.

Looking back, I see that exchange as the missing piece in my encounter years earlier with Delilah. The system at that time had me tied so firmly into a lockstep curriculum that I could not touch the students' real personal needs without feeling I had abandoned the revered traditional teacher role.

I'm glad those days are past.

Chapter 4

Perplexities

> The core challenges of teaching are rarely taught in colleges of education, rarely acknowledged by administrators or policy makers, and yet essential if teaching is ever to be more than clerking. . . . We [teachers] are the instruments of our teaching, and knowing ourselves is essential. (Ayers, 1997, p. x)

The stories in this chapter explore the complexities of the student-teacher relationship, school policies, and the general culture of schooling. Each author provides a glimpse into the personal struggle of a teacher trying to meet the needs of particular students. The first story, "The One Who Got Away" by Jeanne Buckingham, tells the story of Sabrina, a student in her high school classroom whose actions prompt Jeanne to examine her own teaching practice in an effort to meet the changing needs of her students.

Ruth Givens tells us that she wrote "Teacher Lure: An Anecdotal Analysis of Boundary Issues in Pedagogical Studies" in an effort "to understand how the events in [her] experiences can provide a better understanding of the teacher-student relationship, particularly as it applies to establishing boundaries in that relationship." In "The Dam Breaks: A Story of Culture Wars in the Classroom" John Parbst explores the challenges of trying "to cultivate a better sense of enlightenment and understanding" among his students amid society's racial and ethnic tensions. He also reflects on his need to talk with colleagues, which provides a chance for "group interaction and discussion to understand and clarify the thoughts in my head."

John Piirto grapples with the difficult issues teachers must face when giving grades to students in "Low Grades and the Student/Teacher Relationship."

"When one must place a judgment—a grade—upon another, the answers are not as simple, nor are they detached," he writes in the introduction to the story. In "Sally's Story" Carolyn Thomas writes about the troubled life of one student, Sally, and the lack of support Sally experiences from the school and community. Thomas talks about teaching as a "holy undertaking" that comes with the responsibility to educate all children. Bonnie Voth writes about what she learned from her struggle with one young student's special needs in "As Through a Looking Glass."

REFERENCE

Ayers, W. (1997). Foreword. In G. Larson. *Making conversation: Collaborating with colleagues for change.* (pp. ix–x). Portsmouth, NH: Boynton/Cook.

The One Who Got Away
Jeanne Buckingham

That was the thing about Sabrina Rogers. She certainly could write. I remember looking over an early essay and being startled by the vividness with which she described a chance meeting with some older boys in Ocean City. Her self-assured script told of their flattering comments: she had to be older than 14! Sabrina referred to the strictness of her folks, as she realized she wouldn't be able to see these fellows back home. Her ending was a willful declaration that she would move into her own place when she was 15. I read the piece twice just to be certain that the tone of a 20-year-old was coming from a ninth-grader.

Now here it was again—that bold voice—only this time it was December, and Sabrina was describing her fantasy of killing me. Quite unsuspecting, I had scooped the stack of rough copies from my desk, clutched them to my chest, and dashed to the computer lab. My plan had been to read only those papers on which students had asked for feedback. Sabrina's draft was on the top and stated clearly, "Please read and check mistakes."

The piece began innocently enough. She had written, "I knew on the very first day at City High that this year would be like all the rest." As I read on, however, I began to feel edgy. "Sooner or later one of these damn teachers will give me detention and I will refuse to serve it." I followed her to-be-continued arrow to the back side where I saw, "I am going to kill her. I want to smother her with a pillow and then stab her."

Neither life nor methods courses had prepared me for this death threat. Like a box turtle retracting all appendages into its protective shell, my reflex reaction to danger is to retreat to the comfort of the known. As I read Sabrina's words, even though I knew I had given her detention, I couldn't believe she was threatening me. She didn't mean it. It was a joke. I was over-reacting.

How had our relationship deteriorated so drastically? Sabrina was a student in my period four freshman English class, a nightmare of hormones and hyperactivity. Would-be boxers threw punches as they danced around the room. Adversaries shouted taunts across the aisles, each determined to have the last word. Restless souls cruised to the pencil sharpener while managing a kick here and there along the way. A typical class reminded me of trying to put out all the little grease fires that pop up on my grill when I barbecue chicken. As soon as I quell one flame, another flares from a distant corner. I had already constructed three or four seating charts so as to disconnect the live wires, but there were just too many! Early on, however, Sabrina had not been one of the problems.

Sabrina had ingratiated herself in those warm September weeks. When I circulated among the students to collect homework, she was one of the few to hand a paper to me. She sat in the front of the room and made friends with two other young women. They chatted as they worked and I looked forward to their cheerfulness. They were curious about my seating assignments. "You're not going to change our seats, are you? See how well we work together here. We don't waste time like these other immature jerks." Sabrina glanced from me to her approving friends.

"Well, I'll see. I usually change everyone's seat at the end of each quarter. I do like the way you get your work done." I hedged, knowing my preference for variety.

First quarter ended, and I did change everyone's—including Sabrina's —seat. Though mindful of her plea, my need to be seen as "fair" allowed me to dismiss easily what I saw as a harmless attempt to gain a privilege. With the move, however, I observed another side of Sabrina. She had begun to bait the boys who sat around her in a manner I didn't understand. One day she was a coquette, fluttering her lashes at little Josh Mosley, who panted in the desk opposite. Another day, if her books slid off her desk, she would whirl around, eyes snapping and voice threatening, and smack Josh on the arm.

Sabrina was much too grown up for these ninth grade twerps. Besides, she was lovely. She had skin like a cinnamon-colored nectarine, perfectly smooth. Her eyes were hazel, large and piercing. When she spoke, her full lips, usually tinted with maroon, parted around even white teeth. In a paragraph about how to style hair, Sabrina described the daily ritual which produced the auburn bouffant pulled back to reveal two very large gold hoops. She was never in a hurry, and her carriage suggested poise and self-confidence.

Besides this perverse flirtation, the seat changes also seemed to undermine Sabrina's work ethic. Her friend Abby now sat right behind, and Sabrina had started to twist sideways in her seat and use Abby's desk for writing. Now her back faced me, while her head was always turned to the rear. This way she could easily talk to her friend while appearing to follow the lesson. It was inevitable. Sabrina received a detention.

Early in November, I was still struggling to establish a sense of order among these freshmen, so I had distilled classroom rules to three reminders: follow instructions; speak only when directed to; and remain in your seat. Sabrina was having trouble with the first two. One day, when I had ignored her back and talking for what seemed to me to be too long, I called her name, to remind her of her infraction. Sabrina swiveled in her seat and cradled her head on her desk. She didn't like it when I drew attention to her. What was also becoming apparent, however, was that she wanted to lock wills with me. The next day she forgot her book, a convenient excuse for her to share with her friend, and to continue the socializing. This time when I called her name and asked her to turn around, her hostility was tangible. She glared at me through lowered eyelids, sucked her teeth, and continued as she pleased. I added her initials, SR, to the detention list.

In a holiday mood, I later forgave that first detention, but then the very next day she "forgot" her grammar book again. From the chalkboard, I railed against the sins of fragments and run-ons, while Sabrina sat with her back to me and talked.

"Sabrina, please turn around and pay attention to the lesson," I directed.

"Why don't you just leave me alone!" she shouted.

This sounded more like a dare than a request. Since I knew this class would just love a confrontation, I asked Sabrina to "step out into the hall for a minute." Perhaps she could drop the bravado if we had no audience. Although I did not have time for a conference at that moment, I did want her to hear my requirements.

"You have 13 minutes detention, to be served in three days. Please, in the future, face the front of the room during a lesson, whether or not you have your textbook."

Sabrina rolled her eyes and then pointed one of her scarlet nails—the one with the rhinestone on the tip—in my face. "You are just picking on me for no reason. Those boys in there pull all this stuff and you never do anything. All you do is scream at us."

With the certain instincts of a young predator, this teenager knew how to hurt me. I cringed under charges of unfairness and screaming. I swallowed a protest and remembered *Assertive Discipline*.

"Sabrina, you have three days to do the detention. Please bring your book tomorrow."

The following morning I reminded Sabrina as she was leaving the room, "Don't forget the detention."

Her friend Abby snickered. "She said she's not doing it. I'm just kidding. She's going to do it, aren't you, Sabrina?"

Sabrina nodded, and I wondered at the transformation.

I guess you could say I misread the foreshadowing. So I was quite unprepared for the venom I had just read in Sabrina's rough draft. In the three minutes between classes, I raced along the corridors, reviewing options. Show the school psychologist? Call her mom? Confront Sabrina herself? Perhaps warnings to take seriously student references to violence alarmed me. Maybe I simply sensed the need for a mediator. Whatever the reason, I found myself moving quickly to share this writing, not with Sabrina herself, but with a peer. Even as I handed the draft over to Bill Turner, Sabrina's guidance counselor, however, I still believed I was over-reacting.

Two hours later I was heading for a conference with Sabrina, her mother and the counselor. I was nervous. I could not imagine facing anyone who hated me that much. In her brief life, Sabrina had already out-distanced me in her range of emotions, and I felt I was no match for her. She knew how to feel and express her anger. She could imagine herself doing violent acts. I, on the other hand, go out of my way to be sure people love me. I mistake anger for hurt and search for flaws in myself when criticized. To Sabrina, I must appear as I can sometimes picture myself in student eyes: the white lady with the grey straw bob, who wears long skirts and sandals with socks, and spits when she talks too fast. What aspect of me had elicited such a virulent reaction in her?

We squared off in Bill Turner's office. Sabrina's mother was White, and Sabrina's sepia-toned skin added another layer to her complexity. Was her own father Black? Was there a White stepfather? Many students in our building mark X behind "Black" for race with a hand lighter than mine. Others with Negroid features select "Hispanic." I notice constant reminders that identity is convoluted for our students, but I had overlooked that fact in Sabrina until this moment.

Bill began. "Sabrina, why don't you tell Ms. Buckingham what you told us about your reasons for writing the paragraph?"

"I don't see why she even read it—she wasn't supposed to. I didn't give it to her."

I wanted to object. After all, her writing had somehow found its way to the very top of my papers and was marked "Please read." A motive deeper than self-justification, however, must have kept me quiet. On a subconscious level, I was an advocate for Sabrina. I knew that if I made her look worse than she already did, I would lose any chance for reconciliation.

"You told us earlier that you wrote this paper with Ms. Buckingham in mind. Whether or not you intended her to see it is beside the point. Suppose you tell us the problem, as you see it."

"She's just picking on me. She never yells at anyone else. I do my work. I was just sharing a book. She can't even control the class. She just stands up in the front of the room and screams at us. She should do something about those Black guys—they're always saying crude stuff to us. She never does anything to them. No—just me." I heard her lump all the troublemakers into the phrase "Black guys," as if to distance herself from a despised group. I also heard criticism of me, and self-justifications rushed in like antibodies attacking antigens in the blood stream.

I was allowed to speak next. I tried to include Sabrina with my gaze, but she continued to avert her head, cracking and popping her gum at a quick clip.

"Sabrina is usually a responsible student. Her first quarter grade reflects this."

Her mother interrupted. "But you gave her a *C* and said she was not working up to her potential."

"That was my way of letting Sabrina and you know that I believed she could earn a much higher grade if she tried a bit harder. I didn't mean it as a weakness but rather as a recognition of her talent."

"That's not what it felt like," sniffed Sabrina.

"Anyway," I continued, "Sabrina has begun talking in class during a lesson, not paying attention to my directions and forgetting her book. These actions caused her to earn a detention. She had three days to complete the punishment, but she did not report."

Now Ms. Rogers flashed at Sabrina. "Why didn't you serve the detention, Sabrina? You should have. That was wrong. And your book—you have no business forgetting your book."

For a moment I was relieved. The mother would be reasonable. Sabrina protested but her mother was firm.

"I never forget my books. It was just that one time. And I told you, I'm not serving her detention. I don't think I deserve it."

"You'll do what I say, young lady, or you won't leave the house for a long time."

The counselor tried to guide the conversation to a safe channel. "There are two separate issues here, Sabrina. One is the threat of violence and that will have to be handled by your administrator. The other is the detention you owe Ms. Buckingham, and how you will resolve your differences with her so that you can be productive again in her class. I heard Ms. Buckingham say that you have every possibility of doing well."

"She'll serve that detention—don't you worry about that. What I'm worried about now," Ms. Rogers peered at me, "is how things are going to be after this. I know how teachers can be to a student when a parent comes in to talk about a problem. I want to be sure that you won't take it out on Sabrina."

Forgetting that this mother's concern could be seen as natural, instead I heard her question my integrity. Now on the defense, my eyes filled. My response felt impudent, but I was nonplused and maybe even a bit angry. Whose life was being threatened here, anyway? Who needed protection from whom?

I watched myself turn to Sabrina's mom and say, "I don't really know how to answer that question at the moment."

Over the phone that evening, my own daughter's reactions were certain and immediate. "No way, Mom. No way do you have to let that girl back in your class. Don't do it to yourself."

What a radical idea! Have a malcontent transferred? As it turned out, that decision was within my rights. The assistant principal was clear and swift in the adjudication. "Students may be transferred for threatening a classroom teacher. You have a few days to make up your mind. Sabrina's on a ten-day suspension."

I didn't need ten days and my decision surprised me. Neither Sabrina's improved chances for success with a fresh teacher nor my admission of a personality clash graced my choice. I simply took the easy way out. Every time I thought of looking at Sabrina sitting in a desk before me, my stomach lurched. The class was out of control anyway, and I believed I would never establish order if I had to deal with her overt hostility or my memory of it.

Sabrina transferred to a colleague's class, but her specter did not evaporate. All winter I watched for her at the east side lockers where I knew she met friends at lunchtime. Sometimes I'd see her, and we both would avoid each other's eyes. More often I began to read her name—the first name I'd look for each day—on the absentee list. I fretted over what seemed to be a dropping-out pattern, and imagined Sabrina's tempestuous home life: a mom she could control; a stepdad who rejected and perhaps abused her; curfews she ignored; a sexuality too powerful for her age. I saw her writing desperate lines of self-hatred strong enough to invite suicide.

I read somewhere about the power of the negative, and have applied this notion to my experience as a parent. My grown children sometimes recall only the unpleasantness of their early years and allow it to epitomize their entire youth. I'm just as perverse in the case of Sabrina. This year was pretty good. There wasn't one student about whom I had a bad attitude. Even Sabrina had caught me off-guard. I know I was happy in school. I believe some students felt successful. Invariably, however, my mind returns to what I see as my failure, and I question whether I gave up too easily. Teachers *can* save lives, and I had always seen myself as a dedicated professional, eager to make a difference in each one's life, especially the troubled kids. In Sabrina's case, however, I had decided that I lacked the energy to rehabilitate our relationship. My choice to remove her from my class felt selfish, and the thought haunted me.

Sabrina allowed herself to connect personally with me; she dug her bright nails under my skin and I came to care about her. She let me know her potential and her pain, and she's the one who got away.

REFLECTION ON "THE ONE WHO GOT AWAY"

Twenty years ago, when an English professor asked me how I thought I could be effective with high school students, I answered with a platitude in which I believed fervently. I would see each student as a human being worthy of respect and I would strive to convey my regard in the hope of building student self-esteem. I was so certain I could embrace them all, even the most unlovable.

Now I struggle to maintain that idealism, in the face of growing student disaffection. My classes reflect the demographic challenges of large cities, with their transient populations, and exposure to crime, drugs and violence. The relevance of my subject, English, in their chaotic lives, seems difficult for them to perceive. Believing that students would come to understand and appreciate my investment in their success, I had always hoped that this awareness would mitigate any distance caused by the stark contrast in age, race, experience, and in some cases gender between these students and me. The last few school years, however, have ended with a nagging question about my effectiveness, as more and more students were unsuccessful in my classes.

Rather than accept the inevitability of failure, I examined my teaching methods and abandoned many traditional practices. More instruction would be student centered; students would enjoy increased freedom of movement in the class; alternative methods of assessment such as portfolios, group projects, and writing would eliminate most testing. I vowed to be more consistent with discipline, realizing that both my distaste for the record-keeping details of detention, and high tolerance for disruption, often resulted in frustration for me as well as the students. This last resolution led to my conflict with Sabrina.

The story of Sabrina is really the story of my identity crisis. Because I would continue to teach, I needed to examine what my exchange with this young woman elicited from me, and why. The story highlights the very real daily dilemmas of teachers: How do we encourage the positive student? What behavior do we ignore? How long do we tolerate a disruptive student in the hope of "saving" her? When is it more important to help the student learn self-control rather than parts of speech? Are we listening well enough to decode hidden calls for help? When do we intervene in a personal situation? At what point do we need a mediator?

In retrospect, I appear to have been too rigid with Sabrina. In view of the fact that our encounter occurred precisely during a year when I was consciously committed to reforming my practices, the incident is ironic, regrettable and painful for me to recall. I am a different person, however, from the naive student teacher who so glibly answered her professor. I continue to care about the young men and women with whom I meet 180 days a year, and I hope I can help each to grow in mind and spirit, but I know I won't "save them all." The trouble with Sabrina, however, and perhaps the reason she continues to haunt me, is that maybe she was asking for help and I didn't hear her plea.

Teacher Lure: An Anecdotal Analysis of Boundary Issues in Pedagogical Studies
Ruth Givens

As teachers we all have stories that help affirm our identities in the classroom and clarify our purpose in education. During my twenty-five years of teaching I have amassed memories of students and classes that seemed to transcend the routine of school life, where we established an immediate rapport and maintained a synchronized momentum throughout the year. I have a drawer full of notes and letters from students who have taken the time to tell me that my efforts made a difference in their lives. However, we also have experienced failures in the classroom when some students, for some reason or another, were lost as we lacked the understanding to deal with them or the energy to press them on. Even more unsettling are the dark stories that find us unwittingly involved in the cross fires of events in our students' lives. These experiences are among our stories, but they baffle us—for we cannot find where things went wrong, nor can we figure out how to fix these untidy endings.

One such experience for me has been the obsessive student whose over-attachment forced me to evaluate the boundaries I had established in the teacher-student relationship. Not just early in my career, but later as well, I had two experiences in which my simple gestures of friendliness fueled a loyalty that was beyond a student's typical admiration; rather, it seemed as if the student was completely focused on me. These events were never resolved, nor am I even certain of my own interpretation of them. Perhaps my rationale for telling this story is to provide a kind of catharsis for the emotions that have resided within me for these years, but I wonder if the stories that fill the annals of teacher lore have their own shadow or dark side . . . teacher lure.

Teachers are basically nurturing creatures; otherwise they would have chosen a more lucrative or less demanding profession. I am no exception. As an English teacher, I often learn more about my students than they realize because their essays often reflect the joys and pains of their personal lives. In my earlier years as a teacher, I saw my role as a means to aid their wounded psyches in any way I could. Although I tried not to be intrusive, my heart was an open door for them if they needed someone to listen to them. Consequently, I often found myself in precarious roles of confidentiality as my students sought me out to listen to the details of their lives. The natural affinity that resulted from my openness and their vulnerability created a kind of hubris within me that made me believe that I had the power to affect their decisions and change their lives significantly.

Because I taught in a Christian school, I felt I had an even greater responsibility to be involved in my students' lives, not only by attempting to right the wrongs in their lives, but also by loving the unlovable. In addition, I was often drawn to the causes of the rebels and the underdogs, perhaps because I had always been a bit of a rebel myself. One student, whom I will call Pat, was particularly alienated from her peers. Pat always sat at the back of the room and never had anything to say during or after class. One day I talked with her and encouraged her to try to become more of a part of her surroundings by participating in class. The next day she was in my office crying, telling me her life's story of rejection, abuse, and misunderstanding. This quickly developed into a pattern: Pat would wait for me in my office after class to relate the past and ongoing tragedies in her life.

My "solution" was to offer her relationships with people who would accept her, so I invited her to my home. She began babysitting for me and some of my friends. She became a part of nearly every aspect of my life, but it was a duty-bound relationship because her deep-rooted anger kept a genuine friendship from forming. She would say, "God makes up the rules and we are only his pawns," or accuse the school of collaborating against her. I attempted to dispel her pervasive hostility, to reason with her about her anger, or sympathize with her sense of alienation. She resented the presence of my children or friends or anyone who took my attention away from her, and she interrupted them or excluded them whenever she could. I thought she needed someone so desperately that I "owed" her part of my comfortable life as if it would make hers better.

This relationship continued to demand more and more of me, and all the while Pat would make remarks about her values that were repugnant to my way of thinking. I can still hear her say "there are no rules" to my children, then six and four. Her anger deepened and her life began to unravel as she bought things and didn't pay for them, ran up huge phone bills, failed classes, and began to steal from my friends. Within a few months Pat was committed to the psychiatric ward at a hospital after attempting suicide. During her treatment, Pat told the psychiatrist that I was the only person of value to her and she needed me to be at her bedside for her recovery. My response, however, was that I was quickly becoming afraid of her and I wanted to begin distancing myself. When I asked the psychiatrist if Pat's feelings were out of proportion, she admitted that they were. Nevertheless, the psychiatrist convinced me to "at least spend some time with her," so I reluctantly agreed to meet her during my lunch hour. As we were pulling out of the parking lot, Pat's car stalled. Rather than asking for help, she began shouting obscenities at the passers-by. Her anxiety grew, and by the afternoon Pat was admitted to the hospital. It was then that I was told she had a gun with her. If the car had not stalled, I don't know if she would have used it on me.

I was too afraid to see her again. The psychiatrist warned me to not let my children play alone, in case she wanted to retaliate or hurt me in some way for rejecting her. For years I feared that she would show up in some horrible and threatening way. One of my friends who had been involved got an unlisted phone number, insisting that she had received hang-up calls. So had I.

Never again would I allow myself to be over-involved with a student, I decided. The minute I sensed any kind of mental imbalance or emotional problems I would keep my distance. Until Lisa. Lisa wrote a disclaimer about herself in a paper, and I attempted to reassure her that she had value by writing a positive comment on her paper. The next thing I knew she began bringing me gifts, writing me notes, and waiting for me between classes. In desperation, I decided to try the direct approach. I talked with her after class, telling her that with a hundred students and a family I could not be the friend she needed. She insisted that she wanted nothing from me . . . only to help me. Nothing could dissuade her.

Although I did not give her my phone number or address, she managed to get a job as a student worker in the English department. Placement decisions were made by the university services department, and when she requested to be my teacher's aide they granted her the position, unaware of the dynamics. I had nothing concrete to hold against her; I felt trapped with a student who only wanted to "help" me. When I was in the office, Lisa would tell students that I was too busy to see them. She would bring me gifts and cards that would say things like "your smile makes me melt." I could not convince anyone that this attention was out of bounds, and even I wondered if I were projecting onto this student my fear of another Pat. I had thought that after the first experience with an obsessive relationship, I could control it the next time. After all, the first time I was a naive rookie teacher trying to save the world; this time I had experience and savvy. Why could I not control what was happening to me?

I don't know even today if it was an over-reaction, but I asked to have her removed as my assistant. She then became the aide for the teacher next to my office because the other teachers didn't believe she was causing problems and felt that I had mistreated her. To some, her devotion seemed so innocent, compounding my confusion and guilt for my own actions. Regarding my relationship with Lisa, the atmosphere at work was awkward, but I was determined to hold my ground. However, on my birthday, Lisa decided to "make up," as she called it. She wrote "Happy birthday, beautiful" on my door and had cake, balloons, and streamers throughout the room.

To my great relief, Lisa graduated. But on my next birthday (even though she was no longer a student), Lisa showed up with an even bigger gift, apologizing for the trouble she had caused me the year before. I have never seen her again, and although I've heard that she has told others that she knows she acted inappropriately, I still avoid the prospect of renewing any ties.

For me, the brokenness of these relationships and my inability to resolve them reminds me that the issue of boundaries continues to create perplexing dilemmas. My experiences have left me with more questions than answers. Did I establish appropriate boundaries? Is there such a thing as appropriate boundaries? At times with my students my self-imposed boundaries inhibit me, and at other times I remove my boundaries at my own peril. Each time my decision involves a risk that will affect my students' experiences in my class and my own effectiveness in their lives, which seems to be a proverbial tightrope that I walk in my effort to be a living, breathing part of the event we call education.

REFLECTION ON "TEACHER LURE"

As I stated in my story, the natural proclivity for nurturing makes teachers more vulnerable to those who might abuse their approachability, but it also opens more doors for delightful relationships across generations that would be difficult to build under any other circumstances. In many ways I think relationally oriented people experience the best and the worst of people, and the gains certainly outweigh the losses. My purpose in telling my story is not to warn against the inherent vulnerability of the profession, but rather to understand how the events in these experiences can provide a better understanding of the teacher-student relationship, particularly as it applies to establishing boundaries in that relationship.

Max van Manen (1990) writes that pedagogic situations are always unique and that each situation, each student, creates a distinct case unlike any other, and the pedagogical challenge is to be able to recognize it, search for universal qualities, and apply them to the individual. Since the telling of my story is itself an abstraction, it is by necessity universalized to any reader to some extent. My errors, or the errors of the students I have written about, may have been overlooked by my blind spots or by my earlier inexperience, leaving only partial truth, even if it is unintentional. Nevertheless, the similarities of the two experiences validate a theme or pattern of either their relating or my responding and the boundaries that were established early in the relationship. I have used the term "boundaries" to explain the enigma of the connection we experience with our students in the day in and day out lives of our profession. It is a word that appears to belong to the province of psychologists and therapists when referring to the limits we place on our own approachability. Though the term is by and large neutral by its descriptive nature, it is used more to describe the lack of something than the possession of it. For example, rarely do we hear that one has a great set of boundaries; rather, we hear that one lacks boundaries, although these boundaries are different for each individual, and obtaining them, or at least the right amount, has something to do with establishing independence and autonomy. In some professions, boundary issues may rarely arise, but in professions as people-oriented as teaching, the tensions between intimacy and privacy lurk behind many of our encounters with our students, and the hit-or-miss character of the minute-by-minute decisions teachers make can occasionally take on astronomic consequences. Yet who would deny the chance to affect a life when the opportunity arises?

Certainly those of us who work with young people find our greatest rewards in these opportunities. It has been assumed in the past that our gender significantly affects the way we establish boundaries, but as society continues to relinquish established roles, the uncertainties of establishing boundaries without diminishing relationships has exacerbated the dilemma for both male and female teachers. Women in the profession are often more vulnerable by the very nature of their gender, whether some would claim it is "nurture" rather than "nature" that makes us so. In her studies of women's moral development Carol Gilligan (1993) concludes that the feminine characteristics of fostering social interaction and personal relationships make the formation of ego boundaries more difficult for girls to formulate, but puts them at an advantage in terms of interpersonal relationships. For males who have been rewarded in the past for establishing strong ego boundaries, the demands have been changing to relax those boundaries in favor of interpersonal development. In other words, a precedence no longer exists for men or women, leaving both with unresolved questions.

As the gender gap diminishes, or at least is not as fixed, and as educators move away from a paradigm that insulates them from the students' lived experience, a more indefinite enigma will take its place—albeit a more humane one—but it leaves us with a perplexing question that must be asked: Where are the pedagogical boundaries that separate professional obligations from personal commitments?

As educators we are constantly being made aware that our profession offers questions of meaning daily, even hourly. We have no guide book for each situation; in fact the lack of "right" answers in terms of relational questions sometimes overwhelms us, and we have to go back to those times when it worked—those times when we saw the light dawn or the life change in the lives of our students. Van Manen (1991) writes that meaning questions help us understand the pedagogical significance of a situation, but they "cannot be 'solved' or done away with once and for all. Few pedagogical problems can ever be eradicated on the spot or overnight. Rather, we must learn to get on and get along with these situations and with each other" (p. 108). As we continue to live with the ambiguities that often comprise our interactions with students, our collective insights provided in teacher stories affirm the integrity of a profession that is not afraid to prepare for the future by looking at the past.

REFERENCES

Gilligan, Carol. (1993). *In a different voice: Psychological theory and women's development.* Cambridge, MA: Harvard University Press.

Van Manen, Max. (1991). *The tact of teaching.* Albany, NY: State University of New York Press.

———. (1990). *Researching lived experience: Human science for an action sensitive pedagogy.* Albany, NY: State University of New York Press.

The Dam Breaks: A Story of Culture Wars in the Classroom
John Parbst

> But it will be
> part of you, instructor.
>> from "Theme for English B" by Langston Hughes

Those of us who teach discover very early on in our careers that this profession offers insights into the world that are as much a learning experience for us as for our students. I stumbled upon this discovery quite easily through years of growing up, going to school, and beginning my teaching career in southern California before moving to Long Island, New York, to teach at a community college. My story reflects this move east and one important lesson that moved along quietly beside me before rearing up in a startling way on Long Island.

While growing up in southern California, I marveled at the diversity surrounding me. I loved the physical landscape—the gritty, dry air blowing in off the desert mixing with saturated, cool Pacific breezes, and the vision of high mountain peaks surrounding a basin of valleys and sea-level beaches. There were other, perhaps less attractive, defining characteristics of the landscape as well—a hot cloud of smog hanging in the air, blanketing cracks that opened wider with each passing earthquake. The physical landscape mirrored much of the human culture of southern California. I had the opportunity to experience a wide range of people from diverse cultures. It was often a beautiful mix of people. Unfortunately, the mix proved volatile and ugly at times.

While all of these images and experiences have found a place within me, I remember the students most of all. One year in a writing class, Soon Li expressed her thanks to me for the opportunity to read Lu Xun's short stories again. She traveled back home to Taiwan through his words, and her insights in our writing groups energized the discussion. In another course, Rieko drew parallels between the trickster character in Native American myths and the monkey character she recalled from childhood stories in Japan. Still again, Sandra stood up amid a class of students mirroring our country's European roots and shared some of her experiences growing up African-American. What I recall now is how well the class listened that day. And finally I remember Hao, a political prisoner for six years in a Cambodian P.O.W. camp. Hao loved education and gardening—his captors cheated him of books and the simple pleasure of digging into the earth for far too many years. Amid all these diverse people, I found that reading multicultural literature sparked many powerful remembered thoughts and emotions in my students. I felt good about this rich approach to teaching—and I may have learned more than my students during this time.

I settled into a new teaching job on Long Island during the fall of 1994. The landscape differed noticeably from my old home. As I explored the area, I found that I missed the diverse mountain and desert landscapes of southern California. And I soon noticed I was missing something in the people around me as well. This new college, 60 miles east of New York City, offered very little of the ethnic diversity I had grown up with. Instead, my classes were filled with a homogeneous group of middle-class students from predominantly Italian backgrounds. Yet amid this change, my new community college felt familiar, and this feeling grew more comfortable as I experienced the concerns and desires of my students who shared the same career and educational dreams as my previous students.

These new students seemed to enjoy my teaching style, and I felt very excited about asking students in one of my writing classes to read the novel *Sula* by Toni Morrison. Oh sure, I got lots of those uneasy glances and sullen looks on the first day of class. "We have to read this novel along with all the other writing in the course?" I imagined them all thinking as we discussed the course requirements. "It's O.K.," I thought back at them, "we'll make it through the book and all the writing." Our silent exchanges that day would surely lead to more open discussions once Toni Morrison's powerful, striking prose entered into our class. I eagerly awaited their reactions to the book.

I considered myself lucky with that class. They were a lively, honest group comprised of an intimate number of 15 students. The majority of my students had been in high school the previous year, but a few carried the label "returning student." Eric was one such returning student who worked construction and other odd jobs before giving college a try. Eric also established himself early on as that one student who would challenge my influence over the class during the semester. He sat in the back of the room, as most rebels do, and would on occasion usurp my control over the class and draw everyone into his agenda for a moment. One minute the class would be listening attentively to my introduction of our next project, and the next minute half the class would be hanging out of the windows peering at Eric's idea of the hottest car on campus. But Eric was always good-natured during his interruptions, so these occasional distractions didn't bother me much. However, an event at about the mid-point of the semester shocked me. Eric came into my office before class and said he would rather not read *Sula* because he didn't like Blacks.

I found myself struck dumb. A long and uncomfortable silence. I'm sure the pause between our words didn't really last too long, yet, of course, it seemed to me that Eric and I were opening up a widening hole between us with this silence. What struck me most at the time was how easily Eric was able to articulate that one thought—the words seemed to spill from him like an old habit. I could tell he knew those emotions all too well. Feeling a sudden urge to grab Eric in some kind of pathetic attempt to shake that sentence out from inside him, I realized that I honestly had no idea what to say or do at that point. My hope was to see his words fall and shatter on the floor of my office, but, realizing the futility of that hope, I asked Eric to simply give the book a try and added that I would gladly cover issues and questions about the book very soon in class. Finally, I reminded Eric that our next essay would be based on issues from the book, hoping that my academic bribery would encourage him to make a sincere effort in trying to understand Morrison's poignant message. Eric agreed to read the book and added that he wasn't prejudiced. "I've just had a few personal problems with Blacks, but I don't hate all of them," he remarked before gathering his books and heading off to my class. Eric left, I was alone, and silence again overwhelmed my office—a silence just as uncomfortable as the silence that surrounded both of us after Eric first uttered those words.

I can conjure up images from the novel *Sula* at any time. Sometimes they come to mind without effort—visions of cool, white light; flames engulfing tired, aching bodies; water breaking through to bury a town. Morrison's work joins a body of experiences and emotions that mold the way I think and view my surroundings. But what will this, or any, book mean for my students? In the days following my meeting with Eric I questioned my approaches to teaching this writing course. Why should I require my students to read through this book in what, for most, was their first semester at college? This was, after all, a course defined by the college as "developmental"—a non-credit offering required of these students before the next step down the educational road. Did this book, with its complex language and themes, jump out as a stumbling block on the path to creating clearer pieces of writing for these students? Should I engage my students with the concerns brought up by Morrison in this text when they have so little writing experience? I was beginning to forget the real force of Eric's statement as I questioned my more pedagogical motives and approaches to the course.

Student questions began filtering in about a week before our scheduled discussion of the book. "I don't get it so far." "The language is hard to understand." "Why does everyone celebrate a 'National Suicide Day' in the book?" We talked about some of these issues and some of my answers started with, "You know, I'm not too sure myself, but. . . ." They struggled with the material (and I admitted I did, too), they engaged in conversations, they connected ideas, and they even lost ground in an effort to make some sense of the book. As a group, however, we were making progress in our understanding of this complex novel. I remember once again feeling very good about bringing this novel into our class.

The day of our first *Sula* discussion was one of my few days without some type of structured lesson plan; this day I would let evolve into our direction and into our topics. I knew my students would have something to say about the book based on our formal and informal talks from the previous weeks, but I wondered what thoughts and ideas would actually transpire during the discussion—and in the back of my mind I wondered whether Eric would bring up the discussion we had in my office. However, I also hoped to hear from Janet, who loved to tell us about growing up in South Carolina. And David, who "found" himself at the second Woodstock music festival the previous summer. And Linda, who was doing all she could to save whales and dolphins. I hoped to hear all their voices.

This was a class that usually took some time to "warm up," so the initial silence that greeted me early that class period didn't bother me much. These students were simply reluctant to speak, as many are when faced with difficult material, I reasoned. Surely they must have felt that I held the secret meanings to the book, and I imagined that they were waiting for me to suddenly spill all that I knew about the material. However, after a few questions on rather superficial character information and plot explanation, Janet spoke up. "I don't understand why Blacks today keep bringing up these issues from the past," she announced to the class. David jumped in: "They are already given more advantages than any of us." The dam broke as other voices emerged and thickened in the room. A passionate rage spilled out. I remember hearing words that slashed apart groups of people, and phrases such as "us and them" punctuated the conversation. A few students kept silent, yet for many this was a chance to lash out.

Thinking back as I write this, the day takes on a surreal quality. I heard each of my students speak that semester, but never like this. I remember Janet's frustrations over free writing: "I don't have anything more to say, that's why I've stopped!" I had to continually prod her to keep going through her uncomfortable writing moments. I remember James fighting each assignment, hoping for an easier way out: "Why don't you just tell us what to write and we'll write it," he would groan. He turned out to be one of the class's more imaginative writers that semester. But this day the voices seemed strangely different. Welfare, affirmative action, food stamps, crime, poverty—many in this class could not separate these issues from their vision of Black. These young people felt cheated and tricked beyond tolerance, and it was now time to vent these frustrations.

As you might imagine, this story continually plays itself out in my mind. I did what I could to bring those students and myself to some kind of resolution, but the struggle to blend and calm such volatile emotions is never easy. It is the tentative smiles and uncomfortable glances among students and teachers after such an event that speak quietly of the tensions that exist in our society. As teachers, we often see the crucible ignite in our classrooms and simply do all we can to control the flames.

REFLECTION ON "THE DAM BREAKS: A STORY OF CULTURE WARS IN THE CLASSROOM"

Certainly one of the most pressing concerns in American schools and colleges today is the struggle to nurture a positive environment for learning amid the all too common threats of racism and ethnic tensions that exist in many of our continually growing, diverse classrooms. So many social forces contribute to each person's cultural perspective and awareness that when such issues well to the surface during classroom activities, it is often difficult to know how to begin working through the situation in order to cultivate a better sense of enlightenment and understanding among everyone in the room. My story reflects just such a struggle.

Let me say something about how this story came to be written because this "story behind the story" illuminates an important activity crucial to the breaking down of biased notions in the classroom—creating a feeling of trust among those participating in discussion concerning these sensitive issues. Ironically, the summer before the incident I describe in my story, I participated in a Master Teacher Seminar organized by Suffolk County Community College. This seminar brought together teachers from our multi-campus college as well as teachers from other nearby colleges for a weekend of exploring pedagogical issues. One of the threads of discussion that ran through our weekend together was this idea of cultural tensions in the classroom. A colleague of mine at Suffolk, Barbara Coley, brought to the seminar her idea for a new literature course at our college that would survey contemporary non-western authors. Her driving purpose behind the development of this course was the belief that such non-western voices must be explored within the context of our growing global community.

Along with Barbara's ideas came those of a new acquaintance I would make that weekend—Lisa Whitten from nearby State University of New York College at Old Westbury. Lisa is a psychology professor at Old Westbury who takes a great interest in exploring the ways students react to cultural issues and shared with all of us a recent essay she wrote entitled "Managing Student Reaction to Controversial Issues in the College Classroom" (1993). Lisa's thoughts on this topic were enlightening, yet I must admit it wasn't until after my experience in the classroom the following semester that I looked more closely at the specific discussion techniques Lisa suggests for these situations. For me, however, that summer seminar helped me explore these issues amid the trusting environment of people who grew to be my friends, and it solidified a desire within me to expose my students to such important, yet potentially volatile, ideas.

The summer after the event in my story I was invited to participate in the Long Island Suffolk chapter of the National Writing Project. It was with the help of this group of supportive writers that I was able to collect and arrange my story pieces on paper in a way that helped me to understand myself more intimately and to clarify my approach to teaching within my own mind. Why mention these two gatherings within the context of my story? Because I have learned that I need group interaction and discussion to understand and clarify the thoughts in my head. I feel it is vitally important that teachers embrace this same approach to communication in the classroom. Our students deserve a chance to explore difficult topics within an open and supportive environment, and grappling with these issues in the classroom opens the door for this exploration.

I'd like to hear from readers of my essay who are willing to share comments about it or similar teaching experiences. Write to me c/o English Department, Suffolk Community College, 533 College Road, Selden, New York, 11784-2899 or e-mail <parbstj@sunysuffolk.edu>.

REFERENCES

Rampersad, A., & Roessel, D. (Eds.). (1995). *The collected poems of Langston Hughes.* New York: Knopf.

Whitten, L. (1993). Managing student reactions to controversial topics in the college classroom. *Transformations, 4*(1), 30–44.

Low Grades and the Student/Teacher Relationship
John Piirto

One morning a few days before the start of the fall semester, a young man appeared at my open office door. Blond hair parted in the middle, dark eyebrows, bright blue eyes, he introduced himself and said he would be taking my writing class. "I'm looking forward to it," Jeff told me, "but I want you to know that I'm not a very good writer." He looked me in the eye and kept on. "I'm committed to improving, though. I plan on becoming a software designer, a job where I'll have to do a lot of writing." He went on to say that his goal was to work hard, hard enough to earn an "A."

Jeff radiated an energy and sincerity which I was immediately attracted to. I told him I looked forward to seeing him in class, and encouraged him to work hard. But as a teacher with thirteen years' experience, I also cautioned him, as I do whenever a student has an A grade in mind, about putting pressure on himself and me.

"'A' stands for excellence," I said, "a level difficult to achieve."

His smile was bright. "You'll see," he assured me.

I begin with the above scenario, because it leads to a fundamental question: As teachers, are we prepared to give low final grades to students? But of course. We're professionally trained to make honest evaluations about student achievement. Let us go further, however, and consider that the student has tried hard, has done everything that was asked, yet still failed to achieve. What's more, suppose this student and the teacher have formed a special attachment, become true friends. Will difficulties arise over the low grade? Will the teacher question his or her performance? Will the student feel that the teacher wasn't loyal to their friendship? Ultimately, how does a low grade affect the relationship?

The story that follows reveals two forces at work in teaching: theory and practice. As regards our questions above, theory tells us the answers are simple: any good teacher will attach the proper grade for proper credit earned. In fact, as educators, we would consider it corrupt to apply any other standard. But theory is abstract and impersonal; rarely does it account for emotion, affection, intuitive reaction and response.

The second level asks us to look at the relationship between two people, not only the student/teacher relationship, but the larger one: friendship. When one must place a judgment—a grade—upon another, the answers are not as simple, nor are they detached. The repercussions tug at the heart.

Jeff began by selecting a topic he was interested in, computers, for his first paper. Though he was familiar with his subject and the desire was there, the writing was very poor. We discussed his first draft, reviewing the mechanical and organizational problems. His ideas were sound, though they, too, were problematic as he had only scratched the surface of his thinking. He assumed that no analysis or conclusions were required because, as he explained it, "The reader can figure that stuff out."

For his part he responded well to my suggestions and happily came in three or four times more to let me see what he'd done. Each visit I made sure to admire the effort, but I also told him that the improvement was minimal. "But I am improving," he asked, seeking my verification.

"Yes, you are, Jeff."

His first paper progressed enough that it became "average," and I gave him a C, emphasizing that considering from where he'd started, he had done well to get to this level. Naturally he was disappointed and vowed to do better.

For the next paper, and the next one after that, we went through the same process. There were the continual problems of style and substance. Frustrated, Jeff would ask, "And what should I put right here?" Though I told him I couldn't write the paper for him, on occasion we would write a passage together, so he could see the writing develop, so he could see how an idea could be taken apart and nudged further, so he could see how to make logical connections between sentences.

I pointed to passages other students in the class had written, students who had done well. I gave him passages from published authors, pointing out their writing strategies. I had him consult other teachers, too, so that he could get their input and criticism of his work.

I also gave him grammatical exercises to do, which he would turn in the next day completed, and sent him to the writing lab for extra help. But, I was sad to see, the writing simply did not improve much. His writing was like some kind of circle game, going round and round, from problem to problem and back again.

This "teaching process," however, was only one side of our relationship. The other? We became close friends. Perhaps the relationship could be viewed as a mistake on my part (I'll have more to say about this later), but I think not. Nurturance, empathy, personal warmth, these qualities make up the "heart" of teaching, and should not be overlooked or ignored (Bedwell, Hunt, Touzel, & Wiseman, 1991, p. 13). In fact, this connection is precisely why many of us teach.

Jeff and I discovered a mutual affection for tennis, art, and certain movies, subjects we often discussed in the hall or as prelude to our writing sessions. But it was more than these commonalities which caused us to be friends. I loved Jeff's gumption, his unflagging energy, his charging forward with merry determination in the face of challenge. These valuable qualities are rare and easy to appreciate in any student.

Jeff was also a most active participant in class. With infectious energy he'd lower his thick dark eyebrows and offer a poignant comment, but more often an unwittingly funny one way off the mark. He was a joyful person. Jeff had the ability to lift the class. He was a true "personality." And he tried so hard.

I believed he would be a success at life, no matter what his occupation, designing software or serving ice cream. In fact, I declared this to him as I informed him of his final course grade. In spite of the energy with which he attacked the class, Jeff received a low C. It hurt him. And it hurt me.

REFLECTION ON "LOW GRADES AND THE STUDENT/TEACHER RELATIONSHIP"

From this grade, two failures emerge: his and mine. But let us justify them in the name of education. First, as to Jeff's, if communication is critical to teaching (Seiler, Schuelke, & Lieb-Brilhart, 1984, p. 81), then I must speak with my student.

"Jeff, you may not have reached your goal, but you should not confuse this 'failure' with what you did learn. You certainly did not fail in the enterprises of being a student, the strategies of scholarship, of discovery, and effort. It may be hard for you to accept these as worthy results, as our society places a misguided emphasis on 'winning.' But learning to write is a lengthy undertaking, as is the serious study of any discipline. Guy de Maupassant's writing tutor advised him to write a million words before he ever tried to publish anything. Your writing needs a lot of work. The grade I gave you is the grade you earned."

My failure concerns the lack of ability to educate my student properly. But I justify the grade by talking to myself. "The unequivocal failure on my part would have been to reward Jeff with a higher grade than he earned. This is not to diminish the value of cultivating a student's self-esteem, but what is more dangerous is to build a false sense of accomplishment. Martin Covington (1992) describes for us the horrific downward spiral of academic failure in our schools (pp. 6–9). Ours is a world of grade inflation, declining test scores, students who do not read or write well, nor know how to solve problems. I would have severely let him down—and society—had I graded him on effort and improvement. Anyway, if an evaluation is necessary, and it is in teaching, this evaluation must correlate to the greater world where we grade not on improvement but achievement (Ahmann & Glock, 1981, p. 422)." I conclude by assuring myself that I actually did Jeff and the rest of us a favor by assigning him a low grade.

Terrific. Neat and clean. Justified. But this justification doesn't account for the following repercussions. First, Jeff had set a goal, which he shared with me, and did those things that he believed would take him to that goal. In this particular case, however, he fell far short. He would now feel disillusionment, that he had been lying to himself about his potential for success. He certainly would experience sadness and anger, perhaps self-pity.

What's more is that I contributed to these feelings. Here was a student who did all I asked and more. Here was a student who sought learning and came to me for answers. I helped him seek those answers, or at least I thought I did. As a teacher I want all my students to seek excellence, to aspire to new knowledge, to succeed. But I let him down. Jeff was a special case, I hear myself say, and special cases deserve special attention. As an instructor I am left with guilt, even shame, at my defective teaching ability.

But apart from these academic ramifications, there is something even worse, something that pierces my soul: our friendship deteriorated. Jeff dodged me after the end of the semester, crossing the street when he saw me or taking a different path. When I did come face to face with him, he would offer a curt smile or stiff wave.

One day I stopped him and asked if we could talk. After some polite conversation concerning his new classes, I acknowledged that there seemed to be a distance between us. Could it be the aftermath from the grade I gave him? Oh-no, he assured me. I did what was fair. With a little prodding, however, I found that part of his reticence stemmed from the notion that he'd let me down by not performing well in my class. But he really didn't want to get into any of that with me. I asked him to stop by my office if he got the chance, but that was the last contact I had with him.

Grades are necessary, we as educators hear. Students want them, parents do too, along with colleges, graduate schools and employers. Grades are our measurement. The trouble is, everybody wants good grades. If the grades are bad, well, that's a different story.

When I gave Jeff a low final grade, we lost something. Though we had a relationship built upon trust and mutual sentiments, the final grade violated that trust (Arnett, 1992, p. 220). Jeff felt that I had betrayed him; and since I too felt his hurt, it was as if I did betray him. He was the bad son whom I saw fit to discipline. Yet—and here is where the hurt comes from—he did nothing wrong. His crime was that he could not achieve to a prescribed set of standards, even though he gave it his all.

The situation with Jeff might have hardened me, caused me to keep my distance from students from then on. For isn't this path the safest? To impart knowledge, then disconnect?

Sorry, but many of us can't teach that way. Being involved on a personal level with a student has its challenges, but to keep them "nameless and faceless . . . is to contribute little to the development of competence, autonomy, purpose, and integrity" (Chickering & Reisser, 1993, p. 340). Phillips, Butt and Metzger (1972) tells us that we all attempt to find, through interaction, who we are in relation to other people, and what capabilities we have in evoking responses from them (p. 121). Ponder that idea for a moment and we find that good teaching requires depth and meaning beyond the mere distribution of knowledge and the assignment of grades. It requires contact.

Finally, I can already hear the chorus of those who say if a student/teacher relationship is strong and built upon open communication, then this friendship can survive even a low grade.

Perhaps this is true, but not always.

REFERENCES

Ahmann, J. S., & Glock, M. (1981). *Evaluating student progress: Principles of tests and measurements*, 6th ed. New York: Allyn and Bacon.

Arnett, R.C. (1992). *Dialogic education: Conversation about ideas and between persons*. Carbondale, IL: Southern Illinois University Press.

Bedwell, L. E., Hunt, G. H., Touzel, T. J., & Wiseman, D. G. (1991). *Effective teaching: Preparation and implementation*, 2nd ed. Springfield, IL: Charles Thomas.

Chickering, A. W., & Reisser, L. (1993). *Education and identity*, 2nd ed. San Francisco: Jossey-Bass.

Covington, M. V. (1992). *Making the grade*. New York: Cambridge University Press.

Phillips, G. M., Butt, D. E., & Metzger, N. J. (1972). *Communication in education: A rhetoric of schooling and learning*. New York: Holt, Rinehart and Winston.

Seiler, W. L., Schuelke, D., & Lieb-Brilhart, B. (1984). *Communication for the contemporary classroom*. New York: Holt, Rinehart and Winston.

Sally's Story
Carolyn Thomas

Once upon a time there was a girl named Sally. She lived in a small Oklahoma community where her family had lived for generations. Sally's family were for the most part lower working class, welfare recipients and high school dropouts. When they had jobs, they worked for minimum wage. Their school experiences were less than successful.

Although I had known Sally's family since childhood in school and as a social worker, I first came to know Sally when my daughter, Regan and Sally became friends on the school bus in elementary school. My parents demanded that I end the relationship because of who the family was and the fact that Sally cussed. While I wouldn't allow my daughter to visit Sally in her home, I defended her right to choose her own friends and refused to intervene. It was during this period that my daughter told me that Sally wasn't in school any more.

Weeks passed. One day Regan came home after school, put her hands on her hips and said, "Sally's back. Momma. You won't believe the story she told me! And she expected me to believe it." My daughter went on to relate how Sally's father had chased her, her mother and her brother through the house with a gun and shot at them. The sheriff came, arrested the father and took the family to a shelter for battered families. Sally was back in school because they had returned home to live with their father. My daughter was incensed. "Daddies don't do that!" she insisted. I explained to her as best I could that some daddies do.

When Sally was in the seventh grade, a fifteen-year-old girl was brutally murdered, raped, and the body burned. The day following her disappearance, Sally's father washed his car for the first time in months. Speculation was rife. Finally, Sally's father's cousin was charged with the murder. Sally's father turned state's evidence and testified to his part in disposing of the body. The students and teachers at school talked about the crime incessantly, either not knowing or not caring that Sally could hear their comments.

The next year Sally was one of the junior high cheerleaders that I coached. She worked hard, never missed a practice or a game, and never gave me cause for concern. Other parents didn't want her on the squad. Sally was tainted by the broad brush of her family's sins, real and imagined. She stayed with me one year, but didn't return for a second. The turmoil of the murder trial and the taunts of others proved too much for her.

Sally continued to attend school. She was a mediocre student. School wasn't a place in which she was happy, but then, neither was home.

Six weeks after school started during Sally's sophomore year, her cousin hanged himself in his family's barn. Sally had a difficult time dealing with the death. She continued to stay in school, but her grades, never great to begin with, dropped. After she became ineligible to play basketball, she spent much of her time in the library where I was the media specialist. Sally became invaluable to me as an aide. She worked hard and well. She shelved books, cleaned the library, made bulletin boards, and did a myriad of clerical tasks. She began going to class, getting her assignments and returning to the library. It was months before I learned that no one else knew she was spending most of her time in the library. Her teachers neither knew nor cared where she was as long as she wasn't in their classroom. Sally began spending lunch hours in the library, and she tried to always be present for kindergarten story time. Although I never asked, I suspected that no one had ever read to Sally.

Sally's cousin, Dewayne, a freshman, began to spend time in the library, too. Then Dewayne began missing school because he was in treatment for his long-standing drug and alcohol problems. After he came back to school, he began drinking again. One night, six weeks before the end of school, Dewayne broke into a house and was shot and killed by the homeowner. He was fourteen years old.

Sally and Dewayne were very close and his death was devastating to her. Rightly or wrongly, she blamed the school for many of his problems and hers and didn't want to return to school. I attempted to enlist the help of other teachers in encouraging Sally to return to school.

First, I talked with the math teacher. Not only was she not willing to help, she wouldn't allow Sally to make up any work she had missed since the funeral. Realizing that I had made a mistake, I decided to enlist the help of the one high school teacher that I knew would help me. I went to the teacher and explained that Sally was thinking of dropping out of school with less than six weeks of classes left and that I needed help to get her back in school so that she wouldn't lose her sophomore year. The teacher's response is burned in my memory. She replied, "Good riddance. We don't want her kind anyway." For one of the very few times in my life, I was speechless.

Fortunately, my daughter was able to help me. She called and wrote to Sally who returned to school three weeks before the end of the semester. She failed Algebra I because the math teacher did not let her make up the missed work and the rest of her grades weren't good, but she did finish the school year.

At the end of the year, I resigned my position for reasons unrelated to the incident, and we moved from the community. Shortly before I moved, I ran into Sally's grandfather who told me that he had heard that I had quit my job and was moving away from the community. He said, "But who will stand up for the children if you leave?" I didn't tell him that I had done far too little and was much too late for Sally. Although I felt remorse over Sally, I knew that the other teachers did not. I also knew that had I made them feel guilty, Sally would have paid the price if she returned in the fall. In the end, I remained silent.

I know that you would have preferred reading a story in which the teachers banded together to make Sally's life better. So would I. But I can't tell that story because that isn't the way it happened. I told about the traumas in Sally's life about which I know. Unfortunately, many of the sins against children remain secret so there may be much in Sally's life of which I am unaware. Sally returned to school and graduated. She returned to school, not because of, but in spite of the school and the teachers, because she is a survivor, whether she knows it yet or not. Any hero in this story other than Sally is my daughter who maintained her friendship in spite of great pressure from grandparents, aunts, uncles, teachers and friends. Regan marches to the beat of her own drummer, but with care and consideration for those she meets along the way. Sadly, too many adults in Sally's life turned the other way.

Through the years I have lost contact with Sally. I live elsewhere and have concentrated on my own life during the intervening years. I have not lost contact with the great disappointment I felt with my fellow teachers. I left a more lucrative career in social work because I believed that the only way to truly save our children is in the school system. I am no longer sure. Thoughts of Sally will remain with me as will the callousness of teachers who want only perfect children in their classrooms.

REFLECTION ON "SALLY'S STORY"

Sally is grown now and a mother herself. She continues to live in the same community. Her story has haunted me for years and I have used it many times to illustrate a variety of subjects to preservice teachers in my classes. Rarely do I think of Sally's story without tears.

Perhaps the reason that this incident affects me so strongly is that there are so many Sallys. I spent twenty years in social services fighting a futile battle. I have witnessed unbelievable acts against children. I decided that the only place in which significant differences can be made in the lives of children is in the classroom. I still believe it. The whole idea that "we don't want that kind" reeks of elitism, labeling, disrespect, poverty and a myriad of other injustices.

Perhaps I chose to share Sally's story in an attempt to ease the tremendous burden of guilt I carry as a result of my ineffectiveness. When her grandfather asked me who was going to stand up for the kids when I left, I couldn't answer because I didn't know. There wasn't anyone willing to shoulder the burden. He thought that I was more willing than I was, and I carry my inadequacy with me. All I ever did for his grandchildren was to treat them the same way I treated all the children in the school. Sadly, the grandfather felt that fairness and kindness were exceptional traits as far as his grandchildren were concerned.

I have often wondered if I should have challenged my colleague's comment. Weil (1995) states that one problem in education is teachers' attitudes toward students and that teachers often bring their own biases and egocentric predispositions to the classroom and wittingly or unwittingly allow these attitudes to affect their decisions about who can and cannot learn.

Perhaps I chose to share Sally's story so that each of us would look into our hearts and souls to see if we share some of the same attitudes as the teacher who didn't "want that kind in our school." When we examine who we are, we may see things we don't like, but only then can we change who we are. The task that we have as educators is to educate all children. It appears to me to be a holy undertaking, a way to right the wrongs of the world, to build a better life for our children, all of them.

REFERENCE
Weil, D. (1995). A critical approach to multiculturalism. *Think, 5*(3): 28–37.

As Through a Looking Glass
Bonnie Voth

Benson came into my second grade classroom a few days before the other children were to officially arrive. His mother explained he wanted to meet some of the teachers because he was distraught about school starting. Benson did not say much except to volunteer, "My name is Benson," followed by a half-hearted handshake. His body stance and the fixed look in his eyes revealed a lot. I would come to know this look well in the days ahead.

I had heard various stories mixed with complaints about Benson from other teachers as they gathered in the lounge. I had also had the opportunity to witness his frequent presence in the hall during the latter half of his first grade year. I always try to block preconceived notions concerning the students assigned to me until I have had ample opportunity to interact with them. Benson was to be an exception to my previous methods. When I saw Benson's name toward the bottom of my list of boys, my heart sank.

This was my fourth year of teaching. During the previous three years I had gained confidence in dealing with students and enthusiasm for teaching. Each year's class seemed to be the best I had ever had. I dreaded having to relinquish my class at the end of the last school year because we had come so far together. Last year's class was so eager, so energized, and I looked forward to school each day.

As I began the new school year, though, I had the unmistakable feeling that I was in for an experience that would mold my resolve to teach as no previous year had been able to do. The bell rang that first day of school and Benson presented himself in the doorway with that look in his eyes I had witnessed just a few days before. The challenge was definitely there.

Benson's episodes of misconduct, in the form of tantrums, were mild at first, but disturbing nonetheless. He couldn't sit still very long. And, he did the opposite of what I asked and disturbed the overall atmosphere of the room. He dwelt in his own little world for much of our day. I overlooked his misbehavior to give him time to become acclimated to the class. I revisited all the classroom management theory I had studied in college time and time again in an effort to find the right key. Benson's demeanor in our classroom represented a locked door to me, a door to which I had no key but needed desperately to open.

As the year went on, Benson consumed my every thought. At night I went to bed with thoughts of him. I faced him in the mirror the next morning as I prepared for my day and his physical presence. The harder I tried to find answers, the more his misbehavior escalated. I videotaped Benson on several occasions, thinking I might pick up some kind of clue that I missed by being in the midst of the situation every day. I consulted everyone who had any prolonged contact with him—our school counselor, my principal, his mother, and his private counselor. Everyone agreed there was a problem, but we all perceived him from a different angle. I needed an immediate type of solution that would provide the least amount of interruption to the rest of the classroom.

Benson's private counselor gave me a list of numerous strategies to try. She suggested I praise him for the smallest task he accomplished. For example, "I like the way you picked up your pencil." "You did a good job keeping your feet still." She emphasized that I should avoid giving him any tasks which would make him anxious and possibly bring on an episode. While all of these suggestions were sound, each required one-on-one interaction, and I had 16 other children to share myself with. To further complicate the situation, during the following weeks, at the pinnacle of my "Benson troubles," I received three new students in one week's time. About that time Benson's counselor visited. She told me there would be no quick fix.

I was appalled at the counselor's seeming disregard for what was happening to the other children in the classroom. Some of the children who were less secure in their relationships in the classroom began to act out or withdraw from activities. A few of the boys began to mimic, on a smaller scale, Benson's actions. All at once I had a core of students who began to take on the class and me. I felt outnumbered and desperate. I needed someone with counseling expertise to survey the situation and give me the support I needed to function once again as "The Teacher." I realized that theory is not much good if it cannot be applied to real situations.

Benson's behavior became even more difficult. He refused to do any work at times, defiantly tearing up his papers, removing everything from his desk and breaking any pencils or crayons he could put his hands on. He banged his head on his desk or crawled under it and moaned. I noticed his misbehavior accelerated when I asked students to begin an assignment.

By now other teachers were offering suggestions and prescriptive theories about ways to deal with his behavior. I felt like the mother with her first child, receiving advice from everyone. I was being urged to accept someone else's ready made answers and depend less on my own "teacher instinct." Benson and I began to play off each other.

Out of all this advice one feasible plan surfaced. Our school counselor suggested we try modifying a "card system" she used with older students. Certain consequences were inevitable if Benson had to "turn" his card. He might have to leave the room when he reached a yellow card. A red card meant that the office came for him. At first our school counselor had to assist him in following the plan. While the strategy did not work miracles, within a month we began to notice a definite change in Benson's aggressive behavior. During these respites I had a chance to interact with Benson in more positive ways. The other children responded in kind and began to include him in their play. I wanted so much to peel away the façade and get to the heart of Benson. What made him different from children I had taught previously? What thoughts ran through his mind as he walked into the classroom?

Each day as I reflected on our time together, I found that my thoughts did not simply reside with Benson. Benson became a philosophical mirror. His attitude and behavior were causing me to reflect on a deeper level about my role as a teacher. Maybe the reflection was more revealing about myself that I cared to acknowledge. The earlier confidence I experienced was shaken. This is the type of confidence that Max van Manen (1991) refers to in his text when he speaks to the issue of "fake confidence" (p. 158). I was forced to become introspective. Benson had managed to reveal so much more about me than I had been able to unearth about him.

The whole process I engaged in was painfully slow. It was during this particular semester that I was enrolled in a graduate class focusing on fundamentals of teaching. I was encouraged in this class to reflect on my practice as a teacher, something I had done very little of before. Benson managed to bring to the forefront of my thinking many issues in teaching which are of deeper importance than managing a class or covering necessary curriculum. I had to wrestle with such issues as: Why was I a teacher? What did I hope to contribute to the children in my classroom? What did I hope to learn from this seemingly difficult student that would better prepare me for others students?

Benson indeed presented me with a challenge, the challenge for me to re-evaluate my perceptions of the meaning and practice of teaching. Will he look back in the years ahead and have learned as much about himself as he has managed to teach me about myself?

REFLECTION ON "AS THROUGH A LOOKING GLASS"

The pathway at the university to becoming a teacher is rather predictable. A student participates in a predetermined curriculum and tries to meet the expectations of individual faculty members. Upon graduation students are thrust into a real, but less than perfect, world with their goals focused on trying to change that world into something better.

The novice teacher has the same overwhelming thoughts in the first classroom that a new carpenter must feel when building a first home, or an artist experiences when commissioned to paint a first portrait. The theory must now be put into practice. Teachers have to make decisions based not only on theory but also on direct interaction with students. Those decisions will not only affect the young lives they minister to but will also serve to mold and shape their own resolve to teach.

Memories I have collected throughout my teaching career, those I remember in poignant detail, represent lessons not retrievable from textbooks. Some of them are pleasant and easily adapted to richly embellish the narrative. Others I struggle to put into words because they reflect my inadequacies and are usually accompanied by feelings of guilt or despair. By reflecting on my teaching experiences with children through narrative, I take the initiative in sharing my vulnerability with others. When my reflections are acknowledged and taken to heart by my peers, I will no longer be alone on my journey. Narrative provides not only a means to sort through my thoughts but to allow others to have a voice in my experiences.

The story of Benson is one I have come to cherish. When I decided to write about my year with Benson, I did not imagine that someone else might have also had the same experience. I wrote as a means to capture my thoughts and feelings as if by doing so I could build on them and keep from making the mistakes I made with Benson in the future. I also chose to write about my experience because words give a permanency to experience, and I did not want this particular episode in my life to fade away. In this story the teacher has been reminded of what it mean to be a learner and to remember that the child can be a teacher. Benson taught me to listen more attentively, to become more perceptive, and to love teaching more fervently. I dedicate this story to all the "Bensons" and to all the teachers who have the privilege of teaching them.

REFERENCE
Van Manen, M. (1991) *The tact of teaching*. Albany, NY: State University of New York Press.

Chapter 5

Empowerment

> Caring as we do for our students, our work becomes in a very real sense who we are. When we ponder what it is we value, we are quick to realize that we value our students, their learning, their literacy, and their welfare. We value the relationships that we forge with them every day we are together. (Rief & Barbieri, 1995, p. xi)

The stories in Chapter 5 each show how the authors have taken charge of their own professional development in varied ways. In "A Joyful Noise: The Poetry of Teaching with Two Voices" Joanne Durham and Elizabeth Lauther write about the classroom where they team teach. "Even with 60 children two teachers see twice as much as one," write Durham and Lauther.

In "Writing about Teaching" Elaine Greenspan tells about the rewards and challenges of her professional writing career. She was able to write and teach high school English because she most often wrote about "the real stories in front of me. Nothing is more exotic than the average high school classroom," according to Greenspan. In "Crossing the Highway" Gloria Nixon-John explores both the difficulties she encountered with her colleagues as she learned and grew professionally and the importance of the caring community of professionals she found outside of school. In "Connections" Karen Downing shares her desire to "cushion my students' passage through this stage of their lives by celebrating the writing they do" in her language arts classroom.

REFERENCE
Rief, L., & Barbieri, M. (Eds.). (1995). *All that matters.* Portsmouth, NH: Heinemann.

A Joyful Noise: The Poetry of Teaching with Two Voices
Joanne Durham and Elizabeth Lauther

This story recounts the first year of a team teaching partnership. The
title of our story is taken from *A Joyful Noise: Poems for Two Voices*
by Paul Fleischman, one of our favorite poetry books for children. Set
up for two readers, the book helps children experiment with reading
poetry together.

JOANNE'S STORY

Two years ago I moved from teaching sixth grade to fourth, and with the
change landed in the room next to Lizz Lauther. We didn't talk much past the
exchange of morning hellos. Lizz had a reputation of being a firm disciplinarian,
and, indeed, as I passed her class it always seemed much quieter than mine. I
prided myself on being a successful nurturer, but keeping ironclad control of my
classroom was certainly not my forte. In fact, my perception of the differences
between Lizz and me was so strong that I certainly never suspected that two years
later I would be happily team teaching with her. Yet today our joint classroom is
a place where both of us discipline and both of us nurture. Moreover, it is a place
where both of us teach, and both think we are able to teach 60 students together
better than either of us taught 30 alone.

The story really begins one spring day when Lizz walked into my
classroom and asked me if I was interested in departmentalizing in the fourth grade
the next year. She was planning a move down to fourth grade and wanted to teach
math and science. Since my love is reading, writing, and social studies, her plan
sounded like a perfect fit. I was struggling with how to do a good job of teaching
all subjects, and departmentalizing was something I really wanted to try. After a
few more conversations, we decided to give it a go.

The next year I taught two different groups of students, one in the morning
and one in the afternoon, and Lizz taught each group the opposite time. This
schedule meant working more closely with another teacher than I had done before,
and I liked the arrangement which lessened the stultifying isolation of individual
teaching. Departmentalizing had its down side, too. I hated losing my morning
class each day. The afternoons were discipline wars, and I finished the day battle
fatigued. I teach in a school where three quarters of the students qualify for free
or reduced lunch. Our school is also an ESOL center, with many students new to
the United States. I often felt that my fourth graders needed the consistent attention
of spending the whole day with the same teacher.

One day in March I casually said to Lizz, "You know, the way to really do
this would be to put all the kids in one classroom and teach them together." I was
surprised but pleased when Lizz replied, "Absolutely. Let's do that next year
instead of this changing business." And so our idea was born.

LIZZ'S STORY

I love to teach! I've taught high school, middle school, adults and, of course,
my own children. I returned to the classroom eight years ago, first as a long-term
substitute and then as a sixth grade teacher in a self-contained classroom. What fun

my students and I had! I learned as much from those sixth graders as they did from me. Over the years we struggled together to learn math by using manipulatives. We did hands-on science on the floor, on the window sills, in the corridors and on the playground. We tape recorded our cooperative group activities and when writer's workshop came along, we did that too.

As the years passed, many of my colleagues left Ridgecrest. I realized I really needed someone to talk to about teaching and about my students. I recognized very quickly that Joanne was a person with similar goals and ideals. (She will say we're very different—but we're more alike!) It looked like Joanne was doing the same kinds of things with her students that I enjoyed doing with mine. In fact, she seemed to be having a better time and I wanted to be a part of that!

JOANNE

We now teach 60 children together. All of the desks are in one classroom, and in the other is a rug, tables, chairs, class library, teacher stuff, computers, and coat racks. Lizz plans math, health and science, and I plan reading, writing, and social studies. We each help the other teach. After I do a mini-lesson in reading, Lizz follows up and conferences with students just as I do. Or while she teaches a whole class lesson in math, I walk around the room and individually assess and help students. Sometimes one or the other of us pulls a small group of students into the other room for extra help.

I knew I was going to like team teaching that hectic week before school started when we were putting our rooms together. Usually I hate that time—it seems like an endless process of bulletin board paper flopping on my head for 12 and 14 hour days in the August heat. But this year, two of us putting up two rooms made it so much more palatable. We laughed our way through each crisis, Lizz usually digging up some desperately needed material from her endless "I can't throw it away" collection of junk.

Our August camaraderie extends right into our classroom with our students. We are a team, helping each other out, and so we model all day long what we want from our students. Instead of always telling the students the phrase I have up on my wall in shiny light bulbs, "All of us together are brighter than any one of us alone," we show them everyday the benefits of cooperative learning. If I can't decide the best way to organize ourselves for the next activity, I just stop and ask Lizz in front of the kids, "How do you think we should proceed, Ms. Lauther?" And we have some think/collaboration time right there. One time when Lizz thought up a terrific mnemonic device to remember which group of students go to PE which day, I stopped her and told the class how brilliant that was and we gave her a round of applause.

I learn every day from Lizz. I'm learning that the "magic" of her ability to discipline comes from deceptively simply things, like always meaning what she says, and from deeply profound ones, like how she handles individual conversations with troubled students to help them begin to take responsibility for themselves. And I know that she learns a lot from me, too, like all my positive rituals that set the tone of our class as a joyful place. As we learn from each other, we grow as more capable teachers because of each other, and our mutual respect and friendship grow too.

LIZZ

Even with 60 children two teachers see twice as much as one. There's no question the students benefit from having two of us all day, much the same way that a child can benefit from having two full-time parents. We get to know our students better too, although that may sound strange with 60 of them! Instead of always being busy doing the organizing and logistics of teaching, one or the other of us has time to kid watch, to see what's happening. We didn't miss the day Brian, a struggling reader, couldn't put his book down at the end of the day, sort of hiding it so it wouldn't be collected. I even had time to nudge Joanne so she could catch the moment too. One of us can walk a child suffering from asthma to the nurse's office ourselves, take phone calls from parents or see a parent who just "drops in."

JOANNE

I'll always remember the day Jaime came into class with a look in his eye that told me immediately he was about to hit, poke, push or make fun of whoever was in his path. In a normal classroom I would have tried to talk with him, but the chances of a productive conversation would have been slim in the midst of all the usual morning interactions. Since Lizz was supervising the large group, I was free to take Jaime aside. It turned out that he and his brother had been home alone for two days, and his puppy had gotten out of the house, run over, and killed. Eight year old Jaime had picked him up from the street and buried him in the backyard. He talked with me, cried, and then just stayed with me privately until he was ready to join the rest of the class. We headed off a disastrous day for both Jaime and his classmates by the individual time I was able to spend with him.

LIZZ

An incredible example of how team teaching helped us to grasp any and every opportunity to enrich our students' learning was the mouse episode. In the middle of a parent conference, a mouse ran across the room. The next day, Joanne used the word "mouse" in a phrase instead of the word she meant to say. I immediately started to laugh so we explained to the students what had happened. All of us spent that week finding sayings or titles which included the word "mouse." We even made up our own. During all this silliness, one of our weakest readers found a poem about a mouse and asked Joanne to help him practice reading it. At the end of the week, he stood in front of sixty students and read the mouse poem in a loud, clear voice. The students were so excited that they requested a repeat performance. What a powerful way to attain self-confidence! And none of it would have happened without the teasing and banter between the two adults in the class.

JOANNE

We knew from the many magic moments of the year, like the one Lizz just related, that our students were fine with two teachers and 60 students, but I interviewed a random sample of seven members of our class at the end of the year, to find out their views more directly. For all of them, their first reaction was that they liked our classroom because with a lot of people in the class, "you can have more friends." How easy it is to overlook the importance for the children of their social interactions, but it was clearly the first thing on their minds. The next most common comment was about all the fun activities and projects we did. They liked having two different classroom spaces, too, which allowed the class to divide in different ways. For example, the class members liked the choice of reading silently in one space or reading with friends in the other space. They remembered how Ms. Lauther helped the people writing non-fiction in one room while Ms. Durham helped the fiction writers in the other. They even realized that it's hard for a teacher to be super person. One child commented how the class could move more quickly from one activity to another, because one teacher could be getting the room ready for a project while the other one was teaching the class what to do. A student noted that "It was fun because Ms. Durham knew how to do fun stuff in reading and writing, and Ms. Lauther did fun stuff in math." And another chimed in, "It would be too much work for one teacher." (Amen!) When I pushed for negatives, the voices that had been tripping over each other got quiet. "Did you ever feel more scared, or shy to speak up with so many people, or like you got less attention from the teacher?" I prodded. Blank stares. Silence. "No." Finally one student helped me out. "The only thing was you had to learn to speak very loud so everyone could hear you, and it was easier with so many people to be too noisy and lose our recess."

JOANNE AND LIZZ

Although we were confident this experiment in team teaching would work, we are still constantly awed by how well it works. One day we were reflecting on our classroom, and said, "You know, it's pretty amazing, because neither one of us is a very flexible person." Which is true. We are both highly opinionated about our teaching and have high expectations of ourselves, the administration and colleagues. Many things make team teaching work for us—our particular combination of strengths and weaknesses, likes and dislikes, that complement each other. Underlying similarities in our philosophies about teaching. Honesty with each other. A willingness to take responsibility and carry our own weight. But most of all we think it works because we both believe being a good teacher means constantly learning. We both know that however good we are isn't good enough for our students, who are still not achieving at the levels that will allow them to go out and be leaders in the world they will live in as adults. Teaching alone we each knew we could learn a great deal from our students, but there was only one adult around to pick up the millions of signals they were transmitting every day. Through team teaching there are two points of view on this maze of information, and a much greater chance to turn the information into useful feedback.

Sometimes when people ask about our team teaching experiment, they want to know if any two teachers could work together. We both immediately say no. Certainly there are some criteria that need to be met for a successful team teaching relationship. But we also think back to two years ago, and realize how much our ideas about each other have changed. Our relationship has developed through the act of working together—not passing in the hall, but putting ourselves on the line together with the same goals for the same children. And we wonder how many other colleagues are lurking out there who could be soulmates in this business of teaching if we weren't all locked away in our own little rooms. It's surely worth the risk to experiment more often with the joyful noise of teaching as a poem for two voices.

REFLECTION ON "A JOYFUL NOISE"

How do teachers grow? How do we become better at what we do? Certainly these questions are crucial to efforts at change in our schools. The best ideas in the world can be introduced at workshops, classes, and demonstration lessons. But as teachers we know that when we leave the staff development seminar the real learning is just beginning—the process of implementing an idea and shaping it as it smashes into obstacles and tries to make its way towards success with a specific group of children in a specific environment. For that critical part of learning, there is seldom consistent, hands-on support in the traditional set-up. Without that support, we suspect it is the pre-packaged, "teacher-proofed" materials that are most likely to survive the bumpy road from staff development to the students, while many far worthier but more complex approaches go untried in real classrooms, or are dropped after initial difficulties are encountered.

The expectation that teachers learn in isolation contradicts the experiences both of the authors of this story had in other professions. We were used to learning by collaborating with other adults, learning in the process of feedback from different points of view on a shared situation. Perhaps because of this, we were struck with the difficulty of growing as a teacher while being the only adult in a classroom of children. Our understanding of good pedagogy only heightened the contradiction. How ironic to believe deeply in and utilize cooperative learning with our students, only to have no one to share in the process of our own learning! How strange to build classroom practice on recognition of the social construction of knowledge, only to build knowledge of our teaching alone!

Our perceptions of these contradictions are supported by research into collaboration among teachers. Fullan and Hargreaves (1991) cite a study by Rosenholtz (1989) of 78 elementary schools in Tennessee. "Learning impoverished" schools with low levels of student achievement were compared with "learning enriched" schools performing at higher levels. It was found that teachers in the "learning impoverished" schools usually worked alone, while those in the "learning enriched" schools worked together more. In the latter schools, "it is assumed that improvement in teaching is a collective rather than individual enterprise, and that analysis, evaluation, and experimentation in concert with colleagues are conditions under which teachers improve" (p. 44).

Teacher collaboration comes in many shapes and sizes, and team teaching is undoubtedly not the answer for everyone. But we offer this story of the inception of team teaching in our classroom because for us it has made a difference. It has allowed us to take up greater challenges with fewer frustrations. It has helped us replace "I can't take that on" with "Let's go for it!" And therein we believe lies a tale worth telling.

REFERENCES

Fleischman, Paul. (1988). *Joyful noise: Poems for two voices.* New York: Trumpet Club.
Fullan, M. G., & Hargreaves, A. (1991). *What's worth fighting for? Working together for your school.* Andover, MA: The Regional Laboratory for Educational Improvement of the Northeast and Islands.
Rosenholtz, S. (1989). *Teachers' workplace: The social organization of schools.* White Plains, New York: Longman.

Writing about Teaching
Elaine Greenspan

I taught in the public schools for 27 years, 25 years as an English teacher. Looking back, I can see that what fueled my energy and kept me optimistic was a concurrent writing career. Teaching and writing have always been a braided strand in my life. As a young teacher I published my first article, "How to Get Your Child Ready for First Grade," in *Family Circle* when I was teaching elementary school in Albuquerque's South Valley. Since there was no opening in the high schools, I was teaching first grade for a year. Previously, I had substituted in the Chicago elementary schools so I had some experience.

Years later, with three of my own children growing up and my career as a high school English teacher established, I published a second article in *Family Circle* entitled, "How to Live with a Teenager." I was living with teenagers as well as teaching them. Subsequently I wrote pieces for *English Journal, Learning, McCall's, Executive Educator, House Beautiful* and other magazines. I have also written books and tape cassettes for J. Weston Walch, an educational publishing house. Recently, I published *A Teacher's Survival Guide*, a combination self-help book and memoir of my teaching experiences. First published by Weekly Reader Books in the early 1980's, I rewrote this book for J. Weston Walch and added new chapters.

I tell all this as a background to explain how writing empowered me as a teacher, gave me a strong sense of self, and served as an excellent diversion from the stress of teaching.

It is becoming increasingly difficult to teach for a long time as I did, to become a career teacher. The problems in the schools today are more intense; plus the deadly focus on public education by the media is usually negative and harsh. Even though a recent Lou Harris and Associates survey found that suburban teachers' job satisfaction has jumped in the last decade, urban teachers are more unhappy. Violence, drugs, and diminishing public support have turned the inner-city schools into a battlefield. Despite this gloomy side, I believe with all my heart that teaching is a fulfilling and creative career.

But even if one teaches in a suburban school, as I did, there are difficulties to be encountered as the years pass. The first obstacle is the repetitious nature of teaching, and the second obstacle is the isolation of a teacher within the four walls of the classroom. As I look back, there is no doubt that had I not developed my writing interest I would have probably transferred into administration after 10 or 15 years, or even left the schools. But as one thing led to another, I found the classroom to be a testing laboratory for the materials I was publishing. The articles I wrote led to offers for books, the books led to public speaking requests, which in turn led to leadership in professional groups. I achieved autonomy, even though every morning for 25 years I faced five English classes. The bells rang hourly, week after week, month after month, year after year. Looking back I think it was a miracle that I did this with so much happiness. Teaching satisfied my deepest yearning to be occupied with a job that had value and meaning.

Yet I had always wanted to be a writer, too, but my youthful goals in this area were obscure. The early short stories I submitted to literary magazines came back. I did not have the discipline to attempt novels. But once I began writing about the classroom, almost everything I wrote got accepted because I was writing from first-hand knowledge. I supplied examples, details, incidents, opinions. I also developed my own writing style, one that was informal, first person, humorous when possible, and animated by the strong emotion I felt for teaching. I was telling teaching stories, teacher lore if you will, but I thought I was describing curriculum methods.

The classroom is a perfect microcosm for a writer. Plenty of colorful, even eccentric characters hang out there. The setting is specific. There is always a strong plot because teaching is full of struggle, conflict, and pain, but it is also about growth, accomplishment, and power. The last, power, is often overlooked, but it is indeed from a position of power that a successful teacher operates, and that power seems to heighten one's writing ability. The kind of power I'm talking about is not corrupt but benevolent and careful. From it one develops a new personality which permeates any writing one does. You have to have "an attitude" to forge a unique writing style.

Over the years, thousands of students submitted to my rules and regulations, listened to my lectures and discussions, and through the unspoken but always present threat of grades, usually obeyed me. I think teachers, like politicians, develop strong personalities if they are successful. And like good politicians, teachers enjoy power and try not to abuse it.

No longer a teacher, it is what I miss most, this power. Like a leader voted out of office, I feel that no one listens to me anymore. My family and friends don't look to me for a good grade, so if I am being officious or bossy they tell me so. They are my equals, and they don't take any baloney. If I have a clever thesis on social change or a trenchant critique of a new movie, there is no longer a captive audience First Period to listen to me. My husband continues to work the crossword puzzle and does not look up when I start declaiming.

But in the classroom I was a person with authority, someone presiding over an often tumultuous arena. And through years of talking, I developed the verbal skills which transferred into a writing style. I knew from the beginning I didn't want to write scholarly articles. What I wanted was the freedom and emotion of fiction transmuted into non-fiction pieces about the classroom. I admired Sylvia Ashton-Warner, the New Zealand author of both fiction and non-fiction about teaching. I was also influenced by authors like Bel Kaufman, Jonathan Kozol, Neil Postman, Philip Lopate, and Ken Macrorie.

In recent years I have been strongly affected by two journalists who have written remarkable studies of charismatic high school teachers. Jay Mathews is the author of *Escalante, The Best Teacher in America* and Samuel Freedman wrote *Small Victories: The Real World of a Teacher, Her Students and Their High School.* Both biographies read like novels in their narrative power and rich accumulation of details. No one else has written such detailed biographies of teachers. I have also read Ernest Boyer, Theodore Sizer, Nancie Atwell, and Vivian Gussin Paley. These are all writers who artfully took the materials of teaching and turned them into influential books.

I learned from each writer, but I was able to forge my own style and terrain. The *English Journal* accepted my very first sketches about teaching and was influential in getting me started. Many educational editors and publishers read the *English Journal*, looking for new writers. That was where J. Weston Walch, Publisher found me in the '70's. I had written a piece called "Entrances and Exits," describing my students before and after class, a sort of a non-fiction short story. Eventually I published books for J. Weston Walch about teaching the short story, poetry, and humanities. I also wrote tape cassette packages on study skills and taking class notes. In a piece for *Learning*, I confessed to profound feelings of envy toward my colleagues, discovering that most teachers shared my hidden emotion. That article later became a chapter in my book, *A Teacher's Survival Guide.*

An important bonus that came from all this writing was that it clarified my thinking. When I gave explanations for teaching poetry or fiction, I was forced to examine my own methods. Writing organized my teaching skills. "How do I know what I think until I see what I say," is a famous writer's adage that has a special truth in it for the teacher. It is one thing simply to take an exercise and foist it on a class because you are in a bind and have nothing to do on a dark, sleeting February morning. But if you are constantly writing about the art of teaching, you think more carefully about the work you give students. This doesn't mean you don't grab fillers just like everybody else does. It means that you know why you're doing it. Being a writer made me more aware of my overall philosophy. When I gave speeches about teaching, they, too, forced me to examine my classroom practices. A speech is another form of writing, after all. Both writing and speaking made me very analytical about what I was doing in the classroom. In effect, I was teaching myself the curriculum by writing it down in books, articles, stories, and speeches.

As I gained confidence, writing led to adventures. For example, one year I entered a Scholastic, Inc. contest where I described how I used Scholastic magazines in the classroom. I won the contest, went to an editorial meeting in New York, and became a Scholastic advisor. An editor there encouraged me to try Young Adult fiction and the first story I submitted was accepted. I went on to write many stories for Scholastic magazines, basing my characters on students in my classes.

These activities took my mind off the difficulties of teaching. I could keep boredom and fatigue at bay by focusing on the classroom as a source for materials. "I'm working on this story, class," I'd confide on a Friday afternoon to a restless group of tenth graders. "If I read it to you, will you give me some feedback?" And the students would listen and provide me with tough but valid criticism. (Sometimes the sophomores could be ruthlessly cruel, but then they could also be enthusiastically complimentary.) Later, when the story came out and I distributed copies of the magazine, they enjoyed reading the revised version. It was a joint venture. They hadn't known a writer or seen how one worked, how the material started out shaggy and unformed and required patient tinkering and revision. So that when I asked for rewrites of their work I carried the moral weight of my own efforts. And the students were proud of my stories, recognizing the school setting, details, even some of the characters. They saw how one took the material of real life and transformed it into fiction.

Speaking of pride, I can remember coming back from a New Mexico Council of Teachers of English conference and telling my homeroom I had been elected president for the next year. Spontaneously, they clapped and cheered. Students like to know about a teacher's extracurricular life, and I tried to share parts of it with them.

That leadership position certainly grew out of my writing activities. Teachers had read my articles in the *English Journal*. Many received the J. Weston Walch, Publisher catalogues and ordered my books and tape cassettes. I was starting to speak at conferences, promoting my books. So I had visibility when I was asked to run for state president. I tell all this frankly so that other teachers can see how one develops over the years. I had no idea when I first began submitting articles that writing was going to tug me into other paths that would be important to my professional life.

In this way I kept myself growing and stimulated. In later years my teaching sometimes took a back seat to my writing and organization activities. I admit freely that I was often too preoccupied to teach with the same intensity of the early years. But by now I could do this. I had files replete with lesson plans, tests, and lecture notes. I could recycle old materials with a practiced hand. Too often teachers feel guilty that they aren't creating new materials or teaching with the same enthusiasm of their beginning years. But like a love affair or marriage, one's passion for teaching undergoes a change. It settles down into a mature affiliation, with periods of boredom interspersed with stretches of contentment and serenity. The early excitement is replaced by an equilibrium that is far easier on the nervous system.

Often my energies went into developing new writing projects. Publishing pieces on education gave me the confidence to try other forms of writing. I took courses in film writing and play writing. I wrote several Young Adult novels, none of which has been published, but they occupied my mind and energies so that when I went into the classroom I had other things to think about.

A long teaching career requires staying power. You have to find another outlet to complement the classroom. Most English teachers, and probably teachers from other disciplines as well, have an interest in writing and probably a flair for it. But timidity and lack of self-confidence keeps them from writing. English teachers, alas, have such elevated literary tastes that if they don't sound like Eudora Welty right away, they give up. But a case can be made for teachers writing their stories as an adjunct to the real life of daily teaching. Not only does writing help shape your teaching, but the regular practice improves writing itself. There was no National Writing Project when I began writing about teaching back in the '60's. I found my way through the books I read, writers in the *English Journal* I admired, and professional conferences I attended.

Writing has continued to sustain me once I retired from teaching. When I revised *A Teacher's Survival Guide*, I felt I needed a fresh outlook, so I went into the schools and interviewed teachers and students. At first I thought I would intersperse their comments throughout the book, but listening to my tapes I saw that each teacher unfolded a theme in her or his life. One teacher had found renewal by teaching in Moscow. Another won a Disney teaching award and became locally famous, so I told her story. A band teacher struggled with discipline and solved the problem through research, so I described his ordeal. Because I understood teaching so well, my subjects trusted me and revealed their deepest feelings. This gave authenticity to my book, despite the fact that I was no longer in the classroom. *A Teacher's Survival Guide* is a self-help book, but it is also teachers' stories: mine and the inspiring teachers I interviewed.

My teaching career gave me the material to get published, which I did not know would happen when I first stepped into the classroom. Some writers move to exotic places in order to have material to write about, but nothing is more exotic than the average high school classroom. By exploring the real stories in front of me, I was able to shift to a second career that enabled me to hang on to the first one. It also showed me in a dramatic way that teaching and writing could be co-dependent.

John Steinbeck has said, "I have come to believe that a great teacher is a great artist and that there are as few as there are any other great artists. Teaching might even be the greatest of the arts since the medium is the human mind and spirit." If this is so, then taking the greatest of the arts and writing about it means that you make concrete what is often mysterious and baffling to others. Teachers will find a nourishing source of renewal in telling their stories. And in the act of writing they will find, as I did, that they are creating order out of what seems like the chaos of daily classroom life.

REFLECTION ON "WRITING ABOUT TEACHING"

I wrote this autobiographical account to help teachers find a way into writing. Re-reading my words a few months later, I felt I didn't say enough about the difficulties I encountered. And there were many. It was hard finding time to keep at my writing what with the pressures of teaching, grading papers, and the demands of my family at home. I never could write during the busy weekdays, so I developed the habit of getting up very early every Saturday and Sunday morning to work on writing projects. I would be at my desk at 6:30 and write for an hour or two before the rest of family awoke. I also disciplined myself to write every morning during summer vacations. Again, I never wrote for more than an hour or two, but if I averaged four pages a day that turned out to be 28 pages a week, or over 100 pages a month. During a summer I could block out a book and then revise it during the school year. But it meant a relentless discipline that made me a driven person. And driven persons are not always easy to live with.

And I didn't say enough about the pain of having my Young Adult novels rejected. I don't want my life to sound as if the writing just came effortlessly. It's easy to describe it now in retrospect, but I struggled along the way. Besides, writing the YA novels, even though they were never published, improved my skills. When you produce 200,000 words (counting all the rough drafts) you can't help gaining dexterity in your writing style.

If I were to give advice to teachers who want to write, I'd say: submit articles to the magazines you read or use in the classroom. You may be getting *Learning, Cricket, Elementary English, Weekly Reader, English Journal,* Scholastic magazines, and various other professional journals. If you read them, decide you'll try writing for them. Also consider the women's magazines like *Family Circle, Women's Day, McCall's,* and *Redbook.* They are all looking for articles about schools and children's issues. Also, submit pieces to your local newspaper or state publications. In addition, many school systems have an in-house newsletter that is eager for topical articles. Send them short pieces. People think that if they can read English they ought to be able to write it easily, but writing is an art like any other that takes time to master. So accept rejection without giving up.

Take writing courses at the local community college or university. Join a writing organization. Perhaps a number of teachers will be interested in forming a writing group that meets regularly to read and react to one another's work. Writing, after all, is a unique form of professional development. Anyone who has struggled to write about the experiences of teaching grows in strength and ability. When I wrote about teaching poetry, I gained new insights into what I could do with students that I hadn't been doing. I saw that I could be less timid, less fearful about experimenting. I wasn't afraid to show my emotions in the classroom, to discuss love and death, war and peace, fear and anxiety.

As I continued to write and publish, I also became more outspoken as a professional. I criticized our overcrowded classrooms. I complained about the lack of materials. I condemned wasteful administrative mandates. In English department meetings I spoke up if I thought we should be more traditional about literature choices, or more radical about writing personal narratives instead of formal essays. People who write learn to articulate issues because they have had constant practice with words, sentences, and paragraphs. Verbalizing the incoherent frustrations of teaching can be a catharsis that empowers not only yourself but also the others around you. Once I published an article called "What's Wrong with Central Office?" in the *Executive Educator.* My frank criticism of bureaucratic callousness created quite a stir for several weeks. I learned the power of the written word, how it clarified not just the feelings of teachers but principals who suffered, too. I felt like Tom Paine calling up the troops for the Revolution. There was no revolution, but there were changes. Writing about my jealousy of other colleagues for a *Learning* magazine article also brought me plenty of comments. How could I reveal myself so openly, some teachers wondered. Wasn't I embarrassed? But most felt a relief that I expressed everyone's secret, guilty emotion. They realized they were not alone in envying the success of colleagues, and this was cathartic.

I have always been happy I chose teaching for my life's career, but I also feel fortunate that I found writing as a way of describing that commitment. In *Horace's Compromise*, Theodore Sizer wrote that "A good teacher is self-confident." Where are you going to find that self-confidence after 10, 13, or 20 years in the classroom? I found it by putting my stories down on paper. It was both a liberation and a means of rescue.

Crossing the Highway
Gloria D. Nixon-John

That summer, the driest summer recorded since 1910, giant snapping turtles took to the highways all over Michigan in search of water. Dry enough, I figured, to dry the tears of several painful years of self-doubt, persecution and alienation. And because I marveled that most of those turtles made it from one side of the highway to the next unscathed, I knew I could survive, too. And so, I decided to keep my course and to let the others either swerve to avoid me or run me down. I had chosen a profession—teaching—that made it impossible for even a lateral move to another job. What disturbed me the most was the fact that once I started doing the things that made me feel like I was becoming a more effective language arts teacher, I somehow became more and more alienated from many of my immediate peers—mostly, the other teachers in my department.

If I look long and hard at the possible factors that caused the turmoil that led to the alienation I felt, here is what I come up with. First, and as a result of my mother's death, I began to write in order to sort things out. I started with rather self-indulgent poetry and then moved into personal essays and fiction as well. Secondly, in doing so, I realized how important it is to allow students to write about things that have meaning for them, instead of writing to show that they have learned facts or mastered skills. This realization led me to place my students more at the center of my classes, both physically and emotionally, instead of in rows in front of my desk, where they were once regimented by my ill begotten notion of their needs. What really contributed to my alienation was trying to share the excitement over the changes that were occurring in my classroom with my peers.

Over this period of change, all of my classes became writing workshops of sorts. If Early American Literature was at the center of the course outline, for example, I would let the students decide the focus, be it a particular writer or a genre. For example, one class decided to look at the everyday lives of early settlers, to dig up diaries and other documents which, in turn, led to the writing of their own diary entries, autobiographical stories and poems with future generations in mind as their audience.

Another class—filled with future environmentalists—got stuck on the Transcendentalists and ended up publishing a magazine called *The New Dial*. They also wrote to senators and congressmen about their concerns, letters that adequately traced the history of the environmentalist movement, abundant with historical quotes.

And over this period of change, my attitude about going to work changed, too. Prior to the change, my teaching had become repetitious, the same materials with the same approximate outcomes. But as I changed my methods and focus, the drudgery of force-feeding materials down students' throats was gone. I began to feel like a resource for my students instead of a task master, instead of a disciplinarian. I began to think through and rethink the choices I could offer them. We, teacher and students, seemed to be inventing what happened in the classroom together. I couldn't be quiet about these changes.

At a department meeting in early spring of the second year of "my awakening" and subsequent alienation, I committed the proverbial faux pas. Because there was a spot on the Department agenda for Other Presentations, etc., I asked to use that time to share a technique I had learned at a writer's conference and had then used successfully in my classroom. Part of this technique involved having students respond to each other's papers in groups. I was especially pleased with the progress and excitement I saw in student papers when I instructed them to talk to each other the way that real writers talk to each other, to discuss things like focus, mood, development, the intent of their work, and the audience for their work. Students found this process rewarding and their writing got better as a result, so I felt it natural to celebrate my excitement with my peers. My department listened politely that day, but I caught a few unpleasant downward glances—the kind of glances exchanged when someone takes off their shoes in a crowded room to expose smelly socks. One teacher did ask a question and seemed genuinely interested, but when the others blatantly rolled their eyes at him, when they struck a hellish posture right out of Hieronymus Bosch, he ignored my answer. Still, I rationalized their behavior as part of the end of the day, or end of the year, ebbing of enthusiasm. Until the following year.

Back from a National Council of Teachers of English meeting with a satchel full of new ideas and books, I declared to my Advanced Placement (AP) students that we were going to turn the classroom into a place where "we can believe we are all writers!"

"That doesn't mean we are going to ignore the skills that you need to pass the AP test," I warned them. "It just means we are going to make it all less painful. Furthermore, I am going to write, too," I said, "and I will even let you help me with my writing."

With my declaration, I actually saw my students fluff themselves up into the posture of writers.

One day per week, we did look at past AP tests in order to develop generic approaches for answering AP questions, but for the most part, we became writers and peer conference partners, and I functioned pretty much like a final editor on a magazine staff would function. Although we were thriving in my classroom, I could not ignore the hurtful remarks that made their way to me.

"Miss So and So said that an AP class is not the place for all of this creative stuff," one student said.

"Mrs. X said we are not going to be ready for the AP test until we do some real writing," another said.

I bit my tongue—for a while at least. Then the generations of Italian blood that had been simmering in my veins began to boil up into color in my cheeks and words on my tongue.

"Do you feel as if you are learning in this classroom?" I would respond. "Then what else matters?"

I began to feel waves of cool breezes in the hall when others passed me. I was excluded from department lunches and outings and found that no one really understood my excitement over the new approaches I was trying. I felt very alone in this isolation, so I began to reach out to writing groups and professional organizations. I also began to read everything I could find about teaching writing. It was empowering to learn about the struggles that Nancie Atwell faced in her career and how she reinvented her own classroom, and when I read Tom Romano's first book, I knew that he had been where I was.

Three years into using what has become known as the writing process approach within the larger whole language context, my colleagues made a frontal attack. I remember the day well because I had to recall the details in meeting after meeting with administrators, as well as a local, professional, ethics board.

My students had finished the AP test just before lunch that day. Several of them came to me ecstatic over the ease with which they wrote the test. They overheard other groups of students complaining about the difficulty they had fitting their answers into a formal five paragraph essay and many of my students laughed at the notion.

Once I got to lunch, I couldn't contain myself and blurted out, "My students are so excited about the AP test. They feel that they did very well."

The air fell suddenly still, and three tables of women looked at me, heads tilted up, eyes cast down in an indignant, rather Victorian, pose.

"Gloria, since you know so much about all of this, you really should write a book," one of them instructed.

By the end of the day, I was ordered to the Assistant Principal's office to explain why I had offended my whole department! I was ordered to apologize for my tone of voice or face disciplinary action. Of course, I professed my innocence, but to no avail. I was the Hester Prynne of the English Department. There were even scaffold scenes in which I was told about all of my other offenses. None of the offenses were punishable by any written code of conduct, but serious, nonetheless. What echoed over and over again in the most formal of those scenes of reprisal was the charge that my tone of voice, my excitement over what my students were doing, seemed to suggest that I believed that I was a better teacher than the other members of the department.

Eventually I took my colleagues's advice and began to write about what I was doing in the classroom and have since published articles, essays, stories and poems about my struggle. Beyond the walls of that school, I have found communities of writers and professionals who take joy in the debate and discussion about teaching language arts. I also joined the National Writing Project. As a result of my professional involvement, I do not fear the proposed mandates and assessments that have been tossed around as of late. I see all bureaucratic involvement in the larger, sometimes less important, context, because through my own strength, I know that with the help of the new communities to which I belong, I can fashion change, mandated or not, to meet the needs of my students.

I have since learned more about turtles, too, in an unscientific but appropriate extrapolation of sorts. I know that it is not dexterity, timing or luck that moves them across the highway in times of drought. They are so moved because of their desire for sustenance despite the risks. And their tough exterior is both their burden and their shield on this necessary and dangerous sojourn.

REFLECTION ON "CROSSING THE HIGHWAY"

When I reflect on my essay "Crossing the Highway," I have many of the old painful feelings I had when I experienced the events explained therein. And I must admit that my relationships with other members of my department have not really improved all that much since. I have made a few token efforts in order that I might be welcomed back into the fold, but some part of me never wants to be accepted back into that covenant. I feel there is some hope, however. As new, mostly younger, teachers are hired into the department, I have found ways to open a discussion with them about teaching philosophies and methods. I have also begun to present my ideas at state and national conferences, entered a doctoral program at Michigan State University, and have become involved in a local chapter of the National Writing Project, forums in which I get plenty of encouragement. I must also say, quite honestly, and as either a warning or an ointment to others who find themselves in the situation that I described in my essay, had it not been for the decision to continue my education and to affiliate with other professionals who were looking for answers beyond traditional approaches, I would have surely left the teaching profession some ten years ago.

Even though I survived those painful years, I still find myself trying to justify, then forgive, what my teaching colleagues did. I also spend time reflecting on what happened to me personally and professionally that led me to change, and why the changes in me caused so much turmoil for others. In doing so, I had to look at what I did, how I did it, and how what I did differed from accepted behavior in this group of teachers.

Clearly what happened to me is that I began to write and to think of myself as a writer. In doing so, I learned many things about the process of writing that forced me to change the way I teach writing. I began to feel that writing was not something others do, but something I could do as well. I wanted to share this excitement with my students so that they too would learn to use and manage writing to express their unique experiences and ideas. To do so meant turning my back on many of the traditional approaches that I had previously used in the classroom, and in so doing, I turned my back on the particular approaches agreed upon by my department, primarily the five paragraph essay style, and the taboos about validating personal narrative and more creative forms. And because I needed to justify what I was doing as a writer and a teacher, I turned to texts that gave me permission to continue on my course. One such text was Donald Murray's *A Writer Teaches Writing* (1985). Just recently, I thumbed through this text again and found an underlined passage that I recall as having near religious implications for me at the time:

Non-traditional composition teaching usually reverses the process and emphasizes personal content and personal voice first, working backwards from global concerns to the particulars of language and manuscript presentation. Writing is a product of the interaction of the global and the particular. We use a word to catch a vague idea and it becomes less vague, and so we work back and forth from whole to part and part to whole, each influencing the other, each strand helping the writer weave a pattern of meaning. (p. 4)

In my classroom, I was turning traditional methods upside down. I was also discovering how to implement this approach through open dialogue between students who began to view themselves as writers in a community of writers. I was clearly out of step with the majority of the teachers in my department at the time.

Opportunities to share teaching ideas with colleagues about methods and beliefs were rare in the department. If ideas came up, there was never any dialogue about why the teacher chose to approach a lesson in one way as opposed to another. Most of the exchanges about teaching occurred on the run in the form of slight pats on the back. The day that I approached my whole department in a direct way, at a meeting to share an idea, I was ignoring the accepted informal procedures that had been set up for sharing, and the accepted way was obviously viewed as less judgmental, less threatening than my approach. I may have also turned the mere pedagogical into something perceived as political because I was not only sharing method with my colleagues, I was also explaining how this method helped students make more decisions about writing without the direct interference of the teacher. In so doing, I was initiating a change, however small, in the power structure of the most important part of the school community—the classroom, the only place in which most teachers feel power at all. Then, too, I dared to see myself as a source of information or an authority on a subject, which was obviously viewed as inappropriate because I was not the department chair and was not assigned by administration to suggest methods to my peers. Teachers do not usually empower themselves.

The political structure of schooling makes it difficult for teachers to implement change even when they know change is good for students. Therefore, many decide to root themselves in accepted traditional methods even when those methods do not get the desired results. Others, in order to make change and still survive, plug into national or regional networks as I did. Plugging into acknowledged networks does not automatically lead to more positive reception of new ideas. In my situation, for instance, I sense that I am perceived as more of a threat now than ever before. The difference is that I no longer feel alone or as isolated because I look beyond my immediate workplace for approval and ideas.

Eleven years older now, scarred but wiser for it, I can look at the turtle metaphor with which I started my story for new insight. I realize that my story is about taking risks in the face of serious consequences. Like the turtle, on some level, I must have known that I could have been crushed by the power and velocity of the status quo. But I proceeded just the same. I know also that many are still shaking their heads at my stupidity and others, I like to fantasize, are perhaps secretly cheering my bravery.

In closing, I must confess that I have taken to carrying a pair of thick work gloves in the back seat of my car so that should I see a turtle misjudging its chances to make it across the road, I might stop, pick it up, and carry it to the other side.

REFERENCE

Murray, D. M. (1985). *A writer teaches writing.* Boston: Houghton Mifflin.

Connections
Karen Downing

She's at it again. This is the fourth day in a row she has done this. I'm in front of the class and I've just given the assignment. Most of the students react dutifully, taking out their books and beginning their reading. But Lindsay is another story. She hunches her shoulders over her desk, curling inward. Her notebook paper sits at an angle. Her purple pen flies with intent. If I look closely, I see the tip of her tongue peeking forth from an always silent mouth.

I purposefully plan to approach Lindsay from behind in an attempt to read the cryptic messages that fall from her pen upon the page. I'm close enough to smell the mousse in her hair when she senses my presence. She immediately pulls in the note. Her body hovers over the warm spot on the desk. The pen slips between her tight lips. Her eyes roll toward the ceiling. She waits for me to move on. And I do. Slowly. I'm disappointed. All I could see was "Hey, Jenn." I want to read more. Her invisible words, a testament to existence that is independent of classroom expectations or homework assignments, sustain life. Her silent actions carry weight and worth, validity.

With rusty expertise, I craft the rest of her note in my head while the students read. No doubt Lindsay tells Jennifer she is bored in English class. Certainly she mentions a new boy she stares at as he enters the room. Somewhere in the note she'll ask Jennifer's advice. It will be offered in cursive response, folded for exchange. This much I know intimately.

I don't remember any particulars from notes I wrote, nor do I still have the masses of notes I received in school over the years. What I do remember is the wash of feelings that surround the notes. Intimacy, belonging, eagerness. To catalog or list implies some sort of control or understanding, as if a neat ordering could lend the protection of detachment. Such feelings resist dissection, spared the plight of frogs and cats in endless biology lessons. Even so, there's the curiosity, the desire to know. Opening up those frogs and cats, we might learn something about ourselves.

I started writing notes about the same time I started carrying a purse to school. Now I can see the obvious correlation between those two actions, that of having a place to put the notes, was secondary. No, it was more to do with a rite of passage; notes and purses were tangible signals of the uncertain time of being a teenage girl. Purses were used to carry lunch tickets, Bonnie Bell lip smacker, maxi pads, and notes. By comparison with my purse now, purses in junior high and high school seemed so light, so unnecessary. And yet a girl would never be without one. A purse held secrets, secrets only other girls could know. If a boy ever looked in a purse, it was either a violation or an intimacy. The line between the two existed tenuously, a touch between two people.

When I was in high school, I remember once at lunch watching a couple who had been going out for several months. They were sitting at a table by themselves. At the end of the lunch period, the boy unzipped the girl's purse and took a piece of gum. That gesture of familiarity told me everything about those two. I understood. But I couldn't see myself in a situation like that one, one which spoke of comfort and certainty with a boy, no matter how badly I burned for it and wrote wistfully about the possibility in notes to friends.

Girls were a different story. Friendships with females were always natural, essential. Our notes were written proof of connection. My notes were always eagerly received, wanted. My friends liked my handwriting—they tried to copy my slant or the way I wrote my sevens. I took great care when writing notes—I personalized them with my signature smiley faces, fancy folding and private nicknames. My friends and I did all of this without our teachers knowing, or at least if they did, they never let on. The web of subterfuge pulled tight, protecting us. We needed to believe in our clandestine powers.

Only once did I have a note of mine found by a teacher. He tossed it to me as I passed his door. He said nothing, just smiled. Did I leave it behind in his classroom? Had he read it? Had he examined my confessions and admissions of uncertainty? In a hallway full of people who had no idea of my momentary trauma, I felt the familiar glow of embarrassment. These words meant something to me, something more than the specific contents. For the then shy girl of 14 that I was, those lines formed a so-needed belonging with girls, a belonging that didn't depend on speech, appearance, and actions.

Eventually I began to write to boys. And boys began to write back. It was confusing but somehow okay that Blair didn't talk to me as he handed me a note in the middle of the passing-time crowds. A dichotomy of talk was taking shape, in print, in person. I learned early on that communication between the sexes was different. The written word was somehow more true, more safe. I could be bold and daring between the thin lines of paper. I reveled in the distance and the inherent delay of the message. The only notes I ever saved back then were from boys; those notes somehow had more worth.

I continue to rely on written words—the ease, the control. I felt this most strongly while saying my wedding vows. My husband was visibly moved by the repetition of vows; I, on the other hand, felt tentative and inadequate in speech. I wanted to freeze the moment and reach for my journal. I needed the chance to process on paper, to communicate how I know best, to make the event real. The moment passed, yet still I feel absent from the ceremony.

The familiar end-of-the-period shuffle brings me back, back to my windowless classroom, back to my students. My students. What is mine is given to me with the utmost caution and reserve. I can command the physical presence of students: voices, eyes, ears. But what matters more is what is not offered to me. What matters is the folded-up piece of paper, thick with gossip and uncertainty, that Lindsay has had a chance to finish after all. With my eyes, I follow her out of the room, out into the gentle darkness of the hallway. Jennifer is there. They pull together, hands meeting in the awaited moment of exchange. Standing alone, in an empty classroom, still smelling the sweaty bodies, I feel the triumph of connection.

REFLECTION ON "CONNECTIONS"

When I received a sabbatical to finish my master's degree after eight years of teaching high school language arts, I was certain I would never think about teaching. I would go the bathroom when I wanted, drink cappuccinos mid-morning, and browse through bookstores for hours on end. And I would write. I had been given a year to be totally self-indulgent, free from the volumes of student writing I normally read. I threw myself into my course work for my M.F.A. in Nonfiction. I intended to write about the year I spent living and working in England. But each time I put my fingers to the keyboard, out came stuff about teaching. Pages and pages later, I had a thesis that explored what a teacher's persona meant to me. A little distance from the classroom gave me the space necessary for reflection.

"Connections" is a part of my thesis. It was born from a simple question asked in one of my graduate classes. "What was the most significant writing you did in high school?" I responded instantly. Note writing. Hmm. Not very academic. Definitely not a five paragraph theme with footnotes. If that was true for me as a student, I wondered how that might carry over to my sensibilities as a teacher. An essay that nudged along my insight was "Underlife and Writing Instruction" (1990) by Robert Brooke. In this piece, Brooke explores the concept of an "underlife" in a classroom, "those behaviors which undercut the roles expected of participants in a situation, revealing a more complex personality outside the role" (p. 96). Encountering that term made my experiences as a teacher take on greater clarity. By observing the underlife of my students, I gain a retrospective understanding of my own past.

I see the humanity of my students—the acne, the new haircut, the pre–spring break tanning, the slouched posture, the dark circles, the smile at last free of braces. With each glimpse of this, I am reminded of who I was at 16 and who I am now at 31. There are differences, but they are slight. The shine of a wedding ring, bite marks on my wrist from a new puppy, a stomach growing with a baby inside. The awareness of our shared humanity allows for an unspoken connection, a more even footing. I carry this insight with me as I try to position myself in my classroom.

When I was in high school, I was indirectly taught that the teacher held the magical knowledge, knew the right answer. This forever frustrated me as a student, making education a guessing game and not a learning endeavor. Now I teach. And I try to convey to my students the lack of a "right" answer. I try to place the onus on them to discover their own thoughts and interpretations and be able to support and articulate them. Some students do not like this. They want to be told what to think. It is my job as a teacher to show them how to think. To do this, I use writing as a means of discovery.

I am acutely aware of the vulnerability inherent in the act of writing, the sense of putting oneself into the words on the page. This vulnerability is heightened in the liminal time of adolescence. When I teach, I try to cushion my students' passage through this stage in their lives by celebrating the writing they do. The trick for me has been balancing "celebrating" with "high expectations." I do not think the teaching of writing need be ripe with gushy validation. Students recognize the hollowness of that. Rather, I encourage my students to push themselves to the point of introspection, regardless of the genre they are writing in. I ask question after question in the margins of their drafts. I try to nudge along their understanding by asking them to reflect on the process and the product. I recognize the difficulty of the task. I also recognize how essential it is for growth.

REFERENCE
Brooke, R. (1990). Underlife and writing instruction. In R. L. Graves (Ed.), *Rhetoric and composition: A source book for teachers and writers* (pp. 96–107). Portsmouth, NH: Boynton/Cook.

Chapter 6

Teacher Lore and the Experienced Teacher

We have laid out in Chapters 1 and 8 why teacher lore can and should be a potent means of professional development in an age of educational reform. Here we want to share how this can be done, what such professional development looks like. We do not offer a single model, but rather a variety of ways and ideas. We will examine how teacher lore can aid the experienced teacher through personal journeys, teacher evaluation, teacher research, case studies, college courses, and the National Writing Project. This is not meant to be an exhaustive list. New ways of using teacher lore are emerging, offering exciting new possibilities. These are ways we have found from a number of authorities and with which we are experimenting.

PERSONAL JOURNEYS

For years teacher lore both as shared personal anecdotes or stories and as written literature has inspired teachers. Greenspan in "Writing about Teaching" in Chapter 5 testifies to the influence of authors like Bel Kaufman, Jonathan Kozol, Sylvia Ashton-Warner, and Vivian Gussin Paley on her own career as a teacher and teacher-writer. Through teacher narratives teachers have found affirmation, motivation, and innovation. Recently, the National Council of Teachers of English attested to the power of teacher stories by organizing the annual 1996 Conference (Chicago, November 21–24) around the theme "Honoring All Our Stories." The Call for Proposals (1996) declared, "In our professional lives, stories are significant aspects of our roles as teachers and learners." Increasingly, professional organizations, scholars, and teacher educators recognize the value of teacher lore. Teachers have already created for themselves professional development through teacher narratives.

Isenberg (1994) in *Going by the Book* chronicles her own development as a career teacher under the influence of five teacher narratives: *Teacher* by Sylvia Ashton-Warner, *Up the Down Staircase* by Bel Kaufman, *To Sir, with Love* by E. R. Braithwaite, *How Children Fail* by John Holt, and *36 Children* by Herbert Kohl. Isenberg recounts what these stories meant to her when she first read them and what they mean now. Now, for example, she sees Braithwaite as imbuing "his teaching with the caring that Nel Noddings advocates—caring that makes all the difference. In a sense, he himself becomes part of the curriculum, as his students study him for clues on how to live and learn in a difficult world" (p. 67). Without preaching about caring or offering a caring checklist, *To Sir with Love* shows how caring teachers behave, a valuable reminder for any teacher. This teacher story has helped Isenberg bring together theory and practice with personal understanding. Isenberg discerns other insights on topics ranging from working with at-risk children to challenging the status quo, and she does it in the company of teachers who know—those authors who share their teaching lives in fiction or non-fiction. Isenberg's ultimate purpose, she says, is to situate teaching narratives "in a literary and scholarly framework and validate them as a type of autobiographical research that should not be easily dismissed by literary critics or educational theorists (who are often teacher-educators) as merely popular or pragmatic writing" (p. 103). Although one may disagree with Isenberg that teacher narratives constitute a genre akin to slave narratives, she captures well what many of us have known. Teacher lore makes a difference to teachers. Burke-Hengen (1995), like Isenberg, attests to the power of teacher narrative in her professional life as she has read books like James Herndon's *The Way It Spozed To Be* (1968) and Mary McCracken's *Lovey* (1976), a tale of dealing with an emotionally disturbed child. Many language arts teachers we know, like Burke-Hengen, can witness to the difference Nancie Atwell's *In the Middle*, for example, has made in their teaching, encouraging them to try reading and writing workshops and to trust their students to take more control of their own learning. What does all this say about professional development?

At the least, teacher narratives should be made available for teachers to read and consider on their own. Many experienced teachers remain unaware that such stories as *Teacher* exist, or they have not seen these books as serious since no one mentioned them in college classes. A small investment in teacher narratives, most of which are available in paperback, in every school library might go a long way. Librarians and teachers could offer booktalks to get the faculty interested in teacher lore. The principal could encourage teachers to check out these books. Some teachers might want to start informal reading groups. Without pressure or mandate, more teachers may discover the power of teacher lore as others have done on their own. In addition, many teachers will be inspired to write teacher lore for their own personal use. The authors of the teacher stories in this volume attest to the power of writing to help them clarify their own experiences, questions, and ideas. Bonnie Voth in Chapter 5, for instance, says that she writes as a means to capture her thoughts and learn from her mistakes. Access to models of teacher lore encourage teachers to try writing for their own understanding and ongoing improvement. Simply offering teachers such new reading material can promote professional development as personal journey. Using teacher narratives in more direct, organized ways during dedicated periods of time will be explored further in this chapter.

TEACHER EVALUATION

A renewed emphasis on teacher evaluation arose in the years after *A Nation at Risk* (1983) as another means of professional development for school reform. Ideally, as Fullan and Stiegebauer (1991) argue, "the primary purpose of teacher evaluation should be teacher development" (p. 325). Unfortunately, the most widely used systems of teacher evaluation, like most inservice requirements, remain unproductive if not counterproductive. Hickcox and Musella (1992) characterize the situation as follows:

Traditional performance-appraisal approaches also tend to be narrowly focused, concentrating for the most part on classroom performance rather than on a broad reflective examination of teaching life. Further, traditional approaches almost always mix appraisal for professional-growth procedures with appraisal for making a judgement. In fact, it is common for the same set of procedures to be used for both kinds of appraisal in spite of evidence to show that the hierarchical aspects of the judgmental appraisal blunt any strong sense of collegiality and professional cooperation growing from the effort to bring about growth. The traditional approach is a technical-rational approach with an emphasis on standardization across widely disparate situations, attention to record-keeping, and written reports. . . . The point is that the traditional approach does not seem to fit too well with the ideas of staff development with its emphasis on collegiality, cooperation, and professionalism. (p. 162)

Traditional approaches can include a number of models from the Product Model, in which teachers are appraised on the basis of student achievement (McGreal, 1983), to the more common Effective Teaching Model, based on the work of Madeline Hunter (Schwarz, 1992). In Oklahoma, the Effective Teaching Model remains the basis of teacher evaluation, apparent in the instrument used with the residency or first-year teacher induction program as well as in district models. The Oklahoma Effective Teaching Model includes such indicators as "Provides closure by summarizing and fitting into context what has been taught" and "Uses a minimum of class time for non-instructional routines, thus maximizing time on task." Such an instrumental, behavior-centered, prescriptive approach may have value for beginning teachers, but it offers most veteran teachers very little.

Teacher evaluation still has to achieve its promise as support for professional development given its current top-down structure, inability to meet individual needs of changing and competent teachers, and preoccupation with accountability and judgment. Johnson (1990) describes the problem in the following:

In practice, the assessment and the improvement of teaching tend to be at odds, the first requiring administrators to make tough, summary judgements and the second calling for them to give teachers support. The prospect of assessment promotes caution among teachers, while improvement depends on their taking risks. The teachers interviewed for this study roundly criticized formal supervision and evaluation practices, observing that they are effective for dismissal but not for improvement, that administrators are rarely prepared to offer genuinely useful advice, and the procedures invariably take precedence over the content of supervision, virtually never providing an opportunity for learning. (p. 266)

Glickman (1991) has referred to this situation as the "evaluation boondoggle" (p. 7). Alternative forms of evaluation have been developed, however, and although not widely practiced yet, "personal, multifaceted, and contingent teacher evaluation could *be* staff development" (Schwarz, 1991, p. 232). One such form involves teacher lore.

　　　　Wood (1992) describes a narrative-based teacher evaluation program which offers experienced, competent teachers authentic growth opportunities. Dissatisfied with traditional approaches from goal setting to a variety of checklists, Wood claims, "None of these designs begins, at the core, with the knowledge and experience of individual teachers, which, to my mind, are the richest grounds for educative inquiry and improved practice" (p. 535). Wood prefers a model which contributes to teachers' development by "a) encouraging their reflection on classroom experiences; b) facilitating the articulation of insights gleaned from that reflection; and c) using these insights for problem-solving, development of educative theory, and institutional change" (p. 537). The approach Wood describes combines elements of clinical supervision and goal-setting models with teacher lore. The following are the nine phases of her program:

1) an initial interview between teacher and supervisor, during which the teacher recounts a critical incident or particular memory of his/her teaching or learning experience;
2) a collaborative interpretation of that narrative account by the supervisor and teacher to discover a continuing challenge or theme in the teacher's professional life;
3) reflection by the teacher on this story and its theme, and the eventual selection of professional goals based on the insights that have risen from that reflection;
4) a second interview, during which the supervisor and teacher explore the teacher's professional goals and ways to monitor progress toward these goals;
5) at least one classroom observation conducted by the supervisor . . . through the lens of the teacher's stated goals;
6) feedback to the teacher in narrative style;
7) a written self-evaluation by the teacher;
8) a written evaluation by the supervisor that responds to the teacher's self-evaluation;
9) a discussion before the end of the year of opportunities for further professional growth. (pp. 537–538)

Wood adds that this program came about partly because of her frustration "that teachers' voices were not a central part of what I was hearing and reading about educational reform" (p. 538). She goes on to describe the experiences of several teachers with this program. (Others have proposed similar ideas of supervision/evaluation based on teacher lore, written and oral. See, for example, Yonemura [1982].)

　　　　Clearly, this is a labor-intensive approach to teacher evaluation and not necessarily suitable for inexperienced or less than competent teachers. Part of its

success is also related to its voluntary nature. However, if professional development within the school is really the goal, not merely bureaucratic assurances of
accountability for public consumption, such a system is worthwhile. Teachers
could also work with one another, not just the administrator, to accomplish the
same purposes. Using a teacher story to focus a teacher on his or her own concerns
personalizes the evaluation process and allows the teacher a genuine commitment
to finding and solving the problems and reaching the goals he or she has set. Such
problematizing of one's practice builds on a teacher's sense of vocation and desire
to improve, perhaps even leading to teacher research. Joanne Bergbom's story
about journal writing in Chapter 3 and Jeanne Buckingham's story, "The One Who
Got Away" in Chapter 4 are examples of teacher stories which could well lead to
setting goals for inquiry, a meaningful basis on which to build an ongoing,
educative teacher evaluation process. As Wood says, "For it is across the awful,
sometimes yawning gap between teachers' original ideas and their present practice
that faculty development can construct a bridge of hope and meaning" (p. 540).
Teacher lore has great potential in teacher evaluation for professional development.

TEACHER RESEARCH

Teacher lore lies at the heart of much teacher research, research about and
including teachers and research by teachers themselves. Patterson, Stansell, and
Lee (1990) put it this way:

Every teacher has stories to tell. Every teacher has truths to share. Teachers can learn to see
children in ways that no one else can. Teachers can show us the ways students learn, and the
reasons that learning is sometimes hard. The research process can help teachers explore their
decisions, find their own voices, and tell their own stories. Through those stories based on
disciplined, systematic research many teachers have spoken out and changed the ways in
which schools work. Ultimately, through research, all teachers can do this. (pp. 1–2)

Teacher narrative can be the *source* of research about teaching and learning and
can serve as the *method* of research about teaching and learning for classroom
teachers. Both teacher research about and by teachers is becoming more common
in the form of graduate theses and dissertations as well as in articles in a growing
variety of professional journals. Teacher narrative, stories of real teachers'
classroom and professional lives, exemplifies many of the qualities and benefits of
qualitative research in education. As Fairbanks (1996) says, narrative research
includes " a broad range of accounts, from first-person narratives of experience to
studies that interpret the stories others tell about their lives, a conception that
overlaps other forms of qualitative research methods, such as ethnography." (p.
321). Fairbanks elucidates the difference between this kind of research and traditional, university-based, quantitative research which depends on statistical studies.
She observes:

Unlike positivist research, which draws conclusions through logical propositions and with
which most readers are more familiar, narratives aim to persuade rather than prove their
claims. They offer descriptions and explanations of situations and circumstances from which
readers may cull insights into their own practice. . . . Prescribed rules or succinct and con-

crete steps for the construction or interpretation of narrative accounts run counter to the very nature of stories. (pp. 320–321)

We will avoid the research "paradigm wars" here and simply note that the strengths of this kind of research for professional growth emerge from the strengths of narrative as a way of knowing. Teacher stories are context sensitive, offering rich accounts of actual classroom life; value-laden, opening up the moral and ethical dilemmas educators face; complex and often open-ended, refusing to offer simple answers to difficult problems; and diverse, portraying the realities of school in a pluralistic society. Teacher narrative invites the kind of critical thinking needed to interpret literature; such writing works, not by generalizable evidence but by verisimilitude, by resonating in another's mind and imagination. Teacher lore research invites others to co-construct the meanings it has to offer. Teacher lore offers educators, policy makers, and the public knowledge *about* teaching, first of all.

   Teacher Lore, edited by Schubert and Ayers (1992), offers a number of examples of educational research built on teachers' experiences and voices. Jagla, for example, in Chapter 5 of *Teacher Lore* explores the place of imagination and intuition through teachers' input. Conversations with teachers serve as a basis for research into teachers' perspectives on parents in Chapter 7 by Hulsebosch. Elbaz (1991) observes that stories can be found in many studies of teacher thinking. She summarizes as follows:

The story to be told is either the centrepiece of the research (Gudmundsdottir, 1988, Oberg and Blades forthcoming) or it may be presented as pretext, data, or case study, but it is there nonetheless in, for example, Shulman's (1987) portraits of Nancy and Colleen, Tabachnick and Zeichner's (1986) account of two beginning teachers' experiences during their induction year, as well as Day's (1987) retelling of the process of staff development in a primary school. To those we should add the current body of work on teachers' life histories (Goodson 1980, Woods 1987). (p. 2)

Other examples of educational research based on teacher lore include Grossman's (1990) *The Making of a Teacher*, a comparative study of secondary English teachers with and without professional education courses prior to their first year of teaching; Wasley's (1994) *Stirring the Chalkdust*, subtitled "Tales of Teachers Changing Classroom Practice,"about educational change; and Bullough's (1989) *First-Year Teacher*, a study of teacher development through the case of one beginning teacher. *Teacher Personal Theorizing* (1992), edited by Ross, Cornett, and McCutcheon, also includes research based on teacher lore. Teachers as well as academicians, policy makers, and others can gain much understanding through and from this kind of research. Kelchtermans (1993) uses teacher narrative to examine professional development itself. He concludes, "I believe that this study showed the usefulness of the biographical perspective for a better understanding of why teachers are acting the way they do. . . . This research experience with the biographical perspective only deepened my belief that to understand the lives, one must get the story" (p. 454).

Moreover, the study of education through teacher narratives helps create community, another strength of narrative as a way of knowing. Elbaz (1991) summarizes the importance of teacher voice and states that "The sense of a community of teachers and researchers, working together, listening to one another, is especially important at a time when the work of both groups is being increasingly bureaucratized" (p. 16). Teachers doing their own research, based on teacher lore, is just as important, however, especially as a means of professional development. The research-narrative-development connection is significant.

The first role that teacher narrative may serve is as impetus for teachers' own research. As in the teacher evaluation model discussed before, a story can serve to focus the teacher and problematize some aspect of his or her work, leading to a desire to find out more. Pantier's "Apart from the Rest" in Chapter 3 of this book indicates how such inquiry might work. Telling or writing a story leads to a reflection which requires research, in this case library research. Pantier's story inspired Pantier to look deeper into the issue of inclusion, to bring together theory and her own experience. Stories connect theory and practice; they can lead to new knowledge on which teachers can act. Moreover, narrative can be the method of teacher research.

Cochran-Smith and Lytle (1993) define teacher research as "systematic, intentional inquiry by teachers about their own school and classroom work" (pp. 23–24). The history of teacher research, also called action research, is usually traced back to Dewey, who urged teachers to continue to inquire about and into their work with children, to be lifelong students of learning. Stenhouse and his colleagues in England in the 1960's and 1970's contributed much to the teacher research movement as have a number of Americans since, especially in the study of children's reading and writing. Americans include Goodman (1985), Goswami and Stillman (1987), Mohr and Maclean (1987), and many others in recent years, like Fleischer (1995). The potential for authentic, even radical school reform when teachers become researchers is captured by Cochran-Smith and Lytle (1993) who declare,"When teachers redefine their own relationships to knowledge about teaching and learning, they often begin to reconstruct their classrooms and to offer different invitations to their students to learn and know. When they change their relationships to knowledge, they may also realign their relationships to the brokers of knowledge and power in schools and universities" (p. 52). As teachers become producers of knowledge, no longer passive recipients of others' research, they are empowered to change in many ways; they also serve as inquiring role models for their own students.

Cochran-Smith and Lytle (1993) illuminate the connection between teacher narrative and teacher research in their description of major kinds of teacher research, including journal writing; teacher group oral inquiries into problems with specific students using a descriptive review process; classroom studies which may depend on such teacher lore as anecdotal classroom records, case studies of certain students or other teachers, and so on; and essays which often call on personal stories as well as scholarly theory. Teacher research can fall into the traditional, quantitative mode, but the categories identified by Cochran-Smith and Lytle can or do involve teacher narrative. The format for reporting the results, as well as the method for collecting data, is usually first-person narrative. We have read, from among our colleagues, for example, teacher research into the effects of playing classical music on student writing and case studies of innovative teachers. Pulling's "Imitation of the Living Voice: What I learned from Quintilian and a Few Eighth Grade Student Writers" in Chapter 3 of this book serves as a good example of teacher narrative-research, as does Durham and Lauther's "A Joyful Noise: The Poetry of Teaching with Two Voices" in Chapter 5. Teacher research can be both systematic, intentional inquiry and the story of that inquiry. Stock (1993) discusses the function of teacher narrative or "anecdote" in teacher research. She observes, as follows:

As teachers we avoid abstract theoretical statements when we talk with one another about our professional work because such statements seem disconnected from what actually occurs in our classrooms. Anecdotal accounts, filled with meaning and significance, seem to serve us better as we research the interactions that constitute teaching and learning in our classrooms. . . . My argument for teacher talk, the power of anecdote, the importance of narrative in educational research rests in just these characteristics: in their very occasionality, and in their very particularity. (pp. 185–186)

Because teacher research is practice-oriented, this research offers an excellent means for professional development. Fleischer (1994) quotes Goswami and Stillman (1987) on characteristics of teacher researchers:

1. Their teaching is transformed in important ways. . . .
2. Their perceptions of themselves as writers and teachers are transformed. They step up their use of resources; they form networks; and they become active professionally.
3. They become rich resources who provide the profession with information it simply doesn't have. . . .
4. They become critical, responsive readers and users of current research. . . .
5. They collaborate with their students to answer questions important to both. . . . (Preface)

Engaging teachers with narrative teacher research is surely one way to improve schools and build teacher morale as well. Of course, teacher research has limitations and is not for everyone. It is time consuming for the teacher, it demands another disciplined routine, and it may not be appreciated by others in the school. Still, it offers many teachers new opportunities to be heard and to learn and change. How teacher narrative becomes reflective research is illustrated in Gretchen's use of student teacher capstone papers, discussed in the next chapter.

A caveat here. Teacher research remains controversial in academic circles. Huberman (1996) warns that teacher researchers are vulnerable to many of the same faults to which all researchers are subject—bias, especially since the teacher is the research instrument; lack of robust methods; the tendency to claim too much; the "risk of narcissism" (p. 138). One should be careful about claiming too much for teacher research. However, teacher research is certainly one avenue for professional development. Teachers who decide to study their own classrooms and schools can bring new energy and insights to their own work and can reform the workplace. What better professional development than "intentional inquiry" into the puzzles and problems of practice! Teacher research groups, such as the Philadelphia Teachers Learning Cooperative, Boston Women Teachers' Group, the North Dakota Study Group on Evaluation mentioned by Cochran-Smith and Lytle (1993), and other professional networks offer a particularly powerful method for professional growth as we will see in the section on the Writing Project.

Connelly and Clandinin (1988) argue that curriculum planning is or ought to be an outgrowth of teacher narrative. They see teacher lore as inseparable from curriculum development as they say:

> What is the central idea of our view? It is simply that all teaching and learning questions—all curriculum matters—be looked at from the point of view of the involved persons. We believe that curriculum development and planning are fundamentally questions of teacher thinking and teacher doing. We believe that it is teachers' "personal knowledge" that determines all matters of significance relative to the planned conduct of classrooms. (p. 4)

Connelly and Clandinin offer methods we have seen before, journal keeping and biography, and other methods like document analysis to enable teachers to reflect on and carry out curriculum. They offer case reports of "specific teachers doing specific curricular things" as examples (p. 157). They also tie together narrative, curriculum, and teacher research, demonstrating that "Action research is, therefore, a deliberate way of creating situations and of telling the story of who we are" (p. 153). In professional development, curriculum issues as well as pedagogical concerns and other considerations are all connected. Curriculum development sessions and task forces have long served as professional development opportunities for some teachers. However, as Connelly and Clandinin envision this work, it is something much more than writing scope and sequence charts or lists of objectives, and it is an ongoing endeavor for all teachers. Curriculum development must be based on teacher knowledge, knowledge often presented, explored, and reconstructed in narrative forms.

CASE STUDIES

As we will see again in Chapter 7 of this book, cases are a particular kind of story and basis of inquiry which constitute one method of learning for preservice teachers. Case studies also have a place in the professional development of inservice teachers. Richert (1991) declares, "Working with cases provides a structure for teaching teachers to reflect and thus enhancing teacher understanding" (p. 129). Case study offers teachers the time, opportunity, and support teachers need to change and grow, argues Richert. She continues, "Cases capture the wisdom of practice and allow teachers to examine that practice (and that wisdom) analytically and systematically as well as intuitively. On a case-by-case basis, teachers can examine what other teachers do and why, what they themselves do and why. They can examine what teachers think, what they know, and what they feel as well as what they do" (p. 126). A rich source on the use of cases is *Groupwork in Diverse Classrooms: A Casebook for Educators* (1995), edited by Judith Shulman, who has done much work on case studies. Zeller (1995) explores the case study as research. Again, the uses and kinds of teacher lore overlap. The use of cases in professional development programs is growing, however.

Ackerman, Maslin-Ostrowski, and Christensen (1996), for example, describe their method for employing what they call "case stories" in all-day professional development and leadership institutes, professional development conferences, and graduate courses. They endorse programs that "are increasingly moving away from presentations by experts and toward programs that involve administrators and teachers as facilitators of their own renewal and growth" (p. 21). Their basic model requires a minimum of three hours and involves the following six steps:

Step 1: The freewrite (warm-up).
Step 2: Writing case stories.
Step 3: Telling, listening, and discussing case stories.
Step 4: Small group reflection.
Step 5: Whole group reflection.
Step 6: Conclusion. (pp. 21–23)

This approach is similar to one we took in a graduate extension course which we will describe in more detail. The authors conclude that the "case story helps break down the isolation of practitioners and build a more collegial environment. The process promotes an atmosphere of trust and a sense of participation and well being" (p. 23). The case story approach allows educators to teach one another. The use of cases and other types of narrative is also finding a place in university courses for inservice teachers.

COLLEGE COURSES USING TEACHER LORE

University coursework, leading to advanced degrees or not, has been considered professional development for teachers for years. Teachers in our state can get professional development "points" for college courses and workshops and can move up the salary scale, a situation common across the country. Unfortunately, teachers have often considered university courses too "ivory tower," and we know from experience that university professors have been condescending, as well, communicating the notion that university researchers have the knowledge and classroom teachers do not. The use of teacher lore offers a different experience, one more likely to offer genuinely useful intellectual and professional growth.

One of our colleagues, Dr. Kathryn Castle, uses teacher lore extensively in two graduate courses she teaches. In an interview, Castle shared with Gretchen how and why she uses teacher narrative in her courses, Fundamentals of Teaching and Analysis of Teaching. She has also shared her syllabi. Castle, a constructivist, has always had an interest in teacher beliefs and how these influence teaching. Twenty years ago Castle used belief inventories and literature on teacher efficacy as she developed her courses. She now doubts the usefulness of such approaches and thinks teachers gain more insight into their own teaching through narrative.

In Fundamentals of Teaching, a master's level course, required reading includes Ayers' teacher narrative, *To Become a Teacher* (1995), and optional reading includes Schubert and Ayers' *Teacher Lore* (1992) and Jalongo and Isenberg's *Teachers' Stories* (1995). Castle first communicates to students, through reading and discussing, the notion of teacher narrative. Two major assignments in the course, then, require the use of teacher lore. Students must do a collaborative group case study presentation and discussion, in which they "present an assigned case to the class in an engaging (creative) manner which involves class members in dialogue on relevant pedagogical issues." Students must also do a reflective paper which is a personal teacher story, either of the teacher's own memories of schooling or of a teaching experience. One of the major purposes of these assignments is "reconnection," helping teachers understand what teaching means for the learner. For example, writing about a childhood memory of schooling can take the writer back to being a child, a powerful emotional and educative experience for many. Castle sees these assignments as more reflective activities than memorizing Bloom's Taxonomy or effective teaching principles. Her goal is to have teachers "raise their own questions and find their own answers."

In the doctoral level course, Analysis of Teaching, students move more quickly to writing their own case or story. The text used is Van Manen's *Researching Lived Experience* (1990). The major term project includes such choices as writing a case for beginning teachers or interviewing an experienced teacher and writing an anecdote, vignette, or story from this teacher's experiences. One of the challenges of this course is for teachers to compare and contrast their own experiences to what published research may say about topics like retention or testing. The meaning of educational research is an underlying theme. Castle describes the analysis of teaching in this course as coming from "within and without." Analysis only from within can lead to mere narcissism. Analysis only from without includes traditional observation systems and does little to change how teachers think or feel. Analysis from teacher narrative and questioning that narrative with other teachers and other research, analysis from both within and without, can be truly transformational, according to Castle.

Other colleagues also use teacher lore in graduate courses requiring texts like Tompkins' (1996) *A Life in School* (listed in Teacher Lore Suggestions). Gretchen uses Rouse's (1993) *Provocations: The Story of Mrs. M.* (listed in Teacher Lore Suggestions) to begin her graduate course in language arts. This teacher story offers an engaging starting point for class discussion.

TEACHER LORE FOR INSERVICE TEACHERS: AN ON-SITE EXTENSION COURSE

To take a look at how teacher lore could be used as professional development for inservice teachers, we designed an extension course open to all teachers in the Mid-Del Public Schools, an urban school district of 1,130 certified staff members located about 70 miles south of Oklahoma State University. The objective of the course was simple: to engage teachers in sharing and reflecting on their professional knowledge through narrative. What we found was that this simple notion produced a semester of powerful writing and discussion which affirmed our belief that reading, writing, reflecting, viewing, and discussing teacher lore can provide a generative environment for talking about teaching and learning.

The course, *Teacher Lore: Sharing Our Knowledge*, met for seven, two-hour sessions over the course of the fall semester, 1995. Elementary and junior high teachers from three different school buildings participated, and each received one hour of graduate credit for the course. We met in a conference room at Del Crest Junior High after school. We selected this particular school district as a place to offer the course because of the openness of district administrators to publicizing the course and encouraging teachers to participate. The specific junior high meeting place was a result of one particularly supportive building principal who was eager for teachers in the building to have an opportunity to meet and study together.

We began the course with history and background of the use of teacher lore, watching excerpts from videos such as *Teachers* and *To Sir with Love*. Each participant selected a book of their choice from the following list: *My Posse Don't Do Homework* by LouAnne Johnson; *Up the Down Staircase* by Bel Kaufman; *Among Schoolchildren* by Tracy Kidder; *White Teacher* by Vivian Gussin Paley; and *A Survival Guide for Teachers* by Elaine Greenspan. Teachers also watched a movie of their choice such as *Dead Poet's Society* or *Stand and Deliver*. We then discussed the books and movies.

With this foundation in place and the community established, each participant wrote a teacher story of her own to share with the class. Each story was riveting; each one straight from the real world of the classroom. The teachers wrote about their students: two young men who were struggling to survive within the system; a little boy, brilliant, creative, and constantly in motion; a class that became a community and talked about issues threatening their very lives; and an autistic child who taught his teacher an important lesson about acceptance. On the evening the first stories were finished, each teacher read aloud to the group. At the end of each reading there was silence and then a spontaneous display of affirmation and encouragement, approval and questions. One story inspired a lengthy discussion about a student who had been expelled from school. The teachers struggled together to make sense of a system that sent away a young girl who needed the school to help her. "We lost her today," said the author of the story. "I didn't know what to say when she told me goodbye."

This interaction is just one of the many during the course that illustrates the power of teacher narratives to provide teachers with time and permission to solve problems and support each other. According to Darling-Hammond and McLaughlin (1996), new approaches to professional development connect teachers to one another and offer teachers in-school teams or cross-school networks that work together over time. Although these networks may look different in different settings, they share these common features:

- Connected to teacher's work with their students
- Linked to concrete tasks of teaching
- Organized around problem solving
- Informed by research
- Sustained over time by ongoing conversations and coaching. (pp. 202–235)

Writing teacher lore is more than writing "just" a story. Built into the course was the importance of reflecting on the meaning of the stories. Duckworth (1987) talks about the need for teachers to "take their own knowledge seriously, to be willing to pay attention to confusion, to make an effort to understand each other's ways of understanding . . . to take the risk of offering ideas of which they are not sure" (p. 84). Once the teacher stories were written, each teacher wrote a reflection on the story. Reflection in this case has several purposes, including telling the story behind the story—why the story was written, what else a reader needs to know. Reflection also connects ideas in the story to the broader conversation, perhaps including references to published research. The reflection component of the stories is important to making teacher lore work as meaningful professional development for teachers because it is in the reflection that teachers can take a close look at what can be learned from the story. Reflecting also challenged teachers in this particular course to take charge of their own learning. As one of the teachers wrote on the course evaluation, "This could eventually become an independent group outside of the University after the teachers have gotten some guidance."

With the stories as a base, the group became comfortable raising questions around difficult and complex issues that emerged from the writing. For example, one veteran teacher wrote of a difficult year when her teaching practice was challenged by an administrator. She tried to make sense of the attacks on her professionalism through writing, and the subsequent group discussions helped her and the group sort through teacher/administrator roles and relationships. Another story lead to a realization that there was a lack of trust among teachers in the building and an inability, or at least a reluctance, to share their real concerns with each other.

Through the reflections the teachers in the class identified many issues that were important to them. "You find out things sometimes that you don't want to know about yourself," said one teacher. Another participant told about realizing some patterns about her teaching life from writing and reflecting on stories about her students. "I realized that . . . I have a pattern of choosing to begin new programs, I choose to teach in situations where I'm not required to follow a curriculum, and I choose to work with students outside the norm."

Participants also identified in their stories/reflections connections to issues being discussed in the larger educational community. *Table 6.1* is a list generated by the group near the end of the course when asked to think back over the topics discussed. Focusing on stories written by real teachers about their own students and classrooms provided a relevant connection to these issues that could not be matched by a staff development session provided by an outside consultant. Veteran teachers already know a great deal about teaching and can share their knowledge with colleagues. This course provided a structure for this kind of learning together.

During the semester the writing itself became important. When talking about choosing a topic for a teacher story, one of the participants said, "The incident [about which she wrote] bothered me and I needed to sit down and write about it." On the course evaluation one participant noted, "I enjoyed the class and

Table 6.1
Teacher Lore: Issues and Connections

classroom management/discipline	special needs students
time management	integrated learning
teaching reading and writing	professional development opportunities
learning styles	professionalism
inclusion	language and literacy
multiple intelligences	second language learners
parental involvement	isolation
state-mandated testing	censorship
curriculum development	sex education
relationships with colleagues	constructivist learning
relevancy of textbooks	teachers as researchers
relationships with school administrators	

appreciated the opportunity to have a reason to start writing again. I had forgotten how much I like to write." Newkirk (1992) speaks of the connection writing offers teachers when he states, "If teachers are to write, they must believe that what they do matters to other teachers; so long as they are isolated they will never gain this sense of having something to contribute" (p. xii). Participants in the teacher lore class echoed Newkirk when they compiled the following list of reasons to write teacher lore:

- gives teachers a sense of importance
- provides authentic professional development
- offers affirmation
- allows teachers to model writing for students
- helps teachers discover the questions they have
- motivates teachers to try new methods
- inspires teachers to become better teachers

In addition, the group concluded that writing teacher stories is "good therapy."

One outcome of the course that we had not anticipated was the teachers' use of their stories in their own classrooms. Independently of each other, teacher participants told about reading the stories they wrote to their students. One participant told about reading her reflection to her students who then asked if they, too, could write about the writing they had done for their portfolios. One teacher told about her students wanting to know more about the child she had written about. The students themselves offered an affirming audience for the stories their teachers shared.

The classroom community that was built around the course remains connected. Two of the teachers meet with Gretchen's preservice teachers to share stories and answer questions about real world teaching. We held a reunion meeting and dinner a year after the course began both to get the group together again and to find out what if any lasting impact the study of teacher lore had on the lives of the participants. All of the original participants attended the reunion meeting. Some of them had not seen each other since the year before.

Our reunion gathering had that comfortable feel of seeing old friends again, catching up with each other's lives, and checking in. After the greeting and mingling subsided, we invited each person to write a reflection on "Teacher lore: One year later." Through the writing we discovered that the stories we shared and the community we built during the course have powerfully impacted each teacher both personally and professionally.

In evaluating the teacher lore course, participants identified similar characteristics as helpful to their own learning. Wrote one participant, "Sharing experiences with our colleagues is something teachers seldom have the opportunity to do; the class was supportive, informative, interesting and shed light on the whole picture of education." "What a relief to be treated like a professional!" wrote another. Some excerpts from the reflections follow:

"So much negativism is being spread about the public schools of today, and this group, small though it may be, represents the light that shines through despite the odds."

"The chance to reflect changed some of my behaviors that needed changing. I tend not to bury my head in the sand anymore; I use the voice I found I had. I want to convince kids that through arts and writing *their* lives can be empowered, too."

"The class featured such powerful written accounts of teacher stories. As a writing teacher, shouldn't I be writing too? Our teaching lives seem somehow more important when we write about them."

"It's good to get back together again even to find that school is pretty stressful for everyone. Probably where so many individuals are trying to do so much for so many, it will always be that way."

"I've incorporated reflections in my class for at-risk students. I ask students to write an autobiography and to reflect on what part their individual history plays in who they are and the decisions they make."

"This class and the discussion from the class helped me to revive many of the old inspirations of my first years in teaching. As the years passed, I had lost some of that excitement. This class changed all of that. I now look for new ways to inspire and excite my students."

"It seems that the teacher lore class reawakened my ability to record with words. I had forgotten that writing was a labor of love and growth for me."

"It is the nature of teaching that it is largely done in isolation. Ironically, teachers seem to be people who like being with others. There are so few opportunities for professional sharing."

Newkirk (1992) writes of the importance of making schools productive learning environments for teachers as well as students which "will mean creating opportunities for teachers to teach teachers. It will mean the end of inservice programs that treat teachers as passive receptacles, and it will mean opportunities for them to develop their creative abilities" (pp. xii–xiii). The teacher lore course proved to us that teacher lore can be a catalyst for meaningful, relevant professional development for teachers. Similar courses and workshops inviting teachers to read and write teacher lore can be designed by teachers, staff development coordinators, curriculum specialists, and administrators using the resources described in Teacher Lore Suggestions beginning on page 175. We created this course to fit into the already crowded, demanding lives of teachers by meeting every other week over the course of a semester. Time to read, write, think, and build a community was essential to this course as it is to all meaningful professional development. The power of teacher lore came to life for those of us who participated in the act of writing about and reflecting on our teaching lives among a caring community of professionals.

NATIONAL WRITING PROJECT/OKLAHOMA STATE UNIVERSITY WRITING PROJECT

Our belief in the power of story to encourage teachers to reflect on and change what happens in their classrooms is based on the respect we have for teachers and their knowledge. This respect has deepened as a result of our connection to the National Writing Project network through Gretchen's association with the New Mexico State Writing Project at New Mexico State University, Joye's connection to the Oklahoma Writing Project at the University of Oklahoma, and our work together with the Oklahoma State University Writing Project.

The National Writing Project (NWP), founded by James Gray in 1974 as the Bay Area Writing Project, is a school-university partnership currently made up of 160 sites. The NWP brings together teachers from all grade levels and curriculum areas in summer and school-year programs to share their knowledge about teaching and learning and to examine their teaching practice. New sites are added each year to the NWP network. According to Richard Sterling (1997), Executive Director, "the NWP has preserved and expanded its core work and accomplishments: universities and schools coming together to improve the writing and learning of every student in America. To this end, universities in 45 states have made the NWP part of their mission and over 1.5 million teachers have committed their time and energy to NWP programs" (*Annual Report*, p. 1).

NWP programs are often singled out as models for meaningful profess-ional development (McLaughlin, 1991; Shanker, 1990). The National Commission on Teaching and America's Future (1996) profiles North Carolina's Capital Area Writing Project as a model for professional development that improves teaching (p. 85).

The Oklahoma State University Writing Project, housed at Oklahoma State University (OSU) in Stillwater, is a professional home to teachers who have participated in the site's summer and school-year programs since 1992. Teachers come together each summer at Oklahoma State and other sites of the NWP to participate in invitational summer institutes where they write, share approaches to teaching, and study research in the field. Stories about teaching are read, written, and told throughout the summer. Teacher participants are asked to bring a piece of teacher lore to share in writing response groups on the first day of the OSU Writing Project's Summer Institute. "Apart from the Rest" by Toni Pantier in Chapter 3 is one of the stories originally written for this purpose. Teachers in each Summer Institute are empowered professionally and even personally when they claim the right to write about their teaching lives.

This simple invitation to "share what you know" has a profound impact on teachers who, some of them for the first time, feel like they find their voice when given the opportunity to write stories about what they know.

An important part of the NWP model is the ongoing professional connection that it provides teachers. Other courses or programs end at the conclusion of the semester or summer. Writing projects continue to provide a place for teachers to work together to share their professional successes, challenges, and questions. Research done by Stanford University's Center for Research on the Context of Secondary School Teaching directed by Milbrey W. McLaughlin (McLaughlin & Talbert, 1993) found that "teachers' responses to today's students and notions of good teaching practice are heavily *mediated by the character of the professional communities* in which they work" (p. 8). The study goes on to conclude that "teachers' groups, professional communities variously defined, offer the most effective unit of intervention and powerful opportunity for reform. It is within the context of a professional community . . . that teachers can consider the meaning of the nation's goals in terms of their classrooms, their students, and their content area" (p. 18). The writing project community offers teachers a local network as well as a connection to the entire NWP network of teachers across the country.

As part of an ongoing professional community both locally and nationally, teachers find opportunity and support for publishing what they know in professional journals, books, and newsletters. *Writers & Projects of the OSU Writing Project* is a newsletter edited by Eileen Simmons, a teacher in the Tulsa Public Schools, and published three times a year by the OSU Writing Project. Simmons encourages Writing Project teachers to submit teacher lore and articles about successful teaching techniques, book reviews, poetry, and fiction for publication in the newsletter. The newsletter gives teachers a chance, as Dahl (1992) suggests, to "place themselves in the role of writers . . . become consumers of professional literature and creators of new information about teaching. To participate in the professional conversation is to shape its topics and focus—to change and be changed by its information and differing points of view" (p. 2). The National Writing Project also encourages teacher/writers to publish in *The Quarterly*, the journal of the NWP; *The Voice*, the newsletter of the NWP; and on electronic web pages linked to the NWP homepage. The NWP also publishes books and edited volumes by teachers. For example, *Teacher's Voices: Portfolios in the Classroom* (1993) edited by Mary Ann Smith and Miriam Ylvisaker, features stories by teachers at different grade levels who studied portfolios in their classrooms. In addition to making publishing opportunities available to teachers, the OSU Writing Project and other NWP affiliates encourage teachers to join in the professional conversation by presenting at local, regional, national, and international conferences.

One of the basic assumptions of the NWP as found in the *Model and Program Design* (1996) states that "What is known about the teaching of writing comes not only from research but from the practice of those who teach writing" (p. 2). The OSU Writing Project and many other local NWP sites support teacher research groups made up of teachers who have what Bissex (1987) calls "a wondering to pursue" (p. 3). Teacher researchers study the art and craft of research and design and implement research projects that will help them look closely at students, classrooms, and teaching practices. Groups meet regularly to share resources and findings and to offer support and encouragement to group members. Cochran-Smith and Lytle (1993) state that "Encouraged by the widespread activities of the National Writing Project . . . [among others] the focus of much of the K-12 teacher research of the last decade has been writing" (p. 11). One example of the NWP's support for teacher researchers is evidenced by *Cityscapes: Eight Views from the Urban Classroom,* a book by members of the National Writing Project Urban Sites Network. The book provides insights into classrooms of teachers dedicated to making urban classrooms work and also provides successful models of teacher inquiry. As a part of a new initiative known as "Rural Voices, Country Schools," the NWP is currently attempting "to raise the visibility and impact of exemplary rural teachers" (Rural voices, p. 1). The work is supported by a grant from the Annenberg Rural Challenge. This project will, among other things, give teachers a place to tell the stories of their schools and communities.

Mary K. Healey (1992) writes about the power of writing communities, such as the Bay Area Writing Project, to support teachers as they examine what goes on in their classrooms. "Once a teacher becomes a teacher writer, there is no going back. . . . We become more sympathetic and understanding. . . . Once we write regularly, we also know that nothing will ever happen unless someone actually does put words down on paper" (p. 258). Writing projects and other professional networks invite and encourage teachers to write the stories of their students and their classrooms. This ongoing connection to a community of learners can give teachers a place to examine their own teaching practice and at the same time share their questions and celebrate their successes.

STRATEGIES FOR WRITING TEACHER LORE

We have seen a number of ways for teachers to produce teacher lore. Getting teachers to tell stories is not difficult as long as they feel safe. However, certain approaches may make the experience more worthwhile and useful for the writer and potential reader. We asked our contributors to share a story they needed to write and then we asked them to reflect on that story. Stories may be focused on certain themes, stages of development, or school problems. Jalongo and Isenberg (1995) devote Chapter 8 of their book to strategies for generating teacher narrative, including reflections on an episode of teaching improvement, writing a letter to a person from the teacher's professional life, writing about a mentor or a child "who still haunts me," and writing about a time when expectations were quite different from the teaching reality. Keeping a journal or anecdotal records on students or simply recording conversations are other ways to proceed. Telling the story of action research is a possibility. As long as teachers have choice and the setting is appropriate, many teachers are eager to be heard at last and to have their experiences taken seriously. Jalongo and Isenberg also offer suggestions for teachers interested in getting their stories published.

PROBLEMS AND POSSIBILITIES

Teacher lore is no panacea for professional development, and the last thing we need is another single "super reform" imposed on teachers in the name of progress. We have carefully avoided offering flow charts and organizational tables. Any use of teacher lore for professional development must retain elements of choice and serendipity. Even in Castle's graduate courses, teachers had choices about cases presented and stories revealed. The worst scenario would be for teacher lore to become a method for the manipulation of teachers rather than for the liberation and enlightenment of teachers. How teacher lore is used and by whom remains problematic.

Also a problem, as in all professional development, are the elements of time and support. Teacher narrative requires large chunks of time for writing, reflection, and research. Too little time today is left to teachers during their school days to pursue professional development. Too often teachers are not supported in their efforts by their administrators or colleagues, either, and teacher stories may be seen as trivial by some policy makers. Another difficulty is that of making sure that uses of teacher narrative are intellectually and professionally challenging. Merely telling stories is not enough to generate school reform. Reflection and research are needed. In addition, change is not often linear and sure; teacher lore comes with no guarantees. Clearly, teacher lore as professional development requires ongoing study and rethinking. Which teachers will be best served, when, and by what approach are all questions that remain.

Nevertheless, the possibilities for genuine teacher growth are impressive. We believe that teacher narrative can be used to meet the challenges of the future, the challenges so well expressed by Hargreaves (1994) in the following words:

The challenge of restructuring in education and elsewhere is a challenge of abandoning or attenuating bureaucratic controls, inflexible mandates, paternalistic forms of trust and quick system fixes in order to hear, articulate, and bring together disparate voices of teachers and other educational partners. . . . It is a challenge of opening up broad avenues of choice which respect teachers' professional discretion and enhance their decision-making capacity. It is a challenge of building trust in the process of collaboration, risk and continuous improvement as well as more traditional kinds of trust in people. And it is a challenge of supporting and empowering school cultures and those involved in them to develop changes themselves on a continuing basis. (p. 260)

REFERENCES

Ackerman, R., Maslin-Ostrowski, P., & Christensen, C. (1996). Case stories: Telling tales about school. *Educational Leadership, 53* (6), 21–23.

Ayers, W. C. (1995). *To become a teacher*. New York: Teachers College Press.

Banford, H. (Ed.) (1996). *Cityscapes: Eight Views from the Urban Classroom*. Berkeley, CA: National Writing Project.

Bissex, G. (1987). What is a teacher-researcher? In Bissex, G. L. & R.H. Bullock (Eds). *See for ourselves: Case-study research by teachers of writing* (pp. 3–5). Portsmouth, NH: Heinemann.

Braithwaite, E. (1959). *To sir with love*. New York: Jove Books.

Bullough, R. V. (1989). *First-Year Teacher*. New York: Teachers College Press.

Burke-Hengen, M. (1995). Teaching lives. *Teacher Researcher, 3* (1), 127–139.

Castle, K. (1997). Personal communication, February 2.

Cochran-Smith, M., & Lytle, S. L. (1993). *Inside/outside*. New York: Teachers College Press.

Connelly, F. M., & Clandinin, D. J. (1988). *Teachers as curriculum planners*. New York: Teachers College Press.

Dahl, K. (1992). Introductions: Old habits, new conversations. In K. L. Dahl (Ed.), *Teacher as writer: Entering the professional conversation* (pp. 1–6). Urbana, IL: National Council of Teachers of English.

Darling-Hammond, L., & McLaughlin, M. W. (1996). Policies that support professional development in an era of reform. In M. W. McLaughlin & I. Oberman (Eds.), *Teacher learning: New policies, new practices* (pp. 202–235). New York: Teachers College Press.

Duckworth, E. (1987). *The having of wonderful ideas*. New York: Teachers College Press.

Elbaz, F. (1991). Research on teacher's knowledge: The evolution of a discourse. *Journal of Curriculum Studies, 23*, 1–19.

Fairbanks, C. M. (1996). Telling stories: Reading and writing research narratives. *Journal of Curriculum and Supervision, 11*, 320–340.

Fleischer, C. (1995). *Composing teacher research: A prosaic history*. Albany, NY: State University of New York Press.

———. (1994). Researching teacher-research: A practitioner's perspective. *English Education, 26*, 86–124.

Fullan, M., & Stiegebauer, S. (1991). *The meaning of educational change*. New York: Teachers College Press.

Glickman, C. (1991). Pretending not to know what we know. *Educational Leadership, 48* (8), 4–10.

Goodman, Y. (1985). Kid watching: Observing in the classroom. In A. Jagger & M. Smith-Burke (Eds.), *Observing the language learner*. Newark, NJ: International Reading Association.

Goswami, D., & Stillman, P. (1987). *Reclaiming the classroom: Teacher research as an agency for change*. Upper Montclair, NJ: Boynton/Cook.

Greenspan, E. (1994). *A teacher's survival guide*. Portland, ME: J. Weston Walch.

Grossman, P. L. (1990). *The Making of a Teacher*. New York: Teachers College Press.

Hargreaves, A. (1994). *Changing teachers, changing times*. New York: Teachers College Press.

Healey, M. K. (1992). Writing communities: One historical perspective. In K. Dahl (Ed.), *Teacher as writer: Entering the professional conversation* (pp. 253–260). Urbana, IL: National Council of Teachers of English.

Hickcox, E. S., & Musella, D. F. (1992). Teacher performance appraisal and staff development. In M. Fullan & A. Hargreaves (Eds.), *Teacher development and educational change* (pp. 156–169). London: The Falmer Press.

Huberman, M. (1996). Moving mainstream: Taking a closer look at teacher research. *Language Arts, 73* (2), 124–140.

Isenberg, J. (1994). *Going by the book*. Westport, CT: Bergin & Garvey.

Jalongo, M. R., & Isenberg, J. P. (1995). *Teachers' stories*. San Francisco: Jossey-Bass.

Johnson. L. (1992). *My posse don't do homework*. New York: St. Martin's Press.

Johnson, S. M. (1990). *Teachers at work*. New York: Basic Books.

Kaufman, B. (1964). *Up the down staircase*. New York: Avon.

Kelchtermans, G. (1993). Getting the story/understanding the lives: From career stories to teachers' professional development. *Teaching and Teacher Education, 9*, 443–456.

Kidder, T. (1989). *Among schoolchildren*. Boston: Houghton Mifflin.

McGreal, T. L. (1983). *Successful teacher evaluation*. Alexandria, VA: Association for Supervision and Curriculum Development.

McLaughlin, M. W. (1991). Enabling professional development: What have we learned? In A. Lieberman & L. Miller (Eds.), *Staff Development for Education in the '90s* (2nd ed.) (pp. 61–82). New York: Teachers College Press.

McLaughlin, M. W., & Talbert, J. E. (1993). *Contexts that matter for teaching and learning: Strategic opportunities for meeting the nation's educational goals.* Stanford, CA: Stanford University, Center for Research on the Context of Secondary School Teaching.

Mohr, M., & Maclean, M. (1987). *Working together: A guide for teacher-researchers.* Urbana, IL: National Council of Teachers of English.

National Commission on Excellence in Education. (1983). *A nation at risk.* Washington, D.C.: U. S. Government Printing Office.

National Commission on Teaching and America's Future (1996). A better way: Professional development that improves teaching. In *What matters most: Teaching for America's future.* (p. 85). Woodbridge, VA: Author.

National Council of Teachers of English (1995). Call for Proposals (86th Annual Convention). Urbana, IL: Author.

National Writing Project. (1997). *Annual report 1996–1997.* Berkeley, CA: Author.

———. (1996). *Model and program design.* Berkeley, CA: Author.

Newkirk, T. (1992). Foreword. In K. L. Dahl. *Teacher as writer: Entering the professional conversation.* (pp. xi–xiv). Urbana, IL: National Council of Teachers of English.

Paley, V. (1979). *White teacher.* Cambridge, MA: Harvard.

Patterson, L., Stansell, J. C., & Lee, S. (1990). *Teacher research.* Katonah, NY: Richard C. Owen.

Richert, A. E. (1991). Using teacher cases for reflective and enhanced understanding. In A. Lieberman & L. Miller (Eds.), *Staff development for education in the 90's.* (pp. 113–132). New York: Teachers College Press.

Ross, E. W., Cornett, J. W., & McCutcheon, G. (Eds.). (1992). *Teacher personal theorizing.* Albany, NY: State University of New York Press.

Rural voices, country schools engages NWP rural sites. *The voice, 2* (1), 1, 16.

Schubert, W. H., & Ayers, W. C. (Eds.). (1992). *Teacher lore: Learning from our own experience.* White Plains, NY: Longman.

Schwarz, G. (1992). Let the buyer beware: Alternatives in teacher evaluation. *The Tower Review, 10* (1), 12–18.

Schwarz, G. E. (1991/1993). Philosophical approaches to teacher evaluation. (Doctoral dissertation, University of North Texas, 1991). *Dissertation Abstracts International 54* (1), 122-A.

Shanker, A. (1990). Staff development and the restructured school. In B. Joyce (Ed.), *Changing school culture through staff development* (pp. 91–103). Alexandria, VA: Association for Supervision and Curriculum Development.

Shulman, J. (Ed). (1995). *Groupwork in diverse classrooms: A casebook for educators.* San Francisco: Far West Lab for Educational Research and Development.

Smith, M. A. (1996). The national writing project after 22 years. *Phi Delta Kappan, 77,* 688–692.

Smith, M. A. & Ylvisaker, M. (Eds.). (1993). *Teachers' voices: Portfolios in the classroom.* Berkeley, CA.: National Writing Project.

Sterling, R. (1997). Welcome to the national writing project (p. 1). In National Writing Project *Annual Report 1996–97.* Berkeley, CA: Author.

Stock, P. L. (1993). The function of anecdote in teacher research. *English Education, 25,* 173–187.

Van Manen, M. (1990). *Researching lived experience.* Albany, NY: State University of New York Press.

Wasley, P. A. (1994). *Stirring the Chalkdust.* New York: Teachers College Press.

Wood, D. R. (1992). Teaching narratives: A source for faculty development and evaluation. *Harvard Educational Review, 62*, 535–550.

Yonemura, M. (1982). Teacher conversations: A potential source of their own professional growth. *Curriculum Inquiry, 12*, 239–256.

Zeller, N. (1995). Narrative rationality in educational research. In H. McEwan & K. Egan (Eds.), *Narrative in teaching, learning, and research* (pp. 211–225). New York: Teachers College Press.

Chapter 7

Teacher Lore in Preservice Education

Giroux's (1988) comment on teacher education remains largely true today. "That teacher training programs in the United States have long been dominated by a behavioristic orientation and emphasis on mastering subject areas and methods of teaching is well documented" (p. 123). Current competency-based certification testing and reform efforts, like that of the Holmes Group, to increase subject area mastery continue to impact teacher education. The National Council for Accreditation of Teacher Education (NCATE), the group seeking to dominate and regulate teacher certification nationwide, commonly uses the word "rigor," by which is meant certain knowledge, skills and performances. Certainly, future educators need to master skills and information from punctuation to effective teaching techniques. However, as Noel (1993) argues, "The often used phrase 'teacher training' expresses the emphasis on behaviors. Teachers have not been considered or treated as thinking, critical beings who would have their own unique beliefs, desires, and goals for the educational situation. The teacher's background experiences, personal knowledge, and feelings within education have not been encouraged to bring to bear on their preparation for teaching or on their decisions in the classroom" (p. 1). Moreover, novice teachers continue to complain about the lack of "reality" in their preparation programs as teacher educators struggle to bridge the gap between theory and practice. Teacher lore offers an alternative to reducing preservice teachers to empty vessels who must be filled up with the "right attitudes," "correct experiences," and "best practices." Because teacher lore is personally engaging, concrete, memorable, complex, and open-ended, it can help students make connections between theory and practice, their ways of thinking and others' outlooks, the college classroom and life in the schools. Teacher lore is increasingly used as a tool in preservice teacher education to begin developing habits of reflective practice.

Preservice teachers lack experience as teachers but have a wealth of experience as students. Teacher lore, used in courses in child development, methods, foundations, and field experiences culminating in student teaching, can help students make the switch from involved spectator of teaching to thoughtful participant, building on and challenging the "apprenticeship of observation." Van Manen (1990) indicates the significance of story for preservice teachers. He says "story provides us with possible human experiences, tends to appeal to us and involve us in a personal way, is an artistic device that lets us turn back to life as lived, whether fictional or real . . . yet, stories transcend the particular . . . [making] them subject to . . . analysis and criticism" (p. 70). Griffin (1994), discussing the use of story in teacher education, explains, "Appealing features of story in professional education include the blending of technology with biography, personal theory with grand theory, abstract generalizations with context specificity" (p. 239). He continues:

It is precisely the blend of the biography and professional practice that may have tremendous power for the teacher candidate who is searching to find his or her place in the teaching profession. Is it better to talk or read about abstract or even concrete conceptions of classroom management, for example, than to place those conceptions in the experiences of admired teachers? Is it more effective to conceive of cooperative learning as a linked set of strategic teaching behaviors rather than as a story of how a teacher intellectually negotiates the requirements of subject matter, the character of classroom groups, and expectations of learning? Is it helpful for novice teachers to come to believe that teaching expertise is somewhere "out there" to be found, rather than a long and intricate tale involving ambition, disappointment, renewal, hunching, discovering, inventing? (p. 240)

Griffin goes on to describe the use of cases in teacher education. This chapter will explore concrete uses in teacher preparation programs of fiction and nonfiction stories and films; the tales of experienced teachers; the use of cases; autobiographical writing; the use of narrative in student teaching and as a way to introduce student teachers to teacher research; and teacher stories in textbooks. Many of the uses described in Chapter 6 can also work for preservice teachers although they may serve different functions. Teacher narrative can have as powerful an impact on new as on experienced teachers.

STORIES AND FILMS

In various teacher education courses, from early field observation seminars to methods courses, teacher lore in the form of literature and films can serve useful functions: a way for students to examine the teaching life, even experience it vicariously; an avenue for examining teaching and schooling within social and political contexts; a vehicle for exploring public attitudes toward teachers and how the media inform those attitudes; a means for honoring the reasons students go into teaching. Tama and Peterson, (1991) describe an entire course at Portland State University designed for developing reflective practice through fiction and nonfiction. Students read books and view films like those listed at the end of this book, they write journal responses and discuss stories. The purpose of this course, say Tama and Peterson is "to move students from a technical understanding of teaching to comprehending the big picture of teaching with all its social and moral implications" (p. 22). Stories allow students to see teaching in its full human context, complicated, varied, value-laden, something more than prescribed behaviors and factual knowledge.

Gretchen has described how she uses stories and films in preservice education courses (Schwarz, 1995). Having students in an early field experience course review a film like *Teachers* (1984) or *Dangerous Minds* (1995) stimulates lively discussion of issues ranging from classroom management to the Hollywood version of the lone teacher. Specific teaching methods become vivid and meaningful when students can read about techniques in action in a book like *Small Victories* (Friedman, 1990). In responding to teacher lore such as *Among Schoolchildren* (Kidder, 1989), preservice teachers must reflect on their own feelings about reaching difficult kids and their own commitment to teaching. Gretchen uses Greenspan's *A Teacher's Survival Guide* (1994) in a course which covers discipline, classroom management, professionalism, school climate, and other such issues. This course is taken before student teaching. The book consists of Elaine Greenspan's stories about her own teaching career and her conclusions about teaching, with advice on such topics as organizing, taking care of self, and working with difficult students and declining funding. Greenspan includes interviews with other teachers, stories of her colleagues, as well. This book engages students in ways that dry articles on 35 rules for classroom management cannot. Students are also urged to agree or disagree, to take issue with one real teacher's views. *A Teacher's Survival Guide* also reminds readers why they have chosen teaching and what the rewards can be, a motivating reminder for nervous preservice teachers. Teacher lore taps into the emotional side of teaching.

The teacher stories in this book offer future teachers much to think about, as well, from needy children to difficult colleagues, from experiences in student teaching to experiences of a teacher writer. For example, a story like Karen Downing's "Connections" in Chapter 5 can remind future teachers what adolescents are really like more vividly than most texts on adolescent development. Joseph and Burnaford (1994) summarize, "Teacher education must provide sufficient opportunities to fully imagine what it is like to be a teacher. . . . Interacting with stories, evoking the memories of teachers and those who have been taught, and joining in conversation about film or television portraitures of teachers may give new teachers an added awareness of this profession in this society and its personal meaning as well" (p. 6).

STORYTELLING

Teacher lore in the form of practicing teachers' told stories is another valuable resource for education students. Teachers love to tell their stories, and these stories can be powerful. Gretchen brings in panels of novice teachers—former students—to talk to students nearing their student teaching. Tips shared by teachers who were in the same place the year before, insights expressed in stories of experience, can be much more effective than the professor's lectures. When a peer says to get plenty of sleep during student teaching, it means something! Panels of veteran teachers in the English methods class also share their techniques and lessons in narrative form, communicating the value of student-centered methods or the need for continuing experimentation and change in practice. Stories can actually aid students in remembering terms, approaches, and processes. Egan (1989) argues, "The story insures memorization by investing material to be learned with the qualities that engage the imagination in the process of learning" (p. 457). A practicing teacher's tale of a successful writing workshop, for instance, may stay with a teacher candidate long after abstract definitions vanish from thought. What real practicing teachers have to say carries weight, and fine veteran teachers can do much to inspire and encourage future teachers.

The teacher educator's own stories of experience are useful, too. Gretchen uses her stories from thirteen years in the schools to illustrate points, provoke discussion, carry warnings, and express the frailties of any teacher. It is helpful for novice teachers to know that professors and veteran teachers have had and still have struggles and dilemmas. Students appreciate these stories; they give credibility and convey the sense that teaching does require ongoing learning. Narrative carries content and creates "trust and space" in the community of future teachers, as Pinnegar (1996) puts it. "War stories" are not merely entertaining; narrative helps bridge theory and practice, offering a human context for learning about teaching.

CASES

A growing number of teacher educators utilize various kinds of case studies in teacher education, having students read cases for study and thought and write cases to deepen their understanding of the classroom. Griffin (1994), as mentioned previously, endorses the use of cases. Bullough (1993) presents a study of preservice teachers' use of cases to create a Personal Teaching Text in a teacher education program aimed at developing reflective practitioners. Levin (1996) tells of how 12 elementary preservice teachers "constructed their own dilemma-based cases based on critical incidents experienced during their field placements in Professional Development Schools, and engaged in a process writing seminar based on a Writer's Workshop format while constructing their cases" (abstract). Case studies require active learning according to Silverman, Welty, and Lyon (1992), who have put together a book of cases based on the experiences of actual elementary and secondary teachers. They explain:

At first, case method may seem a strange way of learning . . . It does not present educational theory in neatly organized chapters with carefully designed tables, charts, and explanations. Rather it presents stories about real teachers in real schools and asks that *you* go to the theory and try to apply it to understand the stories and the problems they present . . . Case method requires that you interact with the theory; it requires that you decide how to use theory to analyze classroom situations in order to solve problems. Deciding for yourself—that is really the heart of case-method pedagogy. It is based on the understanding that the most important learning, the most meaningful learning, the most long-lasting learning comes from the work the learner does on his or her own. (p. xix)

The cases offered include such stories as those of a social studies teacher who takes over a high school AP honors class and has trouble communicating with the students he feels are arrogant. Another case explores the situation of a first-grade teacher who finds a new district science curriculum unteachable. Some teacher educators attach specific study questions to cases; others recommend a certain format for analysis. The case method can be used in an introductory education course, methods or curriculum courses, educational psychology, and field exper- ience courses. Cases are versatile.

Gretchen is particularly interested in the cases provided in *The Ethics of Teaching* by Strike and Soltis (1985). These cases challenge students in her course before student teaching to think about professional ethics. One case, for example, describes the dilemma of a new teacher who discovers that his mentor teacher has a drinking problem affecting his teaching. The mentor wastes class time and does not even try to teach all his students. What should the new teacher do? The teaching life consists of many such ethical dilemmas, and there are no sure steps or checklists to make sure one has made the right decision. Future teachers need to perceive the difficulties and moral responsibilities that the calling of teaching involves. As Nash (1987) argues, "The implications of story for ethical training are significant" (p. 70). In the same management and planning course Gretchen also uses *Situations: A Casebook of Virtual Realities for the English Teacher* (1994) by Wagner and Larson. Students are challenged by cases of teachers who cannot maintain control of their classes or who struggle with grading.

The case method has been receiving growing attention in teacher development as the number of books and articles reflect. Other books of possible interest to teacher educators and teachers include:

1) Kleinfeld, J. (1989). *Teaching Cases in Cross Cultural Education Series*. Fairbanks, AK: University of Alaska.
2) Kowalski, T. J., Weaver, R. A., & Henson, K.T. (1990). *Case Studies on Teaching*. White Plains, NY: Longman.
3) McAninch, A. R. (1993). *Teacher Thinking and the Case Method*. New York: Teachers College Press.
4) Shulman, J. (Ed.). (1992). *Case Methods in Teacher Education*. New York: Teachers College Press.
5) Wasserman, S. (1993). *Introduction to Case Method Teaching: A Guide to the Galaxy*. New York: Teachers College Press.

Wasserman (1995) summarizes the benefits of cases, a special kind of teacher lore, in teacher education:

Students are more actively involved in learning. They are motivated to learn more, to seek information they need to understand the issues better. They become more self-initiating. They develop better habits of thinking; become less satisfied with simple and simplistic solutions to complex educational problems . . . have increased tolerance for ambiguity. They become problem solvers, instead of lesson learners. They grow more confident in themselves. . . . Their communication skills are increased; they appreciate others' points of view and learn to listen respectfully to others' ideas. (p. 148)

Cases offer as many possibilities for preservice teacher development as for inservice education.

PERSONAL WRITING

Autobiographical writing, personal narratives—what we call preservice teacher lore—offers yet another resource for growth and development. Knowles and Holt-Reynolds (1994) introduce a journal issue devoted to autobiographical writing with the following comments:

It is because we believe that learning to teach and learning to be a teacher are ongoing, perhaps life-long, processes and practices where intensely human, personal meanings are created and influenced by a myriad of prior experiences that we proposed and developed this special issue of *Teacher Education Quarterly*. Why write about personal histories? Because in one sense, they are teacher education. Teachers' lives as school pupils before they become teachers, their lives as scholars while they prepare to become teachers, their lives as variously contributing members of the workforce and society, and their lives as professionals in a career of teaching present few clear boundaries. . . .What they lived and learned in the past and what they live and learn today becomes a history they reference for their living and learning tomorrow. (p. 6)

To acknowledge and reflect on life histories allows students to connect consciously their personal and professional lives, examining why they want to become teachers, what they believe about how children learn, what knowledge is most important, what kinds of teachers they hope to become. For example, following Posner's lead in *Field Experience: A Guide to Reflective Teaching* (1993), Gretchen asks students in the early field experience course she teaches to write about their own significant learning experiences and experiences with successful and unsuccessful teachers. Posner (1993) explains the reasons for doing such autobiographical writing. "No one's mind is empty . . . We all have some beliefs about what good teaching is, whether or not we have official status as a 'teacher.' Our own beliefs, principles, and ideals . . . function for each of us as a personal 'platform. . . .' By becoming aware of the perspective by which we operate, we can at least become sensitive to the bases for our own approach to teaching, and, at best, become capable of changing our approach as we gain both new ideas and new teaching experiences" (p. 29). Reflection should begin early in teacher education.

Another example is the Future Teachers' Autobiography Club begun by Florio-Ruane (1994) at Michigan State University. A voluntary program for education students, this "club" allows future teachers to read autobiography like Mike Rose's (1989) *Lives on the Boundary* and Vivian Paley's (1979) *White Teacher*. Students also write and share their own life stories. The purpose is to prepare teachers to deal with culturally diverse classrooms. Florio-Ruane maintains that one way "for teacher candidates to appreciate the experiences of diverse learners is to examine their own and others' autobiographies, focusing on issues of ethnic identity, language, and schooling" (p. 55). She adds that "reading personal narrative of schooling and literacy may prompt teacher candidates to ask important questions" about the cultural messages curricula communicate and the effects of pedagogical approaches on diverse students (p. 56). Students may learn emotionally as well as cognitively through others' life histories that there are many ways to learn. Multiculturalism comes alive as in the stories in this book—set in places as diverse as an Indian reservation, Harlem, and rural Oklahoma. One can imagine many such uses in teacher education programs.

Telling teaching stories, stories from new experience, is a key part of any teacher education program, it seems to us. Gomez and Tabachnik (1992) relate their experiences using teaching stories in an elementary teacher education program at the University of Wisconsin–Madison aimed at preparation for multicultural classrooms. Prospective teachers in seminars connected to field experiences "tell personal narratives of classroom life—which we call teaching stories—as a way to understand their teaching practice" (p. 131). Gomez and Tabachnik, report "In shaping their stories for their listeners, they [teacher candidates] must first reflect on those experiences in light of the role they and others in the story play and how their own and others' beliefs and actions lead to success and failure in teaching and learning" (p. 131). Others then react to and ask questions about these stories. Gomez (1996) further explains:

Through storytelling, we aimed to question our teaching goals; to consider effective alternatives to our teaching practices so that we continually focused on who the children were and what strengths as well as needs they brought to school; and to reconsider our role and actions as individual teachers. We tried to see ourselves as members of not only a classroom community of children to whom we were obligated, but also to see ourselves as members of a school community and of larger communities outside of school to which we were obligated for social action and justice. (p. 5)

Gomez shares the stories of a future teacher, Bobby Jo Johnson, stories which led that teacher to question practices of labeling learners, especially those of color. In Chapter 2 of this book, narrative helps a student teacher, Penny Palmer, question school practices that allow troubled adolescents to be written off by the system.

In student teaching, in particular, storytelling is not an extra, a social activity to be tolerated. Teacher lore is essential for student teachers to make sense of their experiences. Maas (1991) reports on the use of storytelling as the base of a student teaching seminar. Sharing stories, written and told, allows new teachers to critique their own methods, reexamine their assumptions about schools and students, question what they have been studying in college courses, and overcome teacher isolation. Maas declares, "The lessons of the seminar, the information, were embedded within the language of stories. . . . We learned about others, and about the worlds that surround them, through our stories. We ultimately learned about teaching" (p. 218). Problem solving can be accomplished as students share what their cooperating teachers do about make-up work or what they tried with students who sleep in class. The supervisor, college educator, can learn as much as the student teachers in this process. Student teacher lore keeps the professor in touch with reality, too.

REFLECTION AND RESEARCH

Using presevice teacher lore to develop reflective practice and to give future teachers experience with teacher research led to a project Gretchen has found valuable during student teaching. The secondary program at Oklahoma State University requires a capstone paper of student teachers, a final paper which connects theory and practice as student teachers do their first real teaching. These papers, while time-consuming for student teachers, have proven an excellent way to initiate new teacher researchers through a variety of formats. At a seminar on the last day of the student teaching semester, all the secondary student teachers gather, and several students from each subject area share their papers with the whole group, providing perhaps the first professional conference for these novice teachers. During the 1997 spring semester, Gretchen's students took a narrative approach to the capstone paper, and the results were exciting. One of the resulting papers has been revised for inclusion in this book, "Awakening the Boy" by Penelope Palmer in Chapter 2.

Gretchen's students were asked to come up with a story of their student teaching experiences—a story or series of anecdotes that caught their attention for some reason. Once they chose and wrote their stories, stories which provoked some kind of need to know more, the student teachers were told to do a researched reflection on their stories. They were to use library sources and/or action research to respond to the issues which emerged in their stories. Some found appropriate books and articles; others did interviews, surveys, or student case studies at their schools. The variety and quality of the final papers was outstanding. One student teacher wrote a moving story confronting her own discomfort with kids who have physical disabilities. Her reflection led her to examine her own prejudices and to find out about cystic fibrosis, the disease which afflicted her student. Another student teacher wrote a story about a difficult seventh-grade girl who refused to write but turned out to be identified as gifted and talented. The frustration of working with this girl motivated the student teacher to interview a gifted/talented teacher and accumulate advice on working with gifted students. One student teacher wrote a story about a student whom she had grown to care about who was in a gang. This student teacher "made the rounds with the juvenile officer" in the city and gathered information on gang dress and symbols from the Oklahoma Department of Corrections. Others wrote and reflected on such issues as tracking, classroom management, and distance learning, all topics which personally involved them as student teachers.

Each capstone paper, story and research, grew from the student teachers' own real concerns in the classroom, and they discovered resources and ways of answering questions and trying to solve problems. The writing was vivid and engaging, and the reflections honest and thought provoking. Such papers make excellent additions to these teachers' professional portfolios, revealing much about who they are and what they believe and how they solve problems. As John Dewey proclaimed, experience plus reflection can equal growth. Teacher narrative research has a place in preservice education.

TEXTBOOKS

That more educators are recognizing the importance of teacher stories is evident, finally, in a variety of textbooks and other materials being published. For example, Cushner, McClelland, and Safford declare in their text for multicultural education, *Human Diversity in Education: An Integrative Approach* (1992):

There are a great many stories in this book, partly because . . . learning should be a meaningful experience in and of itself. Some stories are about people who really lived or are living and events that actually happened . . . others have been created to illustrate certain ideas and concepts . . . we use stories for their power to speak about complex human experiences—in this case, about the experiences people have with the fact of human diversity. (p. 3)

One of our colleagues has included teacher lore in his new foundations text. In *How Teachers Learn* (1994), Teachers College, William Proefriedt includes his own teacher story in his work on teacher education. More subject and level specific texts, such as *Making the Journey: Being and Becoming a Teacher of English Language Arts* by Leila Christenbury (1994), published by Boynton/Cook, are built on teacher lore. Christenbury tells stories of her own high school and middle school teaching as well as stories of her education students in this methods text. Furthermore, many teacher educators are using teacher lore books like Mathews' biography of Jaime Escalante or others listed at the end of this book in a variety of courses from the sociology of teaching to adolescent psychology.

Even in the quest for national standards, professional organizations like the National Council of Teachers of English and the International Reading Association have called on teacher stories to communicate those standards and current thinking about teaching and curriculum. In the *Standards for the English Language Arts* (1996), one can find a number of vignettes of classrooms across the grade levels which illustrate principles of the standards. These stories are not meant to tell everyone how to "implement the standards," however. Reflective practice, not regulation, is the goal. The document says:

Each vignette is followed by two or three questions that frame the learning experiences depicted from a wider perspective. Characteristically, these questions focus on alternatives that might be considered in the activities presented, issues not fully addressed, and possible adaptations of the insights reflected in the classroom samples. The questions posed in these sections, like the vignettes themselves, invite readers to participate in an ongoing conversation about classroom practices. (p. 48)

These vignettes serve as mini-cases, inviting discussion, not declaring "best practices" which all teachers must follow in some lock-step fashion. The *Standards in Practice* series which elaborates on the English Language Arts standards, broken down into grade levels, is also based on teacher lore. As teacher educators include the standards and similar professional materials in their courses, teacher narrative again affects future teachers.

Clearly, there is a need for ongoing research into the use of teacher narrative with preservice teachers. Questions remain. Is teacher lore helpful for all students? How is it most useful? Will teacher lore introduced in preservice education have a long-term effect on actual practice? How can we avoid reducing teacher lore to a list of competencies embedded in narrative form or mere fable? The greatest power of teacher stories, we believe, lies in their contextuality and ambiguity, the refusal of realistic narrative to reduce life—or teaching—to simple models or maxims. Teacher lore supports the notion of teaching as more than a profession or technology; it helps preservice teachers connect to teaching as a vocation, a complex and unpredictable but compelling calling. As Bullough, with Baughman, (1993) says, "Thankfully, the process of becoming a teacher will always remain wonderfully mysterious despite the best efforts of researchers [and administrators and legislators, we would add] to achieve control, just as the ends of education will remain unpredictable, a condition for which we should be grateful" (p. 93).

REFERENCES

Bullough, R. V. (1993). Case records as personal teaching texts for study in preservice education. *Teaching and Teacher Education, 9*, 385–396.

Bullough, R. V., & Baughman, K. (1993). Continuity and change in teacher development: First year teacher after five years. *Journal of Teacher Education, 44*, 86–95.

Cushner, K., McClelland, A., & Safford, P. (1992). *Human Diversity in Education.* New York: McGraw Hill.

Egan, K. (1989). Memory, imagination, and learning: Connected by the story. *Phi Delta Kappan, 70*, 455-459.

Florio-Ruane, S. (1994). The future teachers' autobiography club: Preparing educators to support literacy learning in culturally diverse classrooms. *English Education, 26*, 52–66.

Freedman, S. G. (1990). *Small Victories.* New York: Harper Perennial.

Giroux, H. A. (1988). *Teachers as intellectuals.* Granby, MA: Bergin & Garvey.

Gomez, M. L. (1996). Telling stories of our teaching, reflecting on our practices. *Action in Teacher Education, 18* (3), 1–12.

Gomez, M. L., & Tabachnik, B. R. (1992). Telling teaching stories. *Teaching Education, 4*, 129–138.

Greenspan, E. (1994). *A teacher's survival guide.* Portland, ME: J. Weston Walch.

Griffin, G. A. (1994). Teacher education curriculum in a time of school reform. In M. J. O'Hair & S. J. O'Dell (Eds.), *Partnerships in Education* (Teacher Education Yearbook II) (pp. 224–245). Fort Worth, TX: Harcourt Brace.

Joseph, P. B., & Burnaford, G. E. (1994). Contemplating images of schoolteachers in American culture. In P. B. Joseph & G. E. Burnaford (Eds.), *Images of schoolteachers in twentieth-century America* (pp. 3–25). New York: St. Martin's Press.

Kidder, T. (1989). *Among schoolchildren.* Boston: Houghton Mifflin

Knowles, J. G., & Holt-Reynolds, D. (1994). An introduction: Personal histories as medium, method, and milieu for gaining insights into teacher development. *Teacher Education Quarterly, 21* (1), 5–12.

Levin, B. B. (1996, October). *Dilemma-based cases written by preservice elementary teacher candidates: An analysis of process and content.* Paper presented at the meeting of the American Association for Teaching and Curriculum, San Antonio, TX.

Maas, J. (1991). Writing and reflection in teacher education. In B. R. Tabachnik & K. M. Zeichner (Eds.), *Issues and practices in inquiry-oriented teacher education* (pp. 211–225). London: The Falmer Press.

Nash, R. J. (1987). Applied ethics and moral imagination: Issues for educators. *Journal of Thought, 22,* 68-77.

National Council of Teachers of English & International Reading Association. (1996). *Standards for the English language arts.* Urbana, IL: National Council of Teachers of English.

Noel, J. R. (1993, April). *Practical reasoning: Constructivist theory and practice in teacher education.* Paper presented at the meeting of the American Educational Research Association, Atlanta, GA. (ERIC Document Reproduction Service No. ED 390 835).

Pinnegar, S. (1996). Sharing stories: A teacher educator accounts for narrative in her teaching. *Action in Teacher Education, 18* (3), 13–22.

Posner, G. J. (1993). *Field experience: A guide to reflective teaching,* 3rd ed. White Plains, New York: Longman.

Schwarz, G. (1995). Making connections: Teacher lore in teacher education. *The Teacher Educator, 31,* 34–42.

Silverman, R., Welty, W. M., & Lyon, S. (1992). *Case studies for teacher problem solving.* New York: McGraw-Hill.

Strike, K. A., & Soltis, J. F. (1985). *The ethics of teaching.* New York: Teachers College Press.

Tama, M. C., & Peterson, K. (1991). Achieving reflectivity through literature. *Educational Leadership, 48* (6), 22–24.

Van Manen, M. (1990). *Researching lived experience.* Albany, NY: State University of New York Press.

Wagner, B.J., & Larson, M. (1994). *Situations: A casebook of virtual realities for the English teacher.* Portsmouth, NH: Boynton Cook.

Wasserman, S. (1995). Teaching with cases: Teacher educators and preservice teachers in professional preparation. In M. F. Wideen & P. P. Grimmet (Eds.), *Changing times in teacher education* (pp. 135–150). London: The Falmer Press.

Chapter 8

Change in Professional Development

Learning to be a teacher turned out for me to be much more like learning to be a person. (Proefriedt, 1994, p. 9)

Proefriedt (1994) in *How Teachers Learn* describes, like Powers in Chapter 2, the first year of teaching. He was assigned a "contained" seventh grade class made up of behavior problems and "slow learners." He tells how concerned he was about keeping order and how difficult teaching a number of different subjects was. He tells how he wondered about his own inadequacies in the presence of experienced teachers, and how his teacher community shared stories in the daily car pool, teachers' lounge, and local pub. Proefriedt concludes that this kind of informal but rational discourse about teaching—"a discourse shaped by everyday problems in the classroom and by concerns with educational purpose, with issues in the lives of young people that affect their capacity for learning, with reflections on one's own strengths and weaknesses as a person and as a teacher"—seems a solid basis on which to "prepare teachers to lead reflective work lives" (pp. 9–10). We share this conclusion, and in this chapter we will look at how teacher lore contributes to ongoing, reflective teacher education. First, we will examine the inadequacies of the current prevalent model of professional development for school reform. Then we will develop the argument that teaching is better seen as a vocation than a profession, and a vocation requires different kinds of development opportunities. Finally, we will connect teacher lore and sound principles of teacher development.

THE CURRENT SITUATION AND THE CHANGE PROCESS

Certainly, any improvement occurring in the nation's classrooms happens only with the involvement of teachers. Thus, in 1994 "teacher education and professional development" was added to the original six National Education Goals. Dilworth and Imig (1995) comment that this goal "suggests that practicing teachers are key to the transformation of schools and that in order for teachers to lead the reform efforts, they need to be offered expanded and enriched professional development experiences" (p. 1). Moreover, not only students, parents, and policy makers desire school improvement/change, but so also do teachers themselves. Fullan and Stiegebauer (1991) remark, "Change is needed because many teachers are frustrated, bored, and burnt out. Good change processes that foster sustained professional development over one's career and lead to student benefits may be one of the few sources of revitalization and satisfaction left for teachers" (p. 131). In coping with changing times, many welcome positive change in the schools. As McClure (1991) states, "Professional growth *is* at the heart of school renewal, and, ultimately, the restructuring of American education" (p. 221).

Despite much rhetoric, however, professional development opportunities have not changed. Overall, few schools have experienced a genuine change in culture through staff development. The following description from Hirsch and Ponder (1991) still holds:

Sink or swim beginnings. One-shot workshops injecting all with the same patent medicine. New truths delivered by faraway prophets. This year's episode of "bells and whistles to make our district a lighthouse," sponsored by the same folks who brought you last year's version. The frustration of trying new ideas—alone—while schools and classrooms run on old ones. (p. 43)

We have our share of stories about silly "inservice days," to say nothing of useless admonitions we were told in our teacher education programs. Teachers we know are still subjected to one-size-fits-all training so they can implement the latest reform fad, forced to listen to the newest jargon, and required to spend increasing time on staff development which they have not chosen for themselves and does not help them teach their students. Seldom is professional development sustained over time, either. Lieberman (1995) asserts, "Most of the inservice training or staff development teachers are now exposed to is of a formal nature. Unconnected to classroom life, it is often a melange of abstract ideas that pays little attention to the ongoing support of continuous learning and changed practices" (p. 592). As Johnson (1990) observes, "For teachers, learning and growth are personal rather than institutional responsibilities, occurring largely at the margins of their work. Although most school districts sponsor in-service training for their staff, the teachers in this study generally considered the programs superficial and irrelevant" (p. 249). Consideration of the nature of change or reform and a rethinking of what it means to be a teacher will shed light on why so many professional development efforts have been and continue to be insufficient or even counterproductive.

Traditionally school reform is viewed as planned change, designed by policy makers and carried out by teachers, all of which should proceed in a linear, nonproblematic way. Essentially, the positivist-behaviorist view has held sway.

Change is seen as generic, rational and predictable, and teachers are seen as blank slates on which new ideas can simply be written and then acted upon. Experts outside the classroom prescribe methods, standards, policies, and curriculum. If teachers do not change, it is their own fault; they irrationally refuse to open themselves up to the transmission of new knowledge. Both administrators and "outside experts have often viewed teaching as technical, learning as packaged, and teachers as passive recipients of the findings of 'objective research' " (Lieberman, 1995, p. 592). However, current studies of change in schools indicate that reform is not so simple. First, as Fullan and Stiegebauer (1991) make clear, change is time consuming, multidimensional, and characterized by conflict, anxiety, and struggle—messy; it is a "process, not an event" (p. 130). Fullan and Stiegebauer explain, "All change, including progress, contains ambivalence and dilemmas because, when we set off on a journey to achieve significant change, we do not know in advance all the details of how to get there, or even what it is going to be like when we arrive" (p. 345).   Change, while promising, is at the same time threatening and difficult. Lindsay (1996) observes:

Uncertainty and ambiguity are also evident in the broader literature on innovation and change (e.g., March & Simon, 1993; Martin, 1992; Massarik, 1990; Rogers, 1995). Models of change processes are described less as being planned, goal-oriented, and rationally deliberate and more as being unplanned, undirected, and responsive to other changes in larger social contexts. . . . Successful innovations, finally, are seen increasingly more as systemic and holistic in scope rather than as discrete adjustments or tinkerings in cultures, program, structures, etc. (e.g., Fullan, 1991, 1993; Murphy & Halliger, 1993; Owens, 1991; Rogers, 1995; Sashkin & Burke, 1990). (p. 1)

Contrary to the behaviorist, management-oriented view of school innovation, authentic change cannot be predetermined from the top down. In fact, to ignore the individual realities, the lack of teacher power and voice in the process, and the complexities of school systems leads to what Sarason (1990) calls the "predictable failure of educational reform."

Furthermore, real change requires a "transformation of subjective realities" (Fullan and Stiegebauer, 1991, p. 36). Commands to change, even when rewards are attached (or punishments promised for failure), ignore the special, human situation of the classroom teacher. Fullan and Stiegebauer continue, "Significant educational change consists of changes in beliefs, teaching style, and materials, which can come about *only* through a process of personal development in a social context" (p. 132). Surface changes can be legislated, but lasting changes in how teachers view and do their work, in how they think and feel, must happen on a deeper level, teacher by teacher, community by community. Ironically, at a time when we are coming to new understandings of how students learn, we continue to apply old learning notions to teachers. Lieberman (1995) notes, "The conventional view of staff development as a transferable package of knowledge to be distributed to teachers in bite-sized pieces needs radical rethinking. It implies a limited conception of teacher learning that is out of step with current research and practice" (p. 592). Change in today's schools is very demanding of teachers. The

National Foundation for the Improvement of Education (1996) declares, "Modern teaching and learning are no longer packageable and require sophisticated approaches to teacher development." The report continues:

Today's teachers must take on new roles within the school and be able to teach young people from diverse backgrounds. . . . Teachers now must be sensitive to varying social demands and expectations; must be able to diagnose and address the individual learning and development needs of students, including special emotional, physical, social, and cognitive needs; must be able to use information technologies . . . must make important decisions about what and how much to teach of the overwhelming amount of new knowledge being created in every field; and must reach out more effectively to parents and the community than ever before. (p. 16)

Such roles demand ongoing, authentic, and person-oriented professional development.

    Most staff development, both at the preservice and inservice levels, remains training. Webster's *New World Dictionary* (1991) definition of "train" includes "to condition," "to subject to certain action, exercises, etc. in order to bring to a desired condition," and to "instruct so as to make proficient or qualified" (p. 1418). Preservice college courses in using multimedia or classroom management strategies are largely training. Local inservice workshops on techniques for cooperative learning or materials for creating thematic units are teacher training. National Educational Service is one of many organizations offering training videos on topics from "The Discipline Toolbox: From Obedience to Responsibility" to "How to Get Funding Creatively." ASCD offers training institutes on "Designing Performance-Based Assessment Using Dimensions of Learning." ERIC offers books such as *Teacher Effectiveness and Reading Instruction* by Richard D. Robinson (1991)—for training in "research-based strategies." Ten years ago both Gretchen and Joye were required to take effective teacher training in separate public school districts. Outcome-based education training was required in Oklahoma a few years ago. The list goes on.

    Training is not a bad thing. Teachers need to learn new skills, to find new resources, to practice new techniques, to receive useful tips on practical problems. Teachers will need training at various points throughout their careers. However, training is not enough. Training focuses only on measurable behaviors, on teaching as a technology, not on the complex meanings and relationships which lie at the heart of teaching and learning. Teachers need more in an increasingly complex world. To offer teachers only training is both counterproductive and insulting to teachers.

    Limiting professional development to training has led to what Giroux (1988) has called the "deskilling of teachers" or "proletarianization of teacher work." Giroux maintains that such a technocratic, behaviorist approach includes "a call for the separation of conception from execution; the standardization of school knowledge in the interest of managing and controlling it; and the devaluation of critical, intellectual work on the part of teachers." (p. 123). Adopting others' materials, techniques, and procedures requires little of teachers and offers even less. Little (1993) argues, moreover, that "the dominant 'training' model of teachers' professional development—a model focused primarily on expanding an individual repertoire of well-defined and skillful classroom practice—is not adequate to the ambitious visions of teaching and schooling embedded in present reform initiatives" (p. 1). A better understanding of what teaching *is* should help us alter the training model.

TEACHING AS VOCATION

The root of the word "vocation" means "to call." To view teaching as a calling, something different from an occupation or even a profession, is to begin to understand who teachers are and what they really need for ongoing growth and development. Most of the literature, both that on teacher education reform and that on professional development, has emphasized the view of teaching as a profession. We, like Proefriedt (1994), maintain a view of teaching as a "reflective vocation," instead (p. 7). Arguing that the cry for greater professionalism is based on an inappropriate preoccupation with status and a faith in a reductive notion of knowledge, Proefriedt claims that reflective vocation, on the other hand, acknowledges the altruism essential to teaching and takes "seriously the notion that what is best for the young people we serve is not at all a given, and ought in fact to be part of the sort of inquiry in which teachers are engaged daily" (p. 107). We will further explore teaching as an altruistic vocation with serious moral responsibilities; as a calling that requires care for the whole human being—teacher and student; as a calling which rejects what Proefriedt calls "the notion of teacher knowledge as a set of established, scientific truth claims, the too-often-proclaimed knowledge base" but rather necessitates ongoing inquiry as teachers construct new understandings within learning communities; as a service-oriented undertaking which respects teachers as autonomous, unique, adult learners whose voices should be heard; and as a way of life characterized by uncertainty and ambiguity—all requiring teacher *education* rather than teacher training (p. 107).

Hansen (1995) captures the sense of altruism well in *The Call to Teach*. Teachers are, Hansen notes, public servants highly motivated by the personal meaning and fulfillment they derive from their work. The inner direction and dedication of teachers have been made clear since Lortie's 1975 *Schoolteacher*, a study which revealed that external rewards are not the major motivation of American teachers. Concern about students propels teachers more than any other concern. A National Foundation for the Improvement of Education (1996) survey shows that 73 percent of teachers list improving student achievement as their primary motivation for professional development (p. 15). The stories in Chapters 2–5 of this book demonstrate teachers' deep concern about their charges and about teaching their students well. Westerhoff (1987) concludes, "To be a teacher means more than to be a professional who possesses knowledge and skills. . . . Teaching is a human relationship. It is the teacher as a person who is the key to learning" (p. 193).

Feminist scholars, in particular, have commented on how altruism, the nurturing side of teaching, has been too long ignored. Teachers do focus to a great extent on the personal relationships and emotional connections involved in working with children. McEwan (1995) observes, "Feminist writers, for example, have argued that our conception of teaching is too narrowly rational and Socratic. They propose that it must be tied to moral and affective qualities such as caring and concern for others (Noddings, 1984). Their story seeks to connect teaching to its feminine roots in the relationship that exists between mother and child, rather than placing it in cold logical space" (p. 174). Hargreaves (1994) elaborates that "the dominant paradigms of teacher development research and practice tend to be rational, calculative, managerial, and somewhat masculine in nature" (pp. 24–25). Hargreaves adds that to acknowledge the desires and emotional life of teachers, "their feelings for and in their work," is something "absolutely central to teacher development efforts" (p. 22). Cohn and Kottcamp (1993) also declare that "teachers search for the interpersonal and pedagogical processes to make academics meaningful to their students" (p. 51).

The implication for teacher development is the challenge of eliciting and acknowledging teacher altruism and helping teachers reflect on the best ways to carry out their most benevolent and selfless intentions. Ways for teachers to examine their purposes are all too rare in current staff development programs. Proefriedt (1994) states, "A teacher's education should include opportunities to discuss concrete interactions with students, large- and small-scale curriculum choices, and a variety of other ongoing activities in relation to the forms that altruism might take" (p. 103). Palmer's story "Awakening the Boy" in Chapter 2 reflects the altruism of the eager, novice teacher who believes she can make a difference in student lives. She goes out of her way to relate to a difficult boy. Palmer's reflection touches on important issues. What does the teacher do when the system is not so eager to help students? How do school politics impact altruism? How can teachers be altruistic without exhausting themselves or giving too much attention to just one or a few students? Teachers want to know how to help kids. Teaching is not just a job for most teachers; it is a calling.

Given that serving others is highly motivating for teachers, the whole moral, ethical aspect of teaching remains foundational. Teaching is no neutral technology. Teachers must make hundreds of decisions every day, decisions which are built on their own moral values, decisions which affect students and others. Matters of conscience and caring have emerged in a number of stories in Chapters 2–5, including Weigand's "My, My, My Delilah" and Thomas' "Sally's Story" about caring for the "unlovable," and in Piirto's reflections on the negative aspects of grading. All too often the values and beliefs of teachers and the educational philosophies embedded in various methods and curricula are ignored in teacher training. Teacher education must allow teachers to struggle with the inevitable moral dilemmas they face daily.

Teaching as a vocation then engages the whole human being—the moral, intellectual, emotional, psychological, even spiritual as well as the political and social aspects of being human. Professional development must acknowledge teachers as whole human beings, something which happens now too rarely at either the pre- or inservice level. Boyd (1993) argues that there is a double standard. Teachers have long been admonished to attend to their students' affective and humanistic needs—this is important, they are told, for motivation and personal growth. . . . In staff development planning, however, the idea that teachers have these same needs, rarely emerges" (p. 3). Little (1993) expresses her first principle for staff development as, "Professional development offers meaningful intellectual, social, and emotional engagement with ideas, with materials, and with colleagues both in and out of teaching" (p. 10). Dobson, Dobson, and Kessinger (1980) assert, "If school improvement is to occur, then the uniqueness of all people, old and young, must be entertained. The quality of an institution is a direct expression of the persons who make up that institution . . . concerns for the teacher as person become a holistic approach" (p. 8). Boyd (1993) adds, "professional development is best achieved by first attending to personal and human needs—the need to belong and the need for a level of power normally accorded to others of professional status" (p. 10). Continuing professional education must build on the worries and dilemmas, hopes and fears, commitments and satisfactions of diverse human beings. Professional development must mean teacher self-development. The list of teacher narratives we share at the end of this volume, as well as the stories in this book, reflect the sense of humanity which is essential to vocation. For example, Corcoran's passion for teaching and respect for adolescents is clear in "Monique's Gifts" in Chapter 3, and the complications of ego and idealism and students' psychological problems are communicated in Givens' "Teacher Lure" in Chapter 4. Teachers need much more than training to succeed in their calling.

Teaching is not a profession like law, engineering, or medicine. Proefriedt (1994) notes, "Teaching seems so clearly different from the specialized occupations (such as medicine) to which it is often compared, that one has to wonder whether the notion of the acquisition of a specialized knowledge base is as central to what it means to become a competent teacher as the educational researchers argue" (p. 97). Or as central as most staff developers and teacher educators maintain. The challenges teachers face are so context-dependent and humanly complex that teachers crave the opportunity to examine and discuss their own situations with others who care. There are no prescriptions for making group work successful or for solving the problem of drop-outs—no surefire answers which can be transmitted to teachers. What most supports teachers in their calling is the space and time for ongoing reflection and inquiry. In "Settling In" in Chapter 2, Robbins struggles with such issues as losing control in the classroom, issues for which no single set of strategies will suffice. In "The One Who Got Away" in Chapter 4, Buckingham expresses some of those questions that plague teachers for which there is no tidy "knowledge base." She tells about her own identity crisis and the "real daily dilemmas of teachers"—"What behavior do we ignore? How long do we tolerate a disruptive student in the hope of 'saving' her? Are we listening well enough to decode hidden calls for help? When do we intervene in a personal situation?" Teaching is more like the ministry than it is like engineering or medicine. Teachers do need basic knowledge and skills. Again, training is part of teacher growth. However, as in the ministry, the personal answers each teacher creates to solve problems and teach students transcend information, policies and procedures, and models or "best practices." Teachers need permission to tackle their questions in their own ways.

Clearly, seeing teaching as a vocation rather than a profession enables us to perceive the inherent uncertainty, doubt, and ambiguity in teaching. No bureaucracy, course requirements, or lesson plan format can clearly resolve all the problems and meet all the needs of diverse students, especially in today's schools. Teaching is a complex, risky, moral, emotional, and intellectual undertaking, demanding a great deal of the whole person. Huebner (1987) expresses this notion of vocation:

If teaching is a vocation, being called forth, then we are inherently vulnerable. . . . To accept teaching as a vocation is to acknowledge a fundamental fallibility, and hence a fragility and insecurity . . . covered over by the metaphors of teaching as a profession, as a technology or a method, or an activity of schooling. The search for a method or technology of teaching carries with it the false promise that better methods of teaching can be given to teachers to reduce their insecurity or vulnerability. (p. 24)

Reform itself makes educators vulnerable and insecure; only meaningful, open-ended educational opportunities can help teachers to serve—to take risks—in a turbulent, changing world in which there are few guarantees. Ayers (1993) captures teaching as vocation in the following:

When we characterize our work . . . straightforward images and one-dimensional definitions dissolve, and teaching becomes elusive, problematic, often impossibly opaque. One thing becomes clear enough. Teaching as the direct delivery of some preplanned curriculum, teaching as the orderly and scripted conveyance of information, teaching as clerking, is simply a myth. Teaching is much larger and more alive than that; it contains more pain and conflict, more joy and intelligence, more uncertainty and ambiguity. . . . Teaching is spectacularly unlimited. (p. 5)

The need for *education* rather than *training* becomes clear when teaching is acknowledged to be an unpredictable and vulnerable vocation. Education values the teacher, not as a blank slate, but as a caring and fallible human who brings ideas, experiences, and individual insights and concerns to the professional growth process. The Latin root of the word *educate,* according to Webster's, means "to lead out," and the meanings include "to develop the mind or character" and "to form." Training can make teachers proficient in certain predetermined ways; education can empower teachers to think critically, to act creatively, to *seek* change for the good of students. Widdowson (1993) elucidates the difference in the following observation:

Training is the process of preparing people to cope with problems which can be more or less predicted in advance: its function therefore is to provide a set of routines, techniques, and tactics which can be applied as the occasion requires. It is in this sense formulaic and solution-oriented. Education, on the other hand, is the process of preparing people to deal with the unpredictable: its function is to develop a more general problem-solving capacity in the form of principles and strategies with reference to which problems can be defined. . . . In this sense it is problem-oriented. (p. 268)

The pace and quality of change in society and schools demand education. Veteran teachers, in particular, need support and opportunity to teach better year after year. Teaching is an uncertain and risky undertaking, as expressed in "Teaching Is a State of Mind" by Lain in Chapter 3 and in "The Dam Breaks" by Parbst in Chapter 4. To offer pre- and inservice teachers only training with the illusion that teaching can be made safe and routine is to do teachers a great disservice.

A constructivist philosophy of learning supports the notion of teacher education needed by people with a sense of vocation. Vocation does not allow for passive, hand-me-down changes or reforms. From a constructivist perspective, learners must construct or make new meanings, and they seek this learning in a social context. Henderson (1996) describes constructivist learning as "a complex interaction between students' personal purposes, their prior knowledge and dispositions, and the requirements for specific . . . inquiry" (p. 7). Learning, especially in an era of significant change, means building on what *teachers*, too, already know, offering *teachers* the opportunity to be actively engaged in the learning process, and encouraging sharing of and reflection on ideas. Constructivism recognizes the learner as unique and autonomous, a capable maker of understandings, not just a passive recipient of others' notions. This way of learning is motivating and powerful for *teachers*. Teachers must also experience constructivist learning themselves if they are to respect and engage their students. As Lieberman (1995) remarks, "Drawing on experience and helping to produce new knowledge become as compelling as consuming preexisting knowledge. . . . Being involved as a learner and a participant provides openings to new knowledge and broadens the agenda for thought and action" (p. 593). Osterman (1991) suggests that a constructivist perspective will enable teachers to link theory and practice in ways that allow for change. She endorses a "model of knowledge generation that is constructivist in nature and an assumption that the inquiry process should address the specific needs of the constituency. Professional growth is envisioned as an odyssey whose purpose is not knowledge in an abstract sense, but knowledge of a very personal and purposeful nature" (p. 212). Thus, teachers need the opportunity to reflect on what they already know and think with other teachers in a non-threatening setting; they can then build, discover, understand, reexamine, and challenge the status quo. Lieberman (1994) describes the process as assuming that the teacher is a "*reflective practitioner*, someone with a tacit knowledge base, who continuously builds on that base through ongoing inquiry into practice, constantly rethinking and reevaluating his or her own values and practices in concert with others" (p.15). A constructivist approach to teacher learning and development is exemplified in "A Joyful Noise" by Durham and Lauther in Chapter 5. Professional growth is a major benefit of team teaching for these two educators. The social context of teacher development for school reform is obvious.

The sense of community that comes to mind with the term *vocation,* the idea of people working together for a common and noble purpose, enables teachers to construct school and classroom improvement together. Schools can be transformed by constructivist learning and doing as Sergiovanni (1994) says. Sergiovanni notes that the reflection and dialogue indispensable for school improvement are not "possible when someone in-services and someone else is inserviced. . . . Becoming a community of learners, by contrast, is an adventure in shared leadership and authentic relationships. It requires a certain equality and a certain willingness to know thyself better, to be open to new ideas, and to strive to become. It is an adventure in personal development" (pp. 154–155). Teachers cannot be forced on such an adventure, but they can be invited. It is commonplace to say that teachers should have "input" or choice in professional development. We believe that teachers will only be free to become positive change agents when they can choose education that helps them build on what they already know and allows them to make meaning of their own professional lives in a community of educators.

Basic to constructivist learning then are autonomy, voice, and the uniqueness of each teacher-learner. Teachers must decide what forms of education best meet their needs as adults at varying developmental levels. As Oja (1991) declares, "Teachers who are in the same school, of relatively the same age, and with the same years of experience may think and solve problems differently from one another" (p. 38). Vocation recognizes the various stages and needs of adult learners—one-size staff development does not fit all. Furthermore, teachers, in the words of Neufeld and Grimmett (1994), "merit a personal autonomy, with the assumption that teachers exercise discretion and are self-directed, having the right to decide the specific direction of their own professional development. It is assumed in teacher development theory that growth toward a developed profes-sional state (which we name as an autonomous, self-directed agency) can take place through reflection on the ordinary, day-to-day experience of instructing students in classrooms" (p. 210). Costly outside experts and slick programs are not necessary. Choice and opportunity are. The chance to reflect on the "dailiness" of life in the classroom is key.

Again, children who construct their own knowledge need teachers as models. Brooks and Brooks (1993) note, "When students work with adults who continue to view themselves as learners, who ask questions with which they themselves still grapple, who are willing and able to alter both content and practice in the pursuit of meaning, and who treat students and their endeavors as works in process, not finished products, students are more likely to demonstrate these characteristics themselves" (pp. 9–10). Critically thinking, autonomous students require critically thinking, autonomous teachers.

Teacher autonomy can be threatening to traditional policy makers, administrators, and even teachers. Teachers who change can upset the teacher culture as Gloria Nixon-John describes in "Crossing the Highway" in Chapter 5 of this volume. Autonomous teachers may grow in unexpected ways. Teachers may even question the latest reform initiatives. Greenspan, for example, in "Writing about Teaching" in Chapter 5 tells how she became more outspoken as a professional as she grew in her vocation. Little (1993) dares to propose as one of her six principles for professional development, "Professional development offers support for informed dissent. In the pursuit of good schools, consensus may prove to be an overstated virtue. . . . To permit or even foster principled dissent . . . places a premium on the evaluation of alternatives and close scrutiny of underlying assumptions" (p. 11). Little concludes, "Professional development must be constructed in ways that deepen the discussion, open up the debates, and enrich the array of possibilities for action" (p. 22). The ongoing history of school reform as one bandwagon movement or proclaimed panacea after another must change if genuine reform is to take place. Conforming to one vision is not the goal. As Bell and Gilbert (1994) put it, "Teacher development can be viewed as teachers learning, rather than as others getting teachers to change" (p. 493). The teachers who share their stories in this book are autonomous learners, and they do not all see their work in the same way. We might not even agree with all their conclusions or outlooks nor they with ours. However, each needs to be heard.

The idea of autonomy is connected to the notion of voice that feminist scholars, in particular, have brought forth. Voice suggests that educators who have previously been silenced or marginalized should be heard. Indeed, the voices of teachers have remained largely absent from reform moves and staff development designs. Teachers remain relatively powerless despite all the talk of empowerment; the teaching force continues to be mostly female, while educational administrators and policy makers remain mostly male and white. Teachers' voices must be heard and encouraged in professional development for radical, ongoing school change. Teachers' voices are multiple, as our stories in this book show, expressing outrage, frustration, puzzlement, joy, and their passion for teaching. Neufeld and Grimmett (1994) endorse an "emancipatory theory of teacher development" in which "'Voice' is the sound of an authentic identity—the articu-lation of an autonomous, self-directed moral agency in relation to the solidarity of a collective" (pp. 216–217). To attend to the voices of teachers is to conceive of teaching as a humanistic, holistic, constructivist vocation, something beyond the purview of teacher *training*. We seek professional education that celebrates and challenges the caring voices of teachers through teacher narratives.

TEACHER LORE AND PROFESSIONAL DEVELOPMENT

Teacher lore is one choice, among many, for professional development that offers educational opportunities for growth in a time of change. The connections between teacher narrative and professional development are implicit in Chapter 1. We believe that various uses of teacher lore reflect explicitly the ten principles for inservice education developed by the Conference on English Education (1996), principles congruent with a vision of teaching as vocation. Many of these principles have become commonplace in the recent literature on professional development. Perhaps closest to the principles offered by the Conference on English Education are Lieberman and Miller's (1991) "starting points for considering staff development in a different light" (pp. 107–108). *Table 8.1* shows all of these principles along with the benefits of teacher lore.

Teacher lore is one way to enable teacher reflection. Ambrose (1993), among others, observes, "Writing and reading narrative constitute a dialogue with oneself and others that fosters reflection. This 'teaching conversation,' a personal structuring of the teaching experience, results in practices that promote appropriate learning environments for children" (p. 274). Teacher stories, writing them and/or reading and discussing them, help teachers construct professional knowledge. Huberman (1995) explains how this process works. He says that, "telling the story of one's life is often a vehicle for taking distance from that experience, and thereby,

Table 8.1
Several Principles of Professional Development and Benefits of Teacher Lore

Principles of professional development (CEE)	Professional development (Lieberman & Miller)	Benefits of teacher lore
Reflective and theorized practice	Teaching as craft	Reflective practice
Ownership and agency	Teacher inquiry into practice	Ethical, caring craft
Collaboration	About human development and learning for both students and teachers	Validates teachers as knowers
Sufficient time		
Pluralism and democracy	Culture building	Creates learning communities
School-community partnerships		Offers indepth information about classrooms and schools
Administrative collaboration		
Explicit and tangible support		

of making it an object of *reflection*. Cognitive psychologists call this 'decentering,' and it allows, say, a teacher, to escape momentarily from the frenzied busyness of classroom life—from its immediacy, simultaneity, and unpredictability—to explore his or her life and possibly to put it in meaningful order" (p.131). Huberman goes on to say that this "decentering" can lead to a "sort of emancipation from the grooved ways of thinking about one's work" and ultimately to change in practice. Griffin (1991) summarizes as follows:

Interactive staff development would depend on and account for ongoing reflection, using teacher judgments about their own practices as bases for working toward improving educational opportunity for children and youth. The stories teachers tell, the successes they recount, the frustrations and dilemmas they face would become a significant source of ideas for improvement or change or 'reform' activity. Teachers' thoughts and personal accounts of their work would influence the process of formulating (rather than mandating) ways to act toward school change. (p. 248)

Teacher reflection about practice cannot be separated from reflection about theory. Issues and theories emerge from teacher narrative as we have seen in the stories in this book and in experiences described in the preceding chapters. For instance, the moral-ethical groundings of education can be examined. Hargeaves (1994) says, "Teacher development can help teachers articulate and rehearse resolving these moral dilemmas in their work. By reflecting on their own practice, observing and analyzing other teachers' practice or studying case examples of practice [or personal narrative], teachers can clarify the dilemmas they face and develop principled, practical and increasingly skillful ways of dealing with them (Groundwater-Smith, 1993)" (p. 12). As in our stories, the dilemmas are many, from dealing with a disturbed student turned stalker to working with kids who are rude or smell bad. McEwan and Egan (1995) put it this way:

Stories, it would seem, have a vital role to play in helping us to understand the curriculum, the practices of teachers, the processes of learning, the rational resolution of educational issues, and the matter of practicing how to teach in informed and sensitive ways. To summarize, narratives form a framework within which our discourses about human thought and possibility evolve, and they provide structure and functional backbone for very specific explanations of this or that educational practice. They contribute to our capacity to deliberate about educational issues and problems. (p. xiii)

Not only teachers themselves but administrators, policy makers, parents, and the community can learn about theories, issues, and the ideas that propel school reform from teacher lore. Connelly and Clandinin (1994) declare that "teacher education is a process of learning to tell and retell educational stories of teachers and students. . . . teacher education is a sustained conversation in which we need many responses to our stories in order to be able to tell and retell them with added possibility. Conversations with theory, research, social conditions, different cultural groups, other teachers, students, teacher educators, and children allow for a response-filled environment and encourage more mindful retellings" (p. 150). Teacher lore is rich in content, experience, and theory.

As the Conference on English Education notes, ownership and agency are essential to professional development for change. Teacher narrative offers one option. Rarely in most current, traditional kinds of staff development do teachers have the chance to share what matters most to them in a non-threatening environment, to own the professional development process. Teacher lore validates teachers as knowers and learners in their own voices. Carter (1993) elucidates from a feminist perspective:

Because teaching is largely work done by women, the issue of the use of language for the remote control of teachers by a largely male population of researchers and administrators has been taken up by feminist scholars (see, e.g., Grumet, 1988). Story has played a central role in this discussion in two ways. First, narrative is seen as an especially appropriate form of women's knowing and expression (Belenky, Clinchy, Goldberger, & Tarule, 1986; Helle, 1991). Second, story is used as a frame to undercut the dominant mode of discourse on teaching. (p. 8)

Story allows the expression of emotions, the themes of caring and altruism, the importance of context and the celebration of diversity ignored in the dominant, generic teacher training programs which offer abstractions and general rules on topics from time-on-task to discipline "plans." Teacher lore acknowledges the teacher as human being, uncertain and fallible, as central to school reform.

Narrative is by its nature collaborative. Someone tells a story or writes a story for a group of listeners or readers. Much of the literature on teacher lore notes the growth of community that results. McLaughlin (1994) talks about the importance of enabling professional development by enabling learning communities "characterized by candor, sharing, mutual dependence and support, trust, and high standards" (p. 48). We have talked in Chapters 6 and 7 about specific communities we have experienced through the National Writing Project, through an extension course on teacher lore we offered, and in our own teaching. Moreover, this community may well extend to parents and the wider community. (Parent, administrator, and student lore here emerge as future possibilities in school reform, also). No study presently exists of the effect of teacher lore on those outside the classroom, but the potential for increased understanding and collaboration exists.

Within a community teachers are also enabled to experience and consider diverse viewpoints in a safe environment without an outside mandate hovering over them. Exploring other points of view is fundamental if pluralism and democracy are to flourish. Witherell, et al. (1995) explain in these words:

Narrative allows us to enter empathically into another's life and being—to join a living conversation. In this sense, it serves as a means of inclusion, inviting the reader, listener, writer, or teller as a companion along on another's journey. In the process we may find ourselves wiser, more receptive, more understanding, nurtured, and sometimes even healed. Stories enable us to imagine and feel the experience of the other. (p. 40)

We have seen how teacher narrative can be used to enable diverse viewpoints and to consider diverse practices in Chapters 6 and 7. Greene (1991) claims that when teachers make "an effort to interpret the texts of their life stories, listening to others' stories . . . they may be able to multiply the perspectives through which they look upon the realities of teaching; they may be able to choose themselves anew in the light of an expanded interest, an enriched sense of reality" (p. 12).

Finally, of course, successful professional development requires sufficient time, administrative collaboration, and explicit, tangible support. Building learning communities in which teachers can share and reflect on their stories of failure and doubt as well as their stories of success and accomplishment takes time, the voluntary commitment of participants, and the absence of hidden agendas. In the last two chapters we have looked at examples of how time and support pay off for veteran and student teachers. Teacher lore offers new opportunities for reflective and theorized practice, for ownership and agency, for collaboration, and for pluralism and democracy. Teacher lore—by its respect for the human context, its uncertainty and complexity, its embracing of the passion for teaching—reflects teaching as a vocation, a calling to become a special kind of person.

REFERENCES

Ambrose, R. P. (1993). Personal narratives and professional development. *Childhood Education, 69*, 274–276.

Ayers, W. (1993). *To teach: The journey of a teacher.* New York: Teachers College Press.

Bell, B., & Gilbert, J. (1994). Teacher development as professional, personal, and social development. *Teaching and Teacher Education, 10*, 483–497.

Boyd, B. (1993). *Transforming staff development* (Position Paper). Greeley, CO: University of Northern Colorado. (ERIC Document Reproduction Service No. 362 943).

Brooks, J. G., & Brooks, M. G. (1993). *The case for constructivist classrooms*. Alexandria, VA: Association for Supevision and Curriculum Development.

Carter, K. (1993). The place of story in the study of teaching and teacher education. *Educational Researcher, 22* (1), 5–12, 18.

Cohn, M. M., & Kottkamp, R. B. (1993). *Teachers: The missing voice in education*. Albany, NY: State University of New York Press.

Conference on English Education. (1996). Inservice education: Ten principles. In *Guidelines for the Preparation of Teachers of English Language Arts*, Urbana, IL: National Council of Teachers of English.

Connelly, F. M., & Clandinin, D. J. (1994). Telling teaching stories. *Teacher Education Quarterly, 21*, (1), 145–158.

Dilworth, M. E., & Imig, D. G. (1995). *Professional teacher development and the reform agenda*. Washington, DC: Office of Educational Research and Improvement, (ERIC Document Reproduction Service No. ED 383 694).

Dobson, R., Dobson, J., & Kessinger, J. (1980). *Staff development: A humanistic approach*. Washington, DC: University Press of America.

Fullan, M. G., & Stiegebauer, S. (1991). *The new meaning of educational change*. New York: Teachers College Press.

Giroux, H. A. (1988). *Teachers as intellectuals*. Granby, MA: Bergin & Garvey.

Greene, M. (1991). Teaching: The question of personal reality. In A. Lieberman & L. Miller (Eds.), *Staff development for education in the 90's* (pp. 3–14). New York: Teachers College Press.

Griffin, G. A. (1991). Interactive staff development: Using what we know. In A. Lieberman & L. Miller (Eds.), *Staff development for education in the 90's* (pp. 243–258). New York: Teachers College Press.

Hansen, D. T. (1995). *The call to teach*. New York: Teachers College Press.

Hargreaves, A. (1994, April). *Development and desire: A postmodern perspective*. Paper presented at the meeting of the American Educational Research Association, New Orleans, LA. (ERIC Document Reproduction Service No. ED 372 057).

Henderson, J. G. (1996). *Reflective teaching*. Englewood Cliffs, NJ: Merrill.

Hirsch, S., & Ponder, G. (1991). New plots, new heroes in staff development. *Educational Leadership, 49* (3), 43–48.

Huberman, M. (1995). Working with life-history narratives. In H. McEwan & K. Egan (Eds.), *Narrative in teaching, learning, and research* (pp. 127–165). New York: Teachers College Press.

Huebner, D. (1987). The vocation of teaching. In F. S. Bolin & J. M. Falk (Eds.), *Teacher renewal: Professional issues, person choices* (pp. 17–29). New York: Teachers College Press.

Johnson, S. M. (1990). *Teachers at work*. New York: Basic Books.

Lieberman, A. (1994). Teacher development: Commitment and challenge. In P. P. Grimmett & J. Neufeld (Eds.), *Teacher development and the struggle for authenticity* (pp. 15–30). New York: Teachers College Press.

Lieberman, A. (1995). Practices that support teacher development. *Phi Delta Kappan, 76*, 591–596.

Lieberman, A., & Miller, L. (1991). Revisiting the social realities of teaching. In A. Lieberman & L. Miller (Eds.), *Staff development for education in the 90's* (pp. 92–109). New York: Teachers College Press.

Lindsay, M. (1996, October). *Curriculum, revision, staff development, and education reform through systemic collaboration: A case study*. Paper presented at the meeting of the American Association for Teaching and Curriculum, San Antonio, TX.

Little, J. W. (1993). *Teachers' professional development in a climate of education reform.* New York: Teachers College, National Center for Restructuring Education, Schools, and Teaching. (ERIC Document Reproduction Service No. ED 373 049).

Lortie, D. C. (1977). *Schoolteacher.* Chicago: University of Chicago Press.

McClure, R. M. (1991). Individual growth and institutional renewal. In A. Lieberman & L. Miller (Eds.), *Staff development for education in the 90's* (pp. 221–241). New York: Teachers College Press.

McEwan, H. (1995). Narrative understanding in the study of teaching. In H. McEwan & K. Egan (Eds.), *Narrative in teaching, learning, and research* (pp. 166–183). New York: Teachers College Press.

McEwan, H., & Egan, K. (1995). Introduction. In H. McEwan & K. Egan (Eds.), *Narrative in teaching, learning, and research* (vii–xv). New York: Teachers College Press.

McLaughlin, M. W. (1994). Strategic sites for teachers' professional development. In P. P. Grimmett & J. Neufeld (Eds.), *Teacher development and the struggle for authenticity* (pp. 31–51). New York: Teachers College Press.

National Foundation for the Improvement of Education. (1996). *Teachers take charge of their learning* (Executive Summary). Washington, DC: Author.

Neufeld, J., & Grimmett, P. P. (1994). Conclusion: The authenticity of struggle. In P. P. Grimmett & J. Neufeld (Eds.), *Teacher development and the struggle for authenticity* (pp. 205–232). New York: Teachers College Press.

Oja, S. N. (1991). Adult development: Insights on staff development. In A. Lieberman & L. Miller (Eds.), *Staff development for education in the 90's* (pp. 37–60). New York: Teachers College Press.

Osterman, K. (1991). Reflective practice: Linking professional development and school reform. *Planning and Changing, 22*, 208–217.

Proefriedt, W. A. (1994). *How teachers learn.* New York: Teachers College Press.

Sarason, S. B. (1990). *The predictable failure of school reform.* San Francisco: Jossey-Bass.

Sergiovanni, T. J. (1994). *Building communities in schools.* San Francisco: Jossey-Bass.

Westerhoff, J. H. (1987). The teacher as pilgrim. In F. S. Bolin & J. M. Falk (Eds.), *Teacher renewal: Professional issues, personal choices* (pp. 190–201). New York: Teachers College Press.

Widdowson, H. G. (1993). Innovation in teacher development. *Annual Review of Applied Linguistics, 13*, 260–275.

Witherell, C. S., Tran, H. T. & Othus, J. (1995). Narrative landscapes and the moral imagination: Taking the story to heart. In H. McEwan & K. Egan (Eds.), *Narrative in teaching, learning, and research* (pp. 39–49). New York: Teachers College Press.

Chapter 9

Reflection

Following is a reflection on the writing of *Teacher Lore and Professional Development for School Reform* in the form of a dialogue between Gretchen Schwarz and Joye Alberts. The discussion begins when Gretchen reflects on her early thinking about the importance of reading and writing teacher stories:

G: In my first years of teaching I started collecting materials to write the great exposé about what teaching was really like. Nothing prepared me for teaching, especially emotionally, and at that time teacher bashing was already starting. I thought that people didn't know what teaching was really about, what it was really like. I collected all kinds of journals from kids and experiences and stories and so forth. There was just a felt need there.

Then in 1990 in graduate school I ran across Schubert's article about the Teacher Lore Project that really spoke to me. I thought about the need for such a focus for teachers. I knew in teacher education there ought to be some real stories. Teacher lore reveals the reality of teaching that I certainly hadn't seen in any college textbook.

J: You never did write that book.

G: No, I never did.

J: Now, someone might write that book. At the time you began teaching in 1975 few books by teachers were out there.

G: At least I didn't know about them. Not until more recently did I know that there were classics like Sylvia Ashton-Warner's *Teacher* and Jonathan Kozol's books and James Herndon and so forth. But I didn't know then that any stories existed.

J: It was just your sense that such a book needed to be written?

G: Yes, and of course when I was teaching I didn't have time to do that anyway.

J: It does take time. Writing stories, rather than a book, having an audience and a purpose could help solve the problem of lack of time. A teacher can get at core issues and reflect upon teaching practice without having to write a book.

G: It was a relief to me to find out that writing about teaching did exist and that there were people who valued it. Schubert was the first person I came across in the academic world. It made so much sense, since telling stories is how teachers talk about their work anyway.

J: Telling their stories in the hall! And the stories are not always about problems.

G: Sometimes they are victory stories, celebration stories.

J: And, sometimes they are puzzlements that teachers share with colleagues, asking for help with what is going on in the classroom. It is as if a teacher is asking for another pair of eyes to help her think about a situation or an issue. Teachers are often isolated in their classrooms.

G: I certainly felt that isolation as a beginning teacher. There was no mentoring then, no first-year teacher programs. I was the youngest person on the faculty and I just acted like I knew what I was doing even though I didn't. I wish I had told stories my first year, but I thought I was supposed to know all I needed to.

J: The first time you used teacher lore formally was in your methods classes in 1991.

G: Yes. At the same time I discovered that one of my colleagues, Kathryn Castle, had a similar interest in teacher lore. I showed her a draft of an article I was working on when I first came to Oklahoma State and she was very encouraging. That article never did get published. Then I started doing some research on my own classes.

J: After two OSU Writing Project Summer Institutes, we realized that teachers were sometimes insecure when asked to bring a piece of writing on the first day of the Institute. Sometimes teachers coming to the Institute asked, "What do you want me to write about?" We began asking ourselves how we could better support teachers coming to the institute. We decided to talk about teacher stories as a starting place for writing. You came to the pre-institute meeting to talk about the genre. We invited teachers who so desired to write a piece of teacher lore.

The idea of writing teacher stories in the Summer Institute also had its roots in the story *Confessions of a First Year Teacher* by Kevin Kienholz, a Summer Fellow in 1993. All of us were drawn to this story. As a result of the invitation to write a story about teaching, Toni Pantier's story about Jody, *Apart from the Rest*, which is in Chapter 3, was written for the 1994 Summer Institute.

G: I had also been using teacher lore in observation classes for preservice teachers. But, the idea was more nebulous. I suggested that they do autobiographical writing, have students bring in their own experiences, even at the preservice level. You and I were both playing around with the idea. I was sharing with Kathryn once again about the stories that were coming out of the Writing Project Summer Institute, and she said that we should be collecting these stories for a book.

J: Which is what we decided to do four years ago.

G: Yes, we began by trying to make the book fit a call for manuscripts. It was the wrong call but the right idea.

J: At some point the idea of asking teachers to reflect on their stories as well as telling their stories came into the picture.

G: Some of the other books that we have been reading about teacher lore had the stories, but then they were commented on or explained by the university researcher. If writing stories about the classroom is to be really empowering, then teachers need to interpret the stories for themselves. And, the idea of following the stories with a reflection took the idea further than it had been taken before.

J: We learned during the teacher lore class in Midwest City [see full description of the course in Chapter 6, pp. 127–132] that writing the reflection was a significant part of the process for several reasons. Some time had passed between the writing of the story and the writing of the reflection. Teachers were looking at their own practice. Within the group, the reflections generated some incredible discussions about issues in the daily lives of teachers. And, in the instance of our class, the reflections invited other teachers to help a colleague solve problems and puzzle out solutions.

G: The personal element is key in terms of motivation and understanding. Polanyi (1962) says in his book *Personal Knowledge* that all knowledge is personal knowledge.

J: There are teachers who would say that they don't want to look this closely at their teaching practice or their students.

G: That's okay.

J: Right. But, for those people who would like to take this entreé into looking at their teaching practice, writing and sharing teacher stories is a way to look deeply. When we were getting to know each other in the Teacher Lore class, we read stories by others and watched video clips. These activities built the community that allowed the participants to write their own stories and reflections and think together about their meanings. There has to be time to build a community.

G: Community and trust and a feeling of safety have to be in place.

J: I do think that we have to learn as teachers how to share this kind of thinking with colleagues. Many teachers write and publish their writing, but the writing is not necessarily shared with the teachers they teach with. It would be interesting to do more research to find out whether an outside facilitator, the role we played in the Midwest City class, is necessary to support the group.

G: We don't really know what it takes to make the ideal situation or how to make that last over time. We don't have all the pieces yet.

J: The empowerment of it may be that people find their own connections. I know, speaking from my own experience, that when I felt that I had permission to use the knowledge I had, I approached my job and my life differently. I quit thinking that other people were in charge or were going to tell me what I needed to do. At that point I took charge for myself.

G: It is empowering just to be able to tell a story to your peers and have them listen. Have them be amused or moved. This is the same message we want to send to our students: language is the power to make things happen, to make people respond.

J: You were talking earlier about teacher bashing as a part of your motivation to write in the first place. This point can't be underestimated. We can use stories to look at what goes on in the classroom, with a particular student or a particular practice. Certainly this can help us as teachers. There is also value in giving "outsiders" a glimpse into what goes on in the classroom through reading these stories. Once you know someone, it is hard to bash them. Once you know their struggles.

G: It's like parents who finally teach Sunday school for the first time. It's a different story! The variety of writing in the stories in this book is important because the stories aren't just in that *Dead Poet's Society*, romantic mode. We aren't all heroes in our stories. They don't all end happily.

J: Often there isn't a clear ending.

G: It's ambiguous. It's ambivalent. It's ongoing. Not having an ending drives preservice teachers crazy. They expect to be told everything they need to know to teach. I spend a year telling them that there is no way I can tell them everything they need to know—even if I knew.

J: In addition to writing and reflecting on stories, there is something important about carefully listening to what someone else is trying to say. Sitting around a table, listening to stories, evokes the power of a writing response group when you bring a piece of any kind to a group who is prepared to listen closely to what you have written and offer a response. There is a respect that comes when someone listens to what you have to say.

G: Respect is the word that comes to my mind, too. It helps you get rid of your stereotypes. I have a tendency to say things like, "Oh, he or she is *that* kind of teacher." And then when you hear someone's story from their own lips, you know the emotional weight of the stories, and I can't say that he or she fits into a particular mode anymore. This is a good lesson again to carry over into our own classrooms with kids.

It seems pretty clear that there ought to be something like administrator lore. I think Schubert has been working on student lore. We need other ways for other groups that are involved—parents—to have power in the educational process, to create community.

This idea of community building takes me back to the capstone paper of student teaching where preservice teachers write their stories and reflections. Now I need to find time at the end of the semester for the students to be able to talk about the writing instead of just turning it in and graduating.

J: Having preservice or inservice teachers write and share stories takes time. Something is displaced in order to allow time for writing and sharing to take place.

I was listening to you talk about how many of the issues that come out in these stories aren't easy things to talk about. It takes courage to take that look. We should also hold up as valuable the light-hearted things that happen in our classrooms.

G: Right. I begin the graduate language arts class with short pieces of teacher lore. There are always several pieces that are humorous. That certainly helps build the community—the humor. I remember a few years ago when one graduate student told an embarrassing story about her first year of teaching. An "embarrassing teaching moment" makes a good ice-breaker.

J: So the genre has more of a range than just the serious.

G: And has more of a reason for being, too. Reflection and digging into the issues is part of it but just to start community building, even if you never did anything more with teacher lore, would be valuable.

J: And then you can move into harder issues. You were saying that your graduate students liked *The Wall* (a teacher research narrative) by Jane Juska.

G: Right. When we move into the notion of teacher research, I can have them read a piece like *The Wall* and ask them what they think. They are enthusiastic. They say that this kind of research they can understand, this sounds real, this is engaging, I wanted to keep reading. Hopefully, finally, teachers say, I could do this in my own classroom.

J: There is a later version of *The Wall* that has a reflection. Justa's reflection parallels our thinking that you can go deeper into the same topic rather than having to start on a new one. Five years later she wrote a reflection for an anniversary issue of *The Quarterly of the National Writing Project* which asked all the contributors in the issue to go back and reflect on their earlier pieces.

G: Reflection is natural. There is a tendency after we tell stories to say this is what I learned from that experience. For their capstone papers the student teachers wrote a reflection that was researched in some way. They could talk to other teachers, do library research, a survey or some kind of action research. This way they could learn from their own experience by talking to other teachers and finding out what experts in the field had to say to add to their own experience. For instance, one of the students drove around with a juvenile officer to find out about gangs.

And there are things I would never have thought of. Students end up thinking of things beyond what I could ever assign them to do.

J: In a way we limit the possibilities by not opening the thinking and allowing them to pursue their own ideas. There is something important about being asked to take a careful look at classroom practice in the first place. Watching carefully and making sense of what you see gets preservice teachers into the mode of thinking that this is what teachers do. What a healthy experience to have as a student teacher.

G: I hope this experience is one of the things that will enable them to be agents of change and leaders in the profession eventually. Having students actually do research and get feedback from me makes a difference, too. I commented at the end of one student's paper that he really should be a teacher/writer, that he had so much to say. When I talked with him later, he said he would never have thought that about himself. So, even though I talked about the teacher as writer in general in class, he didn't know that meant him until he had done it himself.

J: It is also important to see what it feels like to write the story. This gives you a sense of the importance of your own thinking which is at the heart of this whole notion. In a way, this kind of writing bursts through the boundaries of a textbook. Our experiences can be the textbook and we can use our experiences to go and find what else there is to learn.

G: And this is certainly real-life writing.

J: This kind of writing has an impact on students in the classroom as well. Most of the teachers in the Teacher Lore class mentioned independently of each other that they had shared the writing they were doing with their students.

G: Some of the student teachers did case studies and told their students that they were writing a paper about them and even the kid who was a difficult case was inspired by that.

J: This illustrates the power of writing on all levels to affirm and empower and give us a feeling that we are important—whoever we are. One of the Midwest City teachers told about her students, upon hearing her reflection on her writing, asking to go back and reflect on their work. The students knew that their ideas must be important and they wanted to write more about them for an authentic purpose. This teacher took advantage of the teachable moment to share an important learning with her students.

G: Thinking about this teacher's classroom makes me pause to see the radical aspect of teacher lore. This is not "the answer." There is no program. This is not a system-wide form that can simply be dropped on top of people. Teachers will be changed in ways we can't even predict as a result of this kind of writing and sharing.

J: There is an element of risk for anyone who goes on this kind of a journey in the first place. In the Teacher Lore class we tried to be as clear as possible about what they would be doing, so the people who came elected to take the risk. This isn't for everyone.

G: Nor is this for every stage of professional life.

J: The invitation needs to be there.

G: And to not only tell stories but to reflect, to do research, to learn. On the other hand, one of the dangers of this kind of thinking is that you could become almost too inward-looking. Again, the community is important for this reason. Invitation is the key.

Teacher Lore Suggestions

Teacher stories go far back. A historical study of teacher lore could itself be interesting and valuable. In this chapter we offer modern titles, fiction and nonfiction, written texts and films, which we have read or seen or about which we have read or heard. The works vary in quality. We have decided to leave out television shows although these, too, from *Mr. Novack* and *Room 222* to *Fame* and *The White Shadow*, may be quite useful. The following is not an exhaustive list. In addition to what we describe here, the reader can find an excellent annotated bibliography of teacher narratives by Maldonado and Winick in Jalongo and Isenberg's *Teachers' Stories* (1995, San Francisco: Jossey-Bass), as well as other lists in several of the articles and books to which we have referred. These texts can be used for private study or for formal teacher education and professional development for practicing teachers. Additionally, these stories are simply enjoyable. We hope the reader will add to this list and that many more teachers will be writing and publishing their own stories.

FILMS (BY YEAR)

Goodbye, Mr. Chips (1939, 1969). Based on the 1934 book by James Hilton. Classic tale of the tough but much-loved British schoolmaster in the traditional British public school.

The Corn Is Green (1945, 1979). Aging woman helps young man achieve academic success.

The Blackboard Jungle (1955). From the 1954 book by Evan Hunter. A new teacher fights to win a place for himself in the urban school in crisis.

Good Morning, Miss Dove (1955). Novel by F. G. Patton. Female Mr. Chips.

Our Miss Brooks (1956). Also a TV series and a 1950 story by R. J. Mann and Perry Clark. Humorous account of high school life in a more innocent time and place.

The Miracle Worker (1962, 1979). Play by William Gibson about Annie Sullivan's struggle to reach and teach Helen Keller.

To Sir with Love (1967). From the book by Edward Braithwaite. New black teacher treats students as adults and wins their respect and appreciation.

Up the Down Staircase (1967). Based on the book by Bel Kaufman. Another new teacher struggles with the bureaucracy and the delinquents in a New York City high school.

The Prime of Miss Jean Brodie (1969). Based on the book by Muriel Spark. Portrait of a non-conformist and demagogue who makes disciples at a British girls' school.

Conrack (1974). Based on the book *The Water Is Wide* by Pat Conroy.

To Serve Them All My Days (1982, BBC). Book by R. F. Delderfield. More muscular Mr. Chips.

Educating Rita (1983). Pygmalion story of a dissipated literature professor mentoring an unschooled hairdresser who outgrows him.

Teachers (1984). Often humorous story of burned out history teacher who recaptures his idealism in the middle of a lawsuit against the typical urban school.

Children of a Lesser God (1986). Based on the play. Teacher becomes emotion ally involved with his deaf student.

The Principal (1987). Another strong principal story but less realistic than *Lean on Me* (1989).

Stand and Deliver (1987). Based on the real life story of teacher Jaime Escalante who shows that barrio kids can master calculus.

Dead Poets Society (1989). Private school students are captured by the romantic, non-conformist spirit of their new English teacher.

Lean on Me (1989). Based on the real life of principal Joe Clark who uses muscle to bring order and learning back to his urban school.

The Browning Version (1994 remake of 1951 film). Retiring classics professor is a disappointed man. Michael Medved says *The Remains of the Day* meets *Goodbye, Mr. Chips*.

The Lion's Den (1994). A documentary video by Oliver Morse.

Renaissance Man (1994). Out-of-work executive teaches eight educationally disadvantaged Army recruits.

Dangerous Minds (1995). Based on *My Posse Don't Do Homework* by LouAnne Johnson. Heroic portrayal of novice urban teacher and former Marine who turns around young lives amid gangs, drugs, and poverty.

Mr. Holland's Opus (1995). Upbeat story of a musician who evolves into an inspirational band director.

187 (1997). Idealistic science teacher struggles to come back in Los Angeles inner-city schools after being stabbed in Brooklyn.

BOOKS

Ayers, William, & Patricia Ford. (Eds.). (1996). *City Kids, City Teachers*. (New York: The New Press). Essays and memoirs about teaching well in urban schools.

Barlow, James. (1962). *Term of Trial*. (New York: Simon & Schuster). Set in industrial England, the story of Graham Wier's teaching experiences.

Bluestein, Jane. (Ed.). (1995). *Mentors, Masters, and Mrs. Macgregor: Stories of Teachers Making a Difference*. (Deerfield Beach, FL: Heath Communications). Famous people from Jimmy Carter to Desmond Tutu tell about important teachers in their lives.

Booth, Wayne. (1988). *The Vocation of a Teacher*. (Chicago: University of Chicago). Well-known literary scholar offers collected speeches/ reflections on teaching.

Braithwaite, Edward. (1959). *To Sir with Love*. (New York: Jove Books). Unemployed engineer tries teaching in downtrodden English school.

Bullough, Robert. (1989). *First Year Teacher*. (New York: Teachers College Press). A research case study of the first year and a half of a seventh grade teacher's experience. Traces teacher development.

Cohen, Rosetta Marantz. (1991). *A Lifetime of Teaching: Portraits of Five Veteran High School Teachers*. (New York: Teachers College Press). Five case studies.

Collins, Catherine, & Frantz, Douglas. (1993). *Teachers (Talking out of School)*. (Boston: Little, Brown). More than 150 teachers from across the nation tell what it's like in America's schools.

Collins, Marva, & Tamarkin, C. (1982). *Marva Collins' Way*. (Los Angeles: J. P. Tarcher). Chicago school reformer tells her story.

Conroy, Pat. (1972). *The Water Is Wide*. (New York: Bantam). New teacher fights bureaucracy to teach poor Black children on an island off North Carolina.

Ernst, Morris L. (Ed.). (1967). *The Teacher*. (Englewood Cliffs, NJ: Prentice Hall). Recollections of influential teachers.

Fedullo, Mick. (1992). *Light of the Feather: A Teacher's Journey into Native American Classrooms and Culture*. (New York: Anchor Books). Stories of a teacher/writer-in-residence from 1979 to 1984 at the Sacaton School District on the Gila River Indian Reservation in Arizona.

Flinders, David J. (1989). *Voices from the Classroom (Educational Practice Can Inform Policy)*. (University of Oregon: ERIC). Case studies of teachers and the implications.

Fox, Mem. (1993). *Radical Reflections (Passionate Opinions of Teaching, Learning, and Living)*. (San Diego, CA: Harcourt Brace). A teacher's views on the language experience approach, etc.

Freedman, Samuel G. (1990). *Small Victories*. (New York: HarperPerennial). A journalist follows the life of a dedicated high school English teacher during the 1987–88 school year in Manhattan's Lower East Side.

Gehrke, Nathalie J. (1987). *On Being a Teacher*. (West Lafayette, IN: Kappa Delta Pi). Tidbits of lore over the lifetime stages of teaching.

Gerson, Mark. (1997). *In the Classroom (Dispatches from an Inner City School that Works)*. (New York: The Free Press). Author tells of his year in a Jersey City Catholic school of mostly minority students.

Godar, John. (1990). *Teachers Talk*. (Macomb, IL: Glenbridge Publishing). Godar spent a year taping interviews with 228 diverse teachers in 10 states. Here are their voices.

Haley, M. A. (1982). *Battleground: The Autobiography of Margaret A. Haley*. (Urbana: University of Illinois Press). Living from 1861 to 1939, a grade school teacher, social reformer, and leader of the nation's most militant teacher organization fights to improve the well being of women teachers in Chicago.

Hawkins, F. P. Lothrop. (1997). *Journey with Children*. (Niwot: University Press of Colorado). Autobiography of a teacher who was part of Open Education, Head Start, and many other educational innovations. Foreword by Nel Noddings.

Herndon, James. (1985). *Notes from a Schoolteacher*. (New York: Simon & Schuster). Herndon's life as a junior high teacher, critical of typical school policies.

Holt, John. (1964). *How Children Fail*. (New York: Pitman). Critique of schooling.

Howe, Quincy. (1991). *Under Running Laughter*. (New York: Free Press). Howe's work at Leake and Watts High School, in which children, mostly black, are in foster care.

Hunter, Evan. (1954). *The Blackboard Jungle*. (New York: Simon & Schuster).

Johnson, LouAnne. (1992). *My Posse Don't Do Homework*. (New York: St. Martin's Press). Film version is titled *Dangerous Minds*.

————. (1995). *Girls in the Back of the Class*. (New York: St. Martin's Press). Continues the saga of ex-Marine urban teacher. Most of the stories are still about boys.

Jones, Ron. (1976). *No Substitute for Madness*. (Covelo, CA: Island Press). Author of *The Acorn People*, Jones shares his stories of working with severely handicapped children at a summer camp, teaching world history, and coaching basketball.

Kane, Pearl Rock. (1991). *The First Year of Teaching*. (New York: Walker & Co.). Real stories of first year teaching on topics/events from plagiarism to graduation.

Kaufman, Bel. (1964). *Up the Down Staircase*. (New York: Avon). Story told through letters, school memos, and such. Captures the reality of New York City schools.

Keizer, Garret. (1988). *No Place But Here: A Teacher's Vocation in a Rural Community*. (New York: Penguin). Daily life of a rural Vermont English teacher.

Kidder, Tracy. (1989). *Among Schoolchildren*. (Boston: Houghton Mifflin). A journalist shadows Mrs. Zajac, a fifth grade teacher in a decaying Massachusetts urban area.

Kohl, Herbert. (1984). *Growing Minds: On Becoming a Teacher*. (New: York Harper & Row). Introduction to the vocation of teaching.

Kozol, Jonathan. (1968). *Death at an Early Age*. (New York: Bantam). Exposes the destructive effects of the Boston Public Schools on the hearts and minds of black children.

———. (1990). *The Night Is Dark and I Am Far from Home,* rev. ed. (New York: Simon & Schuster). Autobiographical critique of American society and school reform.

Kramer, Rita. (1976). *Maria Montessori: A Biography.* (New York: Putnam). Account of Montessori's life and innovative ideas in childhood education such as the value of play.

Kreinberg, Nancy, & Harriet Nathan. (1991). *Teachers' Voices; Teachers' Wisdom.* (Berkeley, CA: Equals). Seven teachers think aloud about their work and professional lives.

Ladson-Billings, Gloria. (1994). *The Dreamkeepers*. (San Francisco: Jossey-Bass). Successful teachers of African-American children.

Landsman, Julie. (1993). *Basic Needs: A Year with Street Kids in a City School.* (Minneapolis: Milkweed). Author tells of her year countering poverty, homelessness, and drugs in a program for at-risk adolescents in Minneapolis.

Lindley, Daniel A. (1993). *This Rough Magic*. (Westport, CT: Bergin & Garvey). The author, a teacher and teacher educator, reflects on his teaching career in light of Jungian psychology.

Logan, Judy. (1997). *Teaching Stories*. (New York: Kodansha International). A middle school teacher in San Francisco for over 20 years sees changes in the neighborhood in which she grew up. Explores a feminist, multicultural curriculum.

Lopate, Phillip. (1975). *Being with Children*. (New York: Doubleday). Life in an elementary classroom.

Lopez, A. H. (1992). *Barrio Teacher*. (Houston: Arte Publico Press). Short biography of a pioneer in urban and bilingual education from San Antonio.

Macrorie, Ken. (1970). *Uptaught*. (New York: Hayden). Macrorie's own reflection on teaching—an "underground success" with thousands of English teachers.

———. (1984). *Twenty Teachers*. (New York: Oxford). Twenty teachers, from first grade to high school shop class, tell about teaching in their own words. Macrorie looks at what they have in common.

Madenwald, Abbie Morgan. (1992). *Arctic School Teacher*. (Norman, OK: University of Oklahoma Press). A white woman's challenges teaching Native Americans in Alaska from 1931 to 1933.

Marshall, Catherine. (1967). *Christy*. Inspirational account of rural school teacher. Also a TV series.

Mathews, Jay. (1988). *Escalante: The Best Teacher in America*. (New York: Holt). Portrait of superstar math teacher in the barrio.

Nehring, James. (1989). *Why Do We Gotta Do This Stuff, Mr. Nehring?* (New York: Fawcett Columbine). Nehring portrays an average day in his life as an English teacher and meditates on what could be better in the American high school.

Paley, Vivian. (1979). *White Teacher*. (Cambridge, MA: Harvard University Press). Paley, author of many books about classroom life, tells how she learned to be a white teacher of black children.

Palmer, Parker J. (1998). *The Courage to Teach*. San Francisco: Jossey-Bass. A college professor explores through stories the "inner landscape of a teacher's life."

Palonsky, Stuart B. (1986). *900 Shows a Year*. (New York: Random House). A field study of teaching from one year in the author's high school teaching experience.

Perl, Sondra, & Nancy Wilson. (1986). *Through Teachers' Eyes: Portraits of Writing Teachers at Work*. (Portsmouth, NH: Heinemann). Various teachers' experiences.

Pratt, Caroline. (1948). *I Learn from Children*. (New York: Simon & Schuster). Portrait of a progressive.

Raphael, Ray. (1985). *The Teacher's Voice: A Sense of Who We Are*. (Portsmouth, NH: Heinemann). Firsthand accounts of 10 teachers.

Rose, Mike. (1989). *Lives on the Boundary*. (New York: Penguin). Rose, a director of UCLA Writing Programs, tells of the struggles of America's educational underclass from which he came.

Rothenberg, M. (1977). *Children with Emerald Eyes*. (New York: Dial Press). Teaching with autistic and schizophrenic children.

Rouse, John. (1993). *Provocations: The Story of Mrs. M.* (Urbana, IL: National Council of Teachers of English). Rouse portrays an offbeat high school teacher who was his own teacher and mentor.

Rubin, Louis D., Jr. (Ed.). (1987). *An Apple for My Teacher*. (Chapel Hill, NC: Algonquin). 12 writers from John Barth to Alfred Kazin tell about important teachers in their lives.

Sacher, Emily. (1991). *Shut Up and Let the Lady Teach*. (New York: Poseidon Press). A reporter turned math teacher spends a year in a New York public school.

Specht, Robert. (1976). *Tisha* (as told to Robert Specht). (New York: Bantam). The story of a young teacher in the Alaska wilderness.

Sterne, E. (1957). *Mary McCleod Bethune*. (New York: Knopf). Biography of the famous black educator.

Stuart, Jesse. (1949). *The Thread That Runs So True*. (New York: Scribner's). Classic story of the author's teaching experience in the mountains of Kentucky.

Tompkins, Jane. (1996). *A Life in School*. (Reading, MA: Addison-Wesley). A Duke University English professor looks at her life and changing teaching.

Welsh, Patrick. (1986). *Tales out of School*. (New York: Viking). A teacher's candid account from the "front lines" of the American high school.

Wigginton, Eliot. (1986). *Sometimes a Shining Moment*. (New York: Anchor Books). Story of the founding of the Foxfire project, also portrayed in a Broadway play.

Wolk, Rondal A. & B. H. Rodman. (1994). *Classroom Crusaders*. (San Francisco: Jossey-Bass). Twelve teachers who are trying to change the system.

LITERARY POTPOURRI

Anderson, Sherwood. (1919). "The Teacher," in *Winesburg, Ohio*. (New York: Huebsch). Frustrations and desires of a small town teacher in this short story collection.

Avi. (1991). *Nothing But the Truth*. (New York: Avon). Young adult novel following a teacher's ruin in the midst of politics and bureaucracy.

Barth, John. (1958). *End of the Road*. (Garden City, New York: Doubleday). Experiences of an English teacher at a state teacher's college.

Caldwell, Erskine. (1950). *Episode in Palmetto*. (New York: Duell). Complexities of student-teacher relationships.

Chaucer, Geoffrey. (1968). *The Canterbury Tales*. (Original work left unfinished in the 1390's). (R. M. Lumiansky, Trans.) (New York: Washington Square Press). See the description of the cleric in the Prologue. "And gladly would he teach."

Duncan, Lois. (1978). *Killing Mr. Griffin*. (New York: Dell). Young adult novel about a group of students who kill their high school English teacher.

Hellman, Lillian. (1934). *The Children's Hour*. One of Hellman's most famous plays about a private school teacher's life and career ruined by a rumor. Also a 1962 movie version.

Irving, Washington. (1899). *The Legend of Sleepy Hollow*. (New York: Putnam). Another classic schoolmaster.

Landau, Elliott D.; Epstein, Sherrie L.; & Stone, Ann P. (Eds.). (1976). *The Teaching Experience: An Introduction to Education through Literature*. (Englewood Cliffs, NJ: Prentice Hall). Includes a variety of pieces and stories by authors including Robert Graves, Jessie Stuart, Irwin Shaw, and Isaac Asimov.

Warren, Robert Penn. (1931). "The Unvexed Isles," in *The Circus in the Attic and Other Stories*. (New York: Harcourt Brace). An English professor is caught in a routine of dullness.

Wilders, Laura Ingalls. (1867–1957). Many titles. Schooling on the frontier is portrayed. Also a popular TV series.

Index

About the
Editors and Contributors

JOYE ALBERTS, a former middle school and high school English teacher, received her B.A. degree from Oklahoma State University and her M. Ed. from the University of Oklahoma. She is co-director of the Oklahoma State University Writing Project and teaches composition courses.

JOANNE BERGBOM teaches English to eleventh and twelfth grade students at H. Frank Carey High School in Franklin Square, New York, where she is also Director of Student Activities. She received her education at Cornell and Hofstra universities. She has been teaching in the Sewanhaka Central High School District for 13 years after taking time out to raise her own four children. She has been a member of the Long Island Writing Project for three years.

JEANNE BUCKINGHAM has taught senior high school English in south central Pennsylvania for 19 years. She is a 1995 National Writing Project Fellow from the Capital Area Writing Project in Harrisburg, Pennsylvania.

MICHAEL BURNS teaches tenth and twelfth grade English and serves as an advisor and resident faculty member at Brandon Hall School, a boarding school in Atlanta.

STEFFIE CORCORAN teaches English and creative writing at Del Crest Junior High School in Del City, Oklahoma. She was named the 1997–1998 Teacher of the Year in her school district, the Midwest City-Del City Public Schools. She also serves as a contributing editor/copy chief for *Oklahoma Today* magazine.

KAREN DOWNING has taught language arts at Valley High School in West Des Moines, Iowa, for eight years. She has an M.F.A. in Nonfiction Writing from the University of Iowa.

JOANNE DURHAM teaches fourth grade at Ridgecrest Elementary School in Prince Georges County, Maryland. Before starting to teach five years ago, she was a union, community, and political organizer for many years. She attempts to use her previous experiences both in her teaching and in helping to develop avenues for change in public education.

RUTH GIVENS received her B.S. and M.A.T. from the University of Tulsa and her Ed.D. from Oklahoma State University. She has taught in high school and college for 25 years. Ruth directs the secondary education and M.A.T. programs at Wheaton College where she is a member of the graduate faculty.

ELAINE GREENSPAN, an English teacher from Albuquerque, New Mexico, for 25 years and now retired, has written many books and articles about teaching. Her most recent book is *A Teacher's Survival Guide*.

SHERYL LAIN has taught English in grades 7–12 since 1968. She is currently Director of the Wyoming Writing Project, an adjunct professor at the University of Wyoming, and K–12 language arts coordinator for Laramie County School District #1. She is a published poet and essayist and is currently working on a book about teaching writing.

ELIZABETH LAUTHER teaches fourth grade at Ridgecrest Elementary School in Prince Georges County, Maryland. She also teaches hands-on science and math and performance assessment at Trinity College in Washington, D.C.

GLORIA D. NIXON-JOHN has taught middle school and high school English for the past twenty-five years in both urban and suburban schools. She is currently working for the Oakland Writing Project in Waterford, Michigan, as a Consultant and Master Teacher. She is also working on a biography of Canadian poet Bronwen Wallace.

PENELOPE PALMER lives in Perkins, Oklahoma. She teaches sophomore English as a first year teacher.

TONI PANTIER, an upper elementary teacher in a magnet program for the gifted, has taught first through sixth grade as well as junior high English. She is a doctoral student at Oklahoma State University in the School of Curriculum and Educational Leadership and an active member of the Oklahoma State University Writing Project.

JOHN PARBST teaches writing and literature courses as well as a training seminar for writing center tutors at Suffolk County Community College in New York.

JOHN PIIRTO'S articles have appeared in academic journals, his stories in literary magazines. His play *The Edge* was produced by the BBC in 1992. He currently teaches in the University Writing Program at the University of Colorado.

LINDA POWERS, a former high school English teacher, is Curriculum Facilitator in the Ponca City, Oklahoma, public schools where she plans and facilitates programs in the areas of curriculum and instruction and professional development for teachers. She is completing a doctorate in the School of Curriculum and Educational Leadership with a focus in language arts at Oklahoma State University with future plans to teach at the university level.

DAVID PULLING holds a B.A. from Louisiana College and an M.A. from the University of Southwestern Louisiana. He has taught English for ten years in St. Landry Parish and Lafayette Parish school districts in Louisiana. He is the Institutional Liaison Officer at Louisiana State University at Eunice and an active teacher consultant with the National Writing Project of Acadiana.

SHARON MCCOY ROBBINS has a B.A. in English Education from the University of North Florida and a master's in English from the University of Illinois at Chicago. She has taught English and humanities for 16 years in urban and suburban schools. She currently teaches English at Beaches Chapel School in Neptune Beach, Florida. She is an active consultant of the National Writing Project at the University of North Florida.

GRETCHEN SCHWARZ has taught high school German and English in New Mexico and Texas. She is a secondary English educator at Oklahoma State University. She supervises student teachers, teaches methods and young adult literature, and enjoys working with teachers at all levels, especially through the Oklahoma State University Writing Project.

CAROLYN THOMAS has been a social worker and a school librarian-media specialist. She is a doctoral student in education at Oklahoma State University.

BONNIE VOTH, a former elementary teacher, is currently working as a Master Teacher in Residence at Northeastern State University in Tahlequah, Oklahoma. She is pursuing a doctorate in Curriculum and Instruction through Oklahoma State University.

CAROLE WEIGAND began teaching in 1969 and has taught sixth through twelfth grades at various times.

ISBN 0-89789-509-6

90000>

EAN

9 780897 895095

HARDCOVER BAR CODE